A Hists
Prisor

A History of Women's Prisons in England:

The Myth of Prisoner Reformation

By

Susanna Menis

Cambridge
Scholars
Publishing

A History of Women's Prisons in England:
The Myth of Prisoner Reformation

By Susanna Menis

This book first published 2020. The present binding first published 2021.

Cambridge Scholars Publishing

Lady Stephenson Library, Newcastle upon Tyne, NE6 2PA, UK

British Library Cataloguing in Publication Data
A catalogue record for this book is available from the British Library

ISBN (10): 1-5275-6711-7
ISBN (13): 978-1-5275-6711-5

Paintings by Noriko Hisazumi, watercolour on paper (2019).
Created for and with reference to the historical sources used in
this study.

Contents

LIST OF ILLUSTRATIONS

Thank you

INTRODUCTION

Invisibility

This book's first object is to present a women's prison history from a criminological perspective that is, as a historical investigation that focuses on the institutional development of women's prisons from the late eighteenth century up to the early twentieth century. Criminology has been considered a discipline that is not much concerned with the subject of women criminals, as its subject matter is male-dominated or, alternatively, treated as a genderless construct.[1] Academic writings criticise the lack of documentation related to the lives and experiences of women prisoners, thus fostering a discourse suggesting that they have been overlooked in a criminal justice system that has had the male offender as its core interest. Feminist criminologists, such as Heidensohn and Silvestri, consider that the 'invisibility' of women offenders is due to the fact that 'women account for a very small proportion of all known offenders, and as a consequence relatively little attention has been given to them'.[2] This 'invisibility' could be understood on a number of levels. For example, Carlen has examined 'the invisible nature of the social control of women'.[3] Zedner and Gelsthorpe have criticised the lack of attention criminology studies have given to assessing the treatment of female offenders.[4] Priestley, for example, suggests that penal practice itself has largely ignored women prisoners because prison is 'a man's world; made for men, by men'.[5] Indeed, Heidensohn further suggests that women have been 'subjected to regimes designed to deal with the larger and more pressing problems of men'.[6] However, the 'invisibility' of women prisoners could also be attributed to the lack of histories written about women prisoners and women's prisons

---

[1] N. Naffine, *Feminism and Criminology* (Cambridge: Polity Press, 1997), p.1.
[2] F. Heidensohn and M. Silvestri, 'Gender and Crime', in *The Oxford handbook of criminology*, ed. by M. Maguire, R. Morgan, and R. Reiner, 5th edn (Oxford: Oxford University Press, 2012), pp.336-361 (p.336).
[3] Carlen, 1983, cited in A. Howe, *Punish and Critique* (London, NY: Routledge, 1994), p.127.
[4] Zedner (2002) and Gelsthorpe (2004) cited in Heidensohn and Silvestri, p.338.
[5] P. Priestley, *Victorian prison lives* (London: Pimlico, 1999), p.69.
[6] F. Heidensohn, *Women and Crime* (London: Macmillan, 1985), p.66.

prior to the 1960s. In 1966, Giallombardo noted that 'the female prison community has been overlooked: it merits study as does any other complex organisation'.[7] Indeed, credit should be given to feminist criminology for spotting a gap in prison historiography; it was only with writings by, for example, Smith (1962), Heidensohn (1985) and Dobash et al. (1986) that a narrative of the history of women prisoners began to develop.

Recognition of women's invisibility in the criminal justice system has brought the issues of sex and gender to the forefront, not only in criminological research but also in penal policy and practice.[8] Historical writings about women prisoners and women's prisons, however, have not been the object of such beneficial progress. In other words, there has been little research shedding new light on or, alternatively, challenging previous claims made by historical studies of women prisoners and women's prisons. Except for Zedner's *Women, Crime, and Victorian England* (1994), the feminist prison historiography has confined its research to a very limited word count (as opposed to books and volumes written on the mainstream [male] prisons and prison population). Additionally, there has been little engagement with primary historical records to understand whether the invisibility of women prisoners represents a real lack of commitment (policy and practical) to addressing women prisoners (and thus scant resources to write histories), or rather, stems from poor criminological historical investigation. The existing work has merely relied upon secondary sources, where one of the latest narratives on women's prison histories in, for example, Carlen and Worrall's *Analysing Women's Imprisonment* (2004) still recites unchallenged historical perspectives formulated in the 1960s, including the discourse of the 'invisibility' of women prisoners.

That women's prison historiographies remain unchallenged has, I argue, brought about stagnation in the discipline. From a historical point of view, drawing upon historical records consulted for this study, I suggest women prisoners and women's prisons would not have been invisible if criminologists had engaged with primary historical sources. This book demonstrates that despite the indisputably small number of women offenders and women prisoners in comparison to their male counterpart, policy and practitioners were just as concerned, at least proportionally, with the woman prisoner as they were with the male prisoner. Different considerations and sometimes separate policies were debated and applied to the female and male prison populations. Of course, research from the 1960s, 1970s and perhaps even

---

[7] Giallombardo, 1966, cited in Howe, p.123.
[8] Heidensohn and Silvestri, p.337.

the 1980s might not have had the luxury of using sources that are now largely available in archives and public databases. Still, the 'invisibility' of women prisoners in history is an unchallenged mantra. Therefore, one of the objects of this book is to unveil the extent of the 'invisibility' of women prisoners and women's prisons.

This book demonstrates that the development of women's prisons can have a history in its own right without needing to compare it with what has been constructed as the mainstream prison history, that is, male prison history. Major women's prison and prisoner histories, such as those by Smith, Dobash et al. and Carlen, have provided the first historical examinations that dedicate their full attention to women's experiences within the context of penal policy. As Howe has observed, these examinations, in turn, have 'fundamentally transformed the critical analysis of punishment regimes'.[9] The problem with these historical analyses, however, has been taking the social construct of the well-established mainstream prison historiography at face value. The writing style of these mainstream histories might have been challenged at times (such as in the case of the Revisionist-Whig dispute), but women's prison histories have been written within the contextual knowledge and boundaries created by these mainstream histories. This approach by criminologists has fostered a theoretical understanding, according to Howe, that women prisoners' small numbers 'have simply not been considered to be a "social problem" warranting close attention' by prison administration.[10]

Indeed, historical sources demonstrate that the question of women prisoners might have been considered unproblematic because prison authorities and reformers thought they knew what was best for the female prison population. However, the narrow approach followed by criminologists has denied the construction of an authentic and independent study on this issue. This, in turn, has led to some conflicting historical accounts; for example, Dobash et al. suggested that women's prison regimes were more repressive than those of male prisons, whereas Zedner's study reveals that this might not have been the case.[11] Scratching beneath the surface of an unchallenged prison history by uncovering primary historical sources that solely address the issue of women prisoners helps us to understand the unique historical dynamic of this specific prison population. It would be misleading to state that the development of women's prisons has been unrelated to the

---

[9] Howe, p.123.
[10] Ibid., p.155.
[11] Ibid., p.154.

development of men's prisons; and yet, denying the development of women's prisons its own historical ownership would be likewise misleading.

Although at the core of this book is the general question of 'prisoners' reformation', the study is contextualised around women's prisons, thus constructing a women's prison history. Inspired by Zedner's work but moving away from other well-established women's prison histories, I have drawn upon primary sources and critically used secondary sources to unfold the question of the historical 'invisibility' of women in penal practice. Indeed, not only do the historical findings cast doubt on the discourse of women's invisibility (or as Zedner puts it: 'to suggest that they [women prisoners] were simply "not foreseen" is patently implausible'),[12] but the historical sources also suggest that the uncritical assertion of women's 'invisibility' has led researchers to neglect the contribution of policy specifically concerning the female prison population in the shaping of mainstream prison policy.

Experiment

The second objective of this book is to expose the experimental nature of the prison penalty and to understand the extent to which it has caused the prison system to be in a constant and permanent state of crisis.[13] Little has been written on the relationship between the two, and historical sources reveal that prison as a primary penalty was lobbied for as a temporary tool, which eventually—and perhaps inevitably—became permanent. It was the state of emergency caused by the shortcoming of the far more popular transportation penalty that advanced the idea of prison as an 'experiment'–until the mid-eighteenth century prisons functioned mainly as detention centres and were classified as a secondary penalty. However, the system of punishment needed to be revised. The death penalty was increasingly seen as morally disproportionate, and judges were never fully committed to it, using their discretion to avert it; moreover, few of those sentenced to death were ultimately executed, thereby casting doubt on the effectiveness of the legal system. Unlike capital punishment, transportation was a morally and economically conducive penalty, and both the government and the judiciary were fond of it. Inconveniently, however, the colonies were less receptive,

---

[12] L. Zedner, *Women, crime and custody in Victorian England* (Oxford: Clarendon Press, 1994), p.100.
[13] The idea of 'crisis' as a concept related to prison discourse is inspired by the perspective of M. Cavadino et al. on 'prison crisis' (*The Penal System*, 5th edn [London: SAGE, 2013]).

first refusing to accept any more women (arguing that they corrupted the morals of the inhabitants mainly because many had to resort to prostitution to survive), then refusing to take any more criminals altogether.

Within this context of uncertainty, suggestions and recommendations were made for a contingency plan, where eventually Parliament had to be persuaded to upgrade imprisonment to function as a primary penalty; Parliament was reassured that this was merely an experiment and that, once the limitations on transportation were lifted, the usual order of things would be restored. However, the plans concerning prison upgrade were not well conceived and lacked coherence and agreement. Indeed, prison as a penalty was born out of a temporary emergency plan where the rationale was not 'confinement' itself, but rather, prisoners' labour and thus imprisonment was perceived as an economic venture. It is exactly this contingency plan which has shaped the foundation of this penalty: on the one hand, imprisonment endured through the centuries and became grounded in the social fabric and penal policy, but on the other hand, the constant search for prison reform from the eighteenth century onwards indicates that the modern prison system has been in a constant state of crisis, which it has never recovered from.

Several authors have explained the state of the prison system as a crisis that began just after the second quarter of the 20th century.[14] Cavadino et al. agree that the prison system has been under a 'moral challenge' and that it is 'now' at a 'critical junction'—where they use the metaphor of an ill person on the verge of either getting better or 'sink[ing] into fatal decline'.[15] It has been suggested that the 'crisis' is an expression of the following: high prison population, overcrowding, poor conditions, understaffing, and poor security;[16] in addition, Carlen highlights the 'legitimacy crisis' of the 1990s in relation to women's imprisonment.[17] However, I maintain that the 'crisis' described by Cavadino and others is not the crisis itself but its consequence. To develop Cavadino's metaphor, a person's illness is a catharsis whereas the actual reason for the illness is the failure of the immune system. Indeed, a critical historical assessment reveals that the modern prison system was

---

[14] See, for example, Fitzgerald and Sim, 1980 and Morris 1989, cited in Cavadino et al., p.9.
[15] Cavadino et al., p.12.
[16] Cavadino et al., p.11
[17] P. Carlen and A. Worrall, *Analysing Women's Imprisonment* (Devon: Willan, 2004), p.16.

born without an immune system – that is, the core aim(s) upon which the prison system should operate.

Hence, the 'crisis' discussed in this book refers to a permanent crisis of existence.[18] This 'crisis of existence' is not necessarily due to imprisonment being essentially an experiment; rather, it is a consequence of the rushed passage of the relevant Acts in Parliament accompanied by little critical elaboration and understanding of what the aims of this penalty ought to be and how these should and could be, if at all, materialised in practice. Thus, the crisis reflects a clash between what was perhaps desirable, conceptualised and expressed in penal and academic discourse against the actual reality and implications of such a penalty. In addition, through an examination of the development of the open prison, the book illustrates how reform of the prison system is inevitably interlinked with and affected by the mainstream orthodox closed prison. Therefore, as this mainstream method has been counter-productive from the outset, any change or reform will be superficial and temporary. Indeed, the discussion of HMP Askham Grange (open women's prison) illustrates this drawback; it demonstrates how this project, being part of a wider plan of prisoners' progression (from closed to open conditions, thereby facilitating future social integration), was nevertheless loosely developed in connection with the core penalty, namely, the closed prison. In other words, the open prison was devised to fulfil the 'training in open conditions' agenda, but its success has been deeply dependent on the (in)effective operation of the closed prison.

Despite experiencing a crisis of existence, the prison system has become firmly embedded in the fabric of society; its durability is puzzling and inconceivable. A concept devised by Carlen offers an explanation of this: 'carceral clawback'. Carlen describes it as the 'power of the prison constantly to deconstruct and successfully reconstruct the ideological conditions for its own existence'.[19] In other words, prison policy will re-justify prison legitimacy by reassigning and reshaping its socio-penal role.

---

[18] Crisis is defined in the Oxford Dictionary as 'a time of intense difficulty', and although this definition suggests a temporal limitation, 'permanent crisis' is not a new concept (despite its ambiguity) in academic discourse. An example for that, which also examines the notion of permanent crisis, is the article by Hont on 'the Permanent Crisis of a Divided Mankind' (I. Hont, 'The Permanent Crisis of a Divided Mankind: Contemporary Crisis of the Nation State', *Political Studies*, 42, (1994), 166-231; 'Crisis', s.1, Oxford Dictionaries, http://www.oxforddictionaries. com/definition/english/crisis 2015 [accessed 24 Jan 2015]).

[19] P. Carlen, 'The Case of Women's Imprisonment in Canada', *Punishment and Society*, 4, 1 (2002), 115-121 (p.116).

The historical investigation in this book demonstrates how, rather than challenging the legitimacy of the use of imprisonment per se, the effective delivery and fulfilment of the aims of imprisonment were tested against and reshaped to reflect 'spur of the moment' socio-political concerns. The carceral clawback concept is critical of the reformation agenda; thus, the use of this concept, as applied in this study throughout the historical development of the prison penalty, also aids in understanding the drawbacks presented by the 'prisoners' reformation' discourse. Indeed, I see the carceral clawback paradigm as one of the driving forces behind prisons' historical development, where the struggle of the government to align policy with practice is exemplified through its periodical need for reform.

Reformation

This leads to the third objective of this book; that is, the evaluation of the concept of 'prisoners' reformation'. With the introduction of the modern prison penalty, the 'reform[20] of the prisoner' was coupled with the prospect of the prisoner re-joining society at the completion of the prison term. Indeed, prison discourses (policy and academic) have developed the understanding that 'reformation' stands for the process through which the prisoner is 'untrained' from her criminal or deviant tendencies, thereby facilitating social integration as a 'new' law-abiding citizen.[21] However, the concept of 'reformation' as aiming to 'improve the offender's character or behaviour'[22] is, in fact, a myth.[23] First, 'reformation' is coupled with the

---

[20] 'Reform' c.1300: to convert into another and a better form. In 1413, it was used to refer to people. Having a strong connotation with European religious movements, it was first used by Martin Luther in the early sixteenth century in the dispute with the Roman Catholic Church ('Reform', *The Concise Oxford Dictionary of English Etymology*, T. F. Hoad, ed. [Oxford: Oxford University Press, Oxford Reference Online, 1996]).

[21] Even in the case of those who maintain the 'nothing works' perspective, the critique still relates to the aspect of reformation, suggesting an assumption that reformation is, after all, the desirable aim (see, for example, Cavadino et al. for a discussion illustrating the 'reformation' discourse).

[22] As defined by Cavadino et al., p.38.

[23] The word 'myth' is used in its etymological meaning, in particular, with reference to these two definitions: a widely held but false belief or idea and an exaggerated or idealized conception of a person or a thing ('Myth', s.2, 2.2, *Oxford Dictionaries*, http://www.oxforddictionaries.com/definition/english/myth?searchDictCode=all [accessed 31 Oct 2015]). The use of 'myth' to exemplify the nonexistence or limitation of a widely held concept is inspired by Garland's paper on 'The Limits of the Sovereign State' (D. Garland, 'The Limits of the Sovereign State: Strategies of

paternalistic assumption that the prisoner suffers from certain criminal or deviant tendencies and that she should be helped to grow out of these. However, merely identifying the offender sentenced to prison as a criminal ignores the substantial impact that life in prison might have on the person; an offender might or might not pursue a criminal lifestyle, might or might not have a criminal character or tendencies, but she will inevitably become a 'prisoner' once imprisoned. In practice, imprisonment as a penalty 'suspends' the offender from society; thus, the 'suspension time' becomes an important factor at the core of this penalty. According to penal and academic discourse, the process of reformation should occur within the 'suspension time', thus within the walls of prison. However, this view has long been identified as controversial: the same tool, that is, imprisonment, which brought about the 'ruin' of the girl (as put by Mary Gordon)[24] is also used as a tool to bring about personal and character 'amelioration' and, thus, effective social integration.

Drawing upon primary historical records, this book demonstrates that despite 'prisoners' reformation' having been a recurring theme in prison policy and prison reform (which it still is), the foundational drawback presented by the prison system has meant that, in practice, an effective implementation of the ethos of reformation was never a feasible task. Prison regimes were routinely reshaped and redesigned to better fulfil this aim of imprisonment; yet, limitations related to ineffective prison management and expensive administration as well as the presence of conflicting social aims and penal policies meant that prisoners' reformation could not be taken beyond its theoretical construction. Such recognition contributes to the understanding that prison policy and prison administration have been less systematic than suggested.[25] Too much credit has been attributed to the prison as a social institution striving for social control; moreover, the anomalous relationship between imprisonment and reformation has been merely tested upon the prison's (un)successful endorsement of new and reshaped policies. Prison discourses and prison studies, as well as social perceptions, have been fixated with the imprisonment aim of 'reformation', but this has been taken at face value.

Instead, the 'myth of reformation' perspective draws attention to prisoners' inevitable adaptation to institutional life, rather than 'reforming' for what

---

crime control in contemporary Society', *British Journal of Criminology,* 36, 4, (1996) 445-471).

[24] M. Gordon, *Penal Discipline* (London: George Routledge & Sons, 1922), p.99.

[25] See, for example, the Revisionist analysis of prison history.

has been deemed desirable, that is, a law-abiding (free citizen's) social life. Historical records indicate that this recognition was acknowledged at times by penal and academic discourses, but it was only with the 1948 Criminal Justice Act that the alternative prison policy of 'training' was proposed (parallel to the orthodox prison system). The 'training for freedom' perspective embraced the understanding that to reform prisoners to become law-abiding citizens, the training must take place outside the prison walls. Hence, borstals and, later, adult open prisons were conceived to facilitate this purpose. It appeared that for the first time, 'reformation' was a feasible prospect, where the discourse encapsulated the idea that prisoners should be trained, rather than reformed, to acquire those social skills lost through the process of institutionalisation. This part of the study explores the relationship between 'reformation' and 'training' by examining the first open prison for women, HMP Askham Grange. The importance of this discussion is twofold. First, in line with the first objective of this book – that is, presenting a women's prison history – this latter part of the study draws close attention to the relationship between the development of penal policy and the development of an open women's prison. The study reveals that the open prison is not without limitations. The process of institutionalisation, as described by Goffman, affects the 'disculturation' of the person, bringing about their 'untraining' from what could be considered 'normal' social skills,[26] thus hindering effective social integration. Thus, the process of institutionalisation is an almost inevitable one, so much so that even the open prison, which was set up as a measure to abate institutionalisation, could be classified as one of Goffman's Total Institutions. Indeed, the examination of the open prison further reveals the controversial nature of the 'prisoners' reformation' concept.

Meanings

I have adopted an interdisciplinary methodological approach, inspired by criminological and historical research methods. The research follows a predominantly desk-based historical and documentary approach; however, I have also conducted field-observations and interviews at HM Askham Grange women's open prison. The general approach is qualitative, hence aiming at understanding meanings rather than focusing on measurements. In this context, I have used thematic, grounded and critical approaches. Although these are three different qualitative methods, they all aim at generating theory from collected data rather than starting off with a

---

[26] E. Goffman, *Asylums* (Middlesex: Penguin Books, 1961; repr 1976), p.23.

hypothesis placed within a theoretical frame to be then tested by the data gathered.[27] More specifically, critical methodology, developed in the 1960s, is understood as aiming at breaking the boundaries of 'formalised domain assumptions', where, according to Scraton and Chadwick, it 'endeavours to locate the experiential realities of individuals [...] within their historical [...] context'.[28] It could be argued that critical methodology reduces the inquiry to smaller levels of analysis, and by doing so the approach over-simplifies the history told. However, the approach allows a move away from set-in-stone historical frameworks which can deny the subjectivity and ownership of history (for example, in the case of women prisoners and women's prisons).

Similarly, the grounded methodology was developed in the late 1960s and aimed to identify 'general concepts, the development of theoretical explanations that reach beyond the known, and offer new insights into a variety of experiences and phenomena';[29] thus, theory becomes a product of data production rather than a preconceived perspective. In other words, the theory produced is grounded upon the observations made, whether empirical (e.g. field-observations) or historical; the observations are tested and re-tested against findings within the context of the research. Finally, a thematic methodology type of research is aimed at identifying themes within 'narratives that reflect the individual perspectives of the research participants'.[30] As opposed to the other two research methodologies, the thematic methodology is relatively flexible because, as Finch and Fafinski note, there is 'no consensus on how you go about doing it'.[31]

---

[27] E. Finch and S. Fafinski, *Criminology Skills* (Oxford: Oxford University press, 2012), pp.384-395.

[28] P. Scraton and K. Chadwick, 'Critical Research', in *The Sage Dictionary of Criminology*, ed. by E. McLaughlin and J. Muncie, 3rd edn (London: SAGE, 2013), pp.107-108. Such research could be seen in the works by Stanley Cohen, Jonathan Simon and David Garland as having as their core objective the investigation of inequality and oppression (in that regard, see the discussion in B. Hudson, 'Critical Reflection as Research Methodology', in *Doing Criminological Research*, ed. by V. Jupp, P. Davies, and P. Francis (London: SAGE, 2000, repr. 2006), pp.175-192).

[29] J. Corbin and A. Strauss, *Basics of Qualitative Research: Techniques and Procedures for Developing Grounded Theory*, 4th edn (SAGE Publications, 2014), p.6. Such research can be identified with the work of Becker on marihuana use (H.S. Becker, 'Becoming a Marihuana User', *American Journal of Sociology*, 59, 3 (1953), 235-252).

[30] Finch and Fafinski, p.385.

[31] Finch and Fafinski, p.385.

The overall process allowed me to deepen the investigation by drawing upon data that had already been gathered. Hence, I looked for further evidence to support the recurrent themes, and eventually, I generated a perspective which was then evaluated in accordance with a theoretical concept. The unusual nature of these tools lies in their extraction of a particular value from a specific experience. Thus, as explained by Hudson in accordance with feminist methodologies (although not wishing to be compartmentalised as a feminist study), the interpretation of this knowledge, these values and experiences will produce a value-based perspective.[32] In other words, the gathering of information and the perspectives generated will be based upon the ways the subjects of research (whether interviewees or authors of documents) make sense of and relate to their world.[33]

Researching prisons: an iron garden gate, a haircut and my sister

Textbooks sometimes discuss the safety aspect of getting into and around prison[34]—presumably a closed prison—but not much is written about getting around an open prison. Anyone who has ever visited a closed prison might find visiting Askham Grange a strange experience, something that the prisoners themselves may experience too. 'Closedness', 'restriction', 'secrecy' and 'security' are so embedded in our cultural understanding of what prisons are that standing in front of Askham Grange's open iron garden gate with no prison officer stopping me from entering indeed made me roll my eyes, wondering whether I was missing something. However, the gate was unattended during all my visits. Thus, I had to find my way to the prison visitors' reception.

Although the reception appeared to be the usual prison reception (officers talking through a glass partition, taking names, checking identification and retaining mobile phones) to my surprise, I was expected to find my way around by myself. As a result, the inevitable question popped into my head: 'Is no one going to escort me?' The answer to this question came in the form of a prison resident (a prisoner) who was on her way to where I was supposed to go; she accompanied me to my interviewee. Indeed, my

---

[32] Hudson, pp.328-342.
[33] L. Gelsthrope, *Doing Prison Research: Doing Interview Research* (Milton Keynes: Open University Press, 1992), p.13.
[34] See, for example, Martin.

experience at Askham Grange challenged my understanding of 'security' and 'safety', placing these in a much wider perspective.

My visits at HMP Askham Grange did not at all resemble Gelsthrope's inspiring account of her experience as a prison researcher. First, unlike Gelsthrope's prison experience in the 1970s, in Askham Grange, I did not feel 'out of place' because of my gender and I certainly did not receive comments such as 'this is not a place for ladies'.[35] Of course, Askham Grange is a female prison, and there is a greater balance between male and female prison staff than there was in Gelsthrope's time. In addition, unlike Gelsthrope's, my research did not involve interactions with the prisoners, and thus, my presence in the prison was less significant. Additionally, it is important to remember that Askham Grange's prisoners are used to laypeople coming in and out, either in relation to the conference facility or the hair salon run in the prison by the prisoners. Thus, whenever I came across prisoners, my presence did not attract particular attention.

One event that exemplifies the unproblematic nature of my presence in Askham Grange was my hairdressing experience. I made an appointment to have my hair cut in Salunique, the hair salon in Askham Grange which is open to the public and run by the prisoners. The salon room was spacious but not particularly large, and it seemed well equipped. The windows facing the luscious garden made me forget where I was, that is, in prison. There were a few trainees in the room, but there was no indication that my presence triggered any interest or was an issue. I had been told that my hairdresser was about to complete the third stage of her training with apparently good grades. We had a brief chat about our studies, as she was doing a sociology degree and was interested in hearing more about my own criminology studies. I said that I was about to meet the prison governor as part of my studies; this did not impress her, and we changed the topic of discussion.

Around the prison, I generally felt welcomed. I certainly felt that my expression of interest to conduct research at Askham Grange was not perceived as problematic, and the smooth access facilitated by the research contact person exemplifies that. In fact, accessibility to Askham Grange (although reaching Askham Grange itself required taking a taxi from York train station) was rather surprising. On my first visit to the prison, I was accompanied by my sister. I left her sitting in a small reception area whilst having my first interview with the deputy governor. To my amusement, on

---

[35] Gelsthrope, 'Feminist methodologies in criminology', p.96.

my return I found out that a member of prison staff had given her a tour of the prison…

*

The book opens with a discussion on *prison historiography*. This provides a critical analysis of several prison historiographies, focusing in particular on the Whigs and Revisionists. This analysis identifies the gap in scholarship that I profess to fill, at least in part, in Part II of this book, *"Reforming" the Prisoner*, which presents a historical account of the development of women's prisons. The chapter assesses penal and prison policies as drafted within the relevant socio-political context of the time; it addresses the experimental nature of the prison system and its state of crisis. The historical time frame ends with an examination of the Prison Commission's contribution to prison policy development under the chairmanship of Sir Edmond Du Cane (1870s). Although Part III of this study, *"Training" the Prisoner*, chronologically follows Part II, it diverts from the development of the orthodox prison system (hence, the closed prison) to instead consider the chronologically parallel development of the borstal system (1900s). The aim of this chapter is to expand the critical examination of 'prisoners' reformation' by examining the trend of 'training' and 'open conditions' as first developed through the borstal system and later through the adult open prison (1930s). The policy of 'training' comes as a striking contrast to the idea of 'prisoners' reformation'; rather than pressing prisoners to grow out of their supposed criminal tendencies, it recognises institutionalisation as a hindrance to social integration, thus working towards its abatement. Part IV of this study, *Understanding Open Prisons: The First Women's Open Prison, HMP Askham Grange*, takes the first open prison for women as a case study and further develops the discussion of the assessment of 'training' and 'prisoners' reformation'. Although the open prison is analysed in its own right, the study critically considers the role and function of the open prison within the wider context of the prison system and how the open prison has been affected by the orthodox closed prison. The understanding of what is an open prison is also tested against the concept of Total Institution.

PART I

PRISON HISTORIOGRAPHY

Critical review of a historiography is typical of historical writing – less so of criminological studies. And yet, the discipline of criminology is grounded in history; most importantly, it has been shaped by different histories written on its various subjects. Criminologists have not engaged much with the representation of that past, that is, with the historiography of a certain subject of study, and it is only in a couple of not-so-recent works by Zedner and Schwan[36] that we see criminologists, rather than historians, tracing the different approaches taken by prison historiography in its aim to explain the relationship between prison and society, the historical variations of this relationship, and the factors that influence it.

The importance of historiographical reviews should not be underestimated. They not only shape a context for reading; they also emphasise the very delicate and controversial history of prison development. Primarily, the aim of such a review is to reveal to the reader that 'reality' might depend upon the type of 'story' told or, alternatively, that 'reality' could be a combination of different 'stories', outlooks, standpoints, beliefs and ideals. However, the sum of these historiographies cannot provide a complete account of prison history because there are as many prison histories as there are people who have left their mark - in one way or another, virtually or physically - on the walls of English prisons. The aim of this chapter is merely to draw attention to the two main stories that prison historiography has told, or better, constructed, and examine how they have affected the way we understand the development of prisons.

*

Prison historiography reveals the manifold aspects of prison 'reality', and the complexity and multiplicity of this 'reality' is what makes the project of writing and reading prison history so fascinating. The 'archaeological

---

[36] L. Zedner, *Women, Crime, and Custody in Victorian England* (1994); A. Schwan, *Representing Female Prisons: Women and Crime in England 1813-1870* (Birkbeck London University: unpublished PhD thesis, 2005).

findings' that inform prison histories are drawn mainly from personal writings, penal policies and reports. The reality described, for example, in personal writings is an end product, constructed through the author's first-hand prison experience; such personal narratives, in turn, shape subsequent historical accounts and their interpretations and critiques, very often leading to revisions of these historical realities. Therefore, the discovery of new historical sources or new interpretations of familiar sources might bring about the reassessment of theoretical and critical perspectives. Such was the case, for example, in Ignatieff's change of heart regarding his 'membership' of the Revisionist prison historiography school. Criticising his own work and that of others such as Foucault, Ignatieff backed down from his original assertion, later arguing that, in fact, 'reformers were more humanitarian than revisionists have made them to be' and that the revisionists' fixation with the centrality of the state was far too exaggerated.[37]

Historians themselves have acknowledged the problematic status of the 'real', claiming that 'absolute historical "truth" (is) a chimera';[38] thus, the competition for 'truth' among different prison histories could undermine the discovery of different 'realities' pertaining to this 'truth'. Moreover, critics have classified, categorised and labelled the different approaches to the writing of prison history; each of these approaches has sought to prove itself the most accurate account regarding historical prison development. And yet, each of these approaches stems from different theoretical grounds reflecting different understandings of human and social interaction, thus representing only 'half of the story'. The prison historiography discussed here concerns two broad approaches: traditional prison history (also known as administrative or reformist) and social prison history (also known as revisionist or social control). Alternatively, Cohen defined them as the 'uneven progress' model and the 'it's all a con' model.[39]

*

---

[37] M. Ignatieff, 'State, Civil Society and Total Institutions: A Critique of Recent Social Histories of Punishment', in S. Cohen and A. Scull ed., *Social Control and the State* (London: Basil Blackwell Ltd, 1983; repr. 1986), p.77.
[38] Tosh, 4th edn, p.200.
[39] Cohen (1985) cited in A. Howe, *Punish and Critique* (London, NY: Routledge, 1994), p.54.

Traditional histories have also been labelled 'Whig' histories. Of course, by definition, the Whig label is typically English,[40] and it aimed at constructing a more English-specific historical account as opposed to the 'Tory' global historical inclusive style, which, it was argued, inevitably lacked accuracy; or alternatively, it simply included too much 'social stuff'.[41] In other words, whilst Tory histories narrated current social developments such as commerce, the arts, the law, customs and manners,[42] Whig history developed a liberal 'optimistic' style, aiming at portraying a positive view of current socio-political developments against the 'primitive' past.[43]

The Whig approach was without doubt the outcome of a desire not only to acknowledge English constitutional history over what appeared to be decaying and troubled France and Germany,[44] but it also sought to emphasise the success of the Protestant Whigs over the Catholic Tories. After all, it has been a popular conviction that the Middle Ages were a period of darkness, whereas the Renaissance and the Reformation represented periods of Enlightenment.[45] Burke explains that this new trend meant to provide a more reliable historical account - because it was based on official records - and it was utilised to promote national unity, citizenship, and nationalist propaganda.[46]

A typical example can be found in Blackstone's *Commentaries on the Laws of England* (1765). In the preface, we can find the following:

> [...] who of late years have attended the public administration of justice, must be sensible that a masterly acquaintance with the general spirit of laws and the principles of universal jurisprudence, combined with an accurate knowledge of our own municipal constitutions, their original, reform, and

---

[40] Although the 'Whigs' were also prominent in America during the reconstruction period (1860s-1870s), Bentley notes that it was only the English 'Whig' historians' writings that were, in retrospective, discredited (p.64).

[41] Bentley, p.64; H. Butterfield, *The Whig Interpretation of History* (NY: AMS Press, 1931; repr. 1978), p.8; and P. Burke, *History and Social Theory* (Cambridge: Polity Press, 2005), p. 6.

[42] Burke, p.3-6.

[43] Tosh, 5th edn, p.20.

[44] Bentley, p.62 (especially related to the period of the second half of the nineteenth century, which included a variety of wars, and constitutional changes from Republic to Imperialism and vice versa).

[45] Butterfield, p.11

[46] Burke, p.5 and Bentley, p.70.

history, hath given a beauty and energy to many modern judicial decisions, with which our ancestors were wholly unacquainted.[47]

However, the labels attached to this historical writing approach, i.e., 'Whig', 'traditional', 'administrative' and 'reformist', are suggestive of the type of criticism attached to it. Bentley notes that the leading doctrines underlying these histories 'were congratulatory', or in other words, 'the story celebrated English liberty and the institutions that it deemed central to the widening of English freedom through the ages'.[48] According to one of its first critics, Henry Butterfield, the Whigs studied the past 'with direct and perpetual reference to the present',[49] and this apparently was counterproductive because it was 'an obstruction to historical understanding'.[50] The 'obstruction' refers to an alleged discretion (abridgement) in choosing the information used to tell the story of history. In addition, this approach excessively and intentionally emphasised the difference between the 'men who furthered progress and the men who tried to hinder it'.[51]

Prison inspector Arthur Griffiths' 1884 work *Memorials of Millbank and Chapters in Prison History* is a good example of this; he chose to depict Elizabeth Fry and the Lady Visitors' work if not pejoratively, then dismissively. According to Griffiths's assessment, Elizabeth Fry's success in the national penitentiary Millbank was not as fruitful as at Newgate; this was because the women prisoners at Millbank had already been well cared for by the prison staff. Hence, Griffiths argued that Elizabeth Fry's work was not only superfluous, but it 'tended to produce hypocrisy rather than real repentance'.[52] Not only this but Griffiths continued to dismiss Elizabeth Fry's work in Newgate by claiming that her 'success' there could be explained by the extremely degrading conditions the prisoners were kept in. It was not surprising that the most microscopic amelioration was immediately noticed, argued Griffiths. The Lady Visitors were 'amateurs, and such as all other unprofessional people, the work they do is imperfect

---

[47] W. Blackstone, *Commentaries on the Laws of England,* Vol I (Oxford: Clarendon Press, 1765), p.ii.
[48] Bentley, p.63.
[49] Butterfield, p.11.
[50] Ibid., p.11.
[51] Ibid., p.11.
[52] In his role as Inspector of Prisons, A. Griffiths, *Memorials of Millbank and Chapters in Prison History* (London: Chapman and Hall, 1884), p.202.

and incomplete'.[53] In his view, they not only wasted 'their energy in the wrong direction' but also caused 'serious injury to (prison) discipline'.[54]

Typical of a Whig history aiming at emphasising the efficiency and success of the present policy and reform, Griffiths' account stated that the prison officers at Millbank (male and female) would never make 'errors' such as the one he ascribed to Elizabeth Fry and the Lady Visitors. Indeed, he argued that in the Millbank penitentiary, 'no fault could be found with their [women prisoners'] treatment generally'.[55] Griffiths concluded by saying, with reference to the Lady Visitors, that he would leave it to the 'reader to decide whether the absence of similar outrageous behaviour now does not at least prove a certain superiority in our modern system of prison administration'.[56] However, historical records indicate that Griffiths's account is biased. First, a quick scan of the newspapers of the time reveals a substantial amount of writing related to the work of Elizabeth Fry and the Lady Visitors, even 30-40 years after Elizabeth Fry's death. For example, the work of the Lady Visitors was featured in women's magazines, such as in *The Woman's Signal* in 1884, with an article by Sarah T. Tooley on 'The Prisoners' Friends'.[57] Additionally, the work of women such as Elizabeth Fry was presented to the young generation by, for example, Marianne L.B. Ker in her article 'The Girl with a Mission' (1885) in the *Young England.*[58] The work of the Lady Visitors was even reported to the Third International Prison Congress in Rome in 1885 by Florence Davenport-Hill, and it was well received.[59]

However, it is for another reason that Griffiths's account is deemed to be biased and to have clearly disproportionately glorified the penal policies and reform prevailing in his own time. In fact, throughout the 1870s-1880s, the work of the Prison Commission, which was responsible for prison policy and its implementation, was heavily and constantly criticised for its lack of success in meeting the targets set in terms of prison reform and prisoners' reformation. It is because of this tendency of the Whig approach to

---

[53] Griffiths, p.204.
[54] Ibid., p.204.
[55] Ibid., p.204.
[56] Ibid., p.205.
[57] S.T. Tooley, 'The Prisoners' friends', *The Woman's Signal*, 1 November 1884, p.280.
[58] L.B.M Ker, 'The Girl with a Mission', *Young England*, 1 June 1885, p.257.
[59] F. Davenport-Hill, *Art II: Women Prison Visitors*, Paper presented by request to the Third International Prison Congress, Rome, reported in *The Englishwoman's Review,* 15 December 1885, p.536.

emphasise only positive historical achievements that Cohen labelled this type of history 'the uneven progress'. In other words, Cohen suggests that the 'correctional progress' identified as such by Whig history is in fact based upon 'a simple-minded idealist view of history' driven by a 'reform vision'[60] and, thus, it is inevitably biased.

Furthermore, Butterfield explains, the Whig tradition of prison history results in the imposition of 'a certain form upon the whole historical story' aiming at producing 'a scheme of general history which is bound to converge beautifully upon the present'.[61] Therefore, in terms of traditional prison historiography, the accounts provided were not only written from the 'top', but they also described stories of continuous grand and optimistic progress. As a consequence, Zedner explains, not only have 'the professed good intentions of reformers' been 'accepted by many historians at face value' as 'uncomplicated', but the actual application of the penal policies has never been put under scrutiny.[62]

*

By the 1960s, history had become an interdisciplinary subject challenging social investigation and theory. The shifting attention to the 'social' has been explained as expressing the need to search for the 'roots' and renew the links with the past. What is known as 'social history' has been developed to rewrite a story 'from the bottom up', examining the 'framework(s) of [...] daily lives'.[63] Within the discipline of (critical) criminology, a new approach was taken by those identified as 'revisionists' in a period when the legitimacy of the repressive state-run institutional regime was contested.[64] Cohen labelled the revisionists' approach as 'it's all a con' reflecting the revisionists' sentiments regarding the exaggerated glorification of Victorian penal reformists and their enterprises. Indeed, the revisionists in general have argued that prison development and reform was never linear or continuous, but most notably, it was all part of a set up plan to control the masses: everyone, including the reformists, was mystified to hear that the changes brought about were fair, human and progressive.[65] Unsurprisingly, these new historical writings did not immediately become popular. For

---

[60] Cohen (1985) cited in Howe, p.54.
[61] Butterfield, p.11.
[62] Zedner, p.93.
[63] Stearns (1980) quoted in Howe, p.50.
[64] Ibid, p.49.
[65] Cohen (1985), cited in Howe, p.55.

example, traditional historians, such as Radzinowicz and Hood, made a point of dismissing this new trend in their seminal work *The History of the English Criminal Law* (1986). Possibly, the revisionists' accusatory and rather contentious tone did not match the Whigs' much more placid approach.

The range of revisionists' views is wide, and Burke suggests that the variety of their approaches and perspectives derives from the different schools of social theory they engaged with.[66] This is also true for penal revisionists, although they all have in common the study of penal and prison regimes within a social context.[67] For example, in the early 1930s, constructing a social history that drew on a Marxist perspective, Rusche and Kirchheimer explored the historical relationship between penal laws, labour markets and class struggle within the context of capitalism.[68] In the 1970s, this perspective was reshaped, especially by Melossi and Pavarini, who adopted a so-called neo-Marxist approach that assessed the variations in penal policies based on 'changes in the mode of production, fiscal crises, phases of unemployment (and) the requirement of capital'.[69] Although Rusche and Kirchheimer's ideas need to be read with caution - indeed, Melossi provides 15 pages of warnings in the preface to Rusche and Kirchheimer's 2003 edition - they nevertheless managed to break away from the usual historical account of prison development: they provided a specific analysis of a very specific topic tackled from an unfamiliar standpoint. Foucault considered it to be a 'great work' because it 'provides a number of essential reference points.'[70] In fact, Melossi thinks that Foucault's appreciation of Rusche and Kirchheimer's work was triggered by the fact that the study of punishment was grounded 'not in philosophical and legal theories and ideas, but in historically concrete practices of punishment'.[71]

Another Revisionist penal view has been broadly identified with the work of Michel Foucault. Cohen and Scull argue that although style and content

---

[66] Burke, p.18.
[67] Howe, p.63.
[68] G. Rusche and O. Kirchheimer, *Punishment and Social Structure* (NY: Russell & Russell, 2003; 1st edn 1968).
[69] Melossi in the preface to the 2003 edition of Rusche and Kirchheimer, p.xxii. See also D. Melossi and M. Pavarini, *The Prison and the Factory: Origins of the Penitentiary System* (MacMillan, 1981).
[70] M. Foucault, *Discipline and Punish: The Birth of the Prison* (London: Penguin, 1979; repr. 1991), p.24.
[71] Melossi in the preface to the 2003 edition of Rusche and Kirchheimer, p.xxviii.

may vary between the many authors associated with this approach,[72] all 'represent a clear advance over the amateurish [...] accounts [...] previously offered'.[73] Revisionism has not escaped critique, possibly because of its heavy political baggage concerning socio-penal control.[74] Nevertheless, its importance lies, once again, in the unfolding of an additional dimension (in my view, specific rather than overly simplistic)[75] for the understanding of penal development. These historiographies brought together the study of crime and the study of the state, drawing mainly upon social control perspectives. Cohen and Scull suggest that the concept of social control in itself might have been an easy target because it was 'the most theoretically impoverished sub-field of sociology' and thus was easy to criticise.[76] However, the revisionists' theoretical framework proved essential in that it broke away from traditional criminology, which interpreted social control as a necessary and positive political function. The 1960s revisionists' historical writings presented instead a story of social control understood as organised repression.[77] For example, for Rothman, the benevolent spirit of the nineteenth century was, to some extent, a delusion and had its own limits deriving from the 'deficiencies and blindnesses [*sic*] of the reform vision'.[78] The revisionists' argument was further elaborated to embrace the perspective that, as Ignatieff put it, 'the prison was thus studied not for itself

---

[72] The most frequently cited are Rothman, with what has been considered the first expression of a revisionist historiography, *The Discovery of the Asylum* (Boston: Little, Brown, 1971); and Ignatieff's English 'version' of Foucault's prison work *A Just Measure of Pain* (NY: Pantheon, 1978).

[73] S. Cohen and A. Scull, 'Social Control in History and Sociology', in *Social Control and the State*, ed. by S. Cohen and A. Scull (London: Basil Blackwell Ltd, 1983; repr. 1986) pp.1-14 (p.3). It is interesting to note that whereas revisionists' reviewers recognise that there are different branches, categories and revisionist approaches, the same specification is not made when discussing the Whig approach. In fact, Bentley argues that what was originally identified by Butterfield as the Whig approach has been applied generically and uncritically, almost as a set model, to all traditional historiographies, creating a generalising misconception (Bentley, p.63).

[74] See Howe, p.44 and Ignatieff, 'State, Civil Society and Total Institutions', pp.76-77.

[75] Ignatieff points to the criticism made against revisionists for 'over-schematizing a complex story' (ibid., p.77).

[76] Cohen and Scull, p.6.

[77] D. Wilson, 'Social Control', in *The SAGE Dictionary of Criminology*, ed. by E. McLaughlin And J. Muncie, 3rd edn (London: SAGE, 2013), pp.421-423.

[78] Rothman (1971) cited in Cohen and Scull, p.4.

but for what its rituals of humiliation could reveal about a society's ruling conceptions of power, social obligation and human malleability'.[79]

*

Although traditional-administrative penal historiographies would mainly, if not exclusively, tell stories of 'great men', it would have been reasonable to expect that the newer penal-social histories would divert at least some attention to the study of women's history. However, in her review, Spongberg notes that although these new studies offered an examination of the lives of ordinary people, these 'people' were, in fact, still men.[80] Furthermore, Naffine argues that revisited historical penal writings (and more generally, critical criminology writings) still take men as 'the natural heartland' of the discipline.[81] The historian Joan Wallach Scott, in her 1985 study on gender and history, suggests that

> by refusing to gender this subject male, historians had produced a system of meaning that not only necessarily excluded women, but naturalised women's subordination to men and normalised their historical marginalisation or invisibility.[82]

Howe highlights an even deeper issue; she criticises these histories for not delivering what 'it says on the tin', i.e., the 'social'.[83] In other words, although the importance of new understandings of the complex social structure of penal regimes is indisputable, questions arise about 'the people on the receiving end of these institutions'. Howe observes that these histories 'had little to say about prisoners of either sex'.[84] Thus, although critics have argued that women were 'invisible' in these penal-social histories, in fact, as better explained by Naffine, even 'men as males have never been the objects of the criminological gaze'.[85] This assertion is important because it emphasises the problematic relationship that new approaches to social histories might then have with the apparently 'male-oriented' benchmark of historical analysis. This is particularly visible in the approach originally taken by Women's Histories.

---

[79] Ignatieff, 'State, Civil Society and Total Institutions', p.77.
[80] M. Spongberg, *Writing Women History since the Renaissance* (Palgrave Macmillan, 2002), p.178.
[81] Naffine, p.2.
[82] Quoted in Spongberg, p.4.
[83] Howe, p.150.
[84] Howe, p.150.
[85] Cain (1990) quoted in Naffine, p.6.

The importance of paying attention to the 'social' aspect of social histories was gaining ground following the women's liberation movement of the 1960s.[86] By drawing attention to the 'invisibility' of women in historical writings, Women's Histories came to be accredited as a historical disciplinary approach. Indeed, Spongberg argues that the establishment of this branch of historiography has much to do with the emergence of feminist consciousnesses since the late nineteenth century.[87] In fact, the importance of Women's Histories lies in the rewriting of another layer of history, albeit within the same context as that previously prescribed by 'standard' (otherwise male-oriented) histories, which draws upon a different experience—that of women. Nevertheless, exactly how these histories should be written has been the subject of a contentious debate. Spongberg argues that Women's Histories have not simply followed either the Whig or the Revisionist style, but they have also further intensified contestation regarding the validity of these historical approaches.[88] Indeed, one of the questions posed by the feminist approach to historical writing, for example, has focused on the problem of constructing a feminine interpretation of history within a historical context that has already been shaped upon 'a masculinist vision of the past'.[89] Thus, it was suggested that one of the core aims for future history writing was 'to assert women's historical subjectivity and to question masculinist historiography.'[90]

The desire to break away from those social histories that were generic in nature, if not biased and male-oriented, also reached the area of penal history with Smith's 1962 work *Women in Prison*. Although Smith's history can be defined as a Whig type of history, soon other contributions followed a more Revisionist-oriented approach, such as Heidensohn's *Women and Crime* (1985) and *The Imprisonment of Women* (1986) by Dobash et al.[91] However, as with early Women's Histories, whether taking a Whig or a Revisionist approach, the theoretical standpoint of women's penal history developed out of an already grounded and undisputable historical knowledge. Perhaps the most significant perspective of these works, which

---

[86] Note that histories written by women are known to have existed since the Renaissance. For a thorough examination, see Spongberg's work.

[87] Spongberg, p.8; see also chapters 6 and 8 of her work in that regard.

[88] Ibid., p.2.

[89] Ibid., p.3.

[90] Ibid., p.8.

[91] A. Smith, *Women in Prison* (London: Stevens & Sons, 1962); Heidensohn, 1985; Dobash et al*., The Imprisonment of Women* (Oxford: Basil Blackwell, 1986) (in that regard, see also Zedner, p.98).

has been carried on by later studies, is the view of the female prisoner as a victim of the 'system' rather than a legitimate subject in her own right. This argument thus prompted the discourse about women offenders and prisoners being 'invisible' within the penal system; that is, their needs being ignored and unmet.[92]

At face value, this discourse is correct; indeed, prison historiographies have dedicated few, if any, pages reporting female prisoners' side of the story. However, once women's prison histories are thoroughly assessed, it becomes apparent that their historical analysis could be problematic. For example, studies by Smith, Heidensohn and Dobash et al. relied upon secondary data and official government documents. Indeed, reading through Smith's research, there is little indication that these secondary data were critically evaluated. Moreover, Heidensohn, for example, used the materials cited by Smith and did little to validate Smith's arguments. A good example of a secondary source used uncritically by the above historiographies is the well-known work by Sidney and Beatrice Webb, *English Prisons Under Local Government*.[93] This study is a critical examination of the political administration of prisons and the criminal justice system; however, whilst this fits nicely with future Revisionist and feminist historical writings about women's prisons and prisoners, the Webbs' focus of interest was pre-national penitentiaries (although also briefly looking at the Du Cane period). Only through later research by, for example, Zedner and McConville was it revealed that the above-mentioned women's prison histories (inspired by the Webbs) might have contributed to some misconceptions related to women's prisons; for example, by differentiating insufficiently between local and national prisons and the pre and post period of the national penitentiaries. In fact, these studies do not appear to reclaim women's subjectivity to any extent; they do little to 'shake' the 'standards' of preconceived notions generated by the available (male-oriented) prison historiographies.

*

The different approaches to historical penal writing undoubtedly have their strengths and weaknesses; these histories might unveil new findings or new historical frameworks, but they can also lead to a misguided understanding of events. One such example is the relationship between religion and

---

[92] In that regard, see Howe's discussion on Carlen's work (p.127-133).
[93] S. Webb and B. Webb, *English prisons under local government*, Vol.5 (London: Longmans, Green, 1922).

punishment, or rather, the reformation of the prisoner. The general understanding fostered by prison historiographers has been the centrality, whether supported or criticised, of religious enterprise in the project of prison and prisoners' reformation. Indeed, the 'penitentiary' itself, by definition and name, meant to play a pivotal religious role in the 1840s master-plan of administrative reform. One of the best examples celebrating this concept is the work by W.J. Forsythe, *The Reform of Prisoners 1830-1900*. Forsythe's analysis is interesting because it aims at rebutting the revisionists' critique of prison management and reformation by shifting attention to the overlooked 'great' evangelical involvement in prison reform, especially during the first half of the nineteenth century.[94] Indeed, history recounts that 'the leagues, associations, speeches and editorials that so invigorated public life in Victorian Britain were often Evangelical in origin'.[95] In fact, the involvement and engagement of evangelicalism, especially by the Quakers, in the penal sphere is indisputable; and yet, caution should be exercised when discussing, on one hand, ideology or policy and, on the other hand, their application.

The actual implementation of ideology and policy generated by the religious enterprise at any time was sporadic, limited, and when applied, inefficient. This is not to undermine the importance of the substantial amount of religious-related writing on the topic of the criminals and their redemption;[96] these writings have certainly contributed to the creation of what Ignatieff called 'the symbolic drama of guilt'.[97] And yet, despite recognising that this symbolic 'triumph of good over evil' constituted a Victorian imagining of 'the reform of the guilty criminal', Ignatieff nevertheless criticised 'Foucault's neglect of the religious vernacular of reform argument'.[98] Hence, the question might be asked whether 'institutional salvation' propaganda had any effect on prison reform and administration, and if so, how much. Certainly, there is a need for a prison history with a focus on religion; this will indubitably reveal a troubling story

---

[94] Forsythe's feelings about the work of the revisionists are expressed in his introduction, p.1-13 (W. J. Forsythe, *The reform of prisoners 1830-1900* (NY: St. Martin's press, 1987).

[95] D. Englander, 'The Word and the World: Evangelicalism in the Victorian City', in *Religion in Victorian Britain: Controversies*, ed. by Parsons, Gerald, Vol 2 (The Open University, 1988; repr. 1997) pp.14-38 (p.16).

[96] Forsythe uses these sources to construct his argument.

[97] Ignatieff, 'State, Civil Society and Total Institutions', p.92.

[98] Ibid., p.92.

of survival and power struggle in the wider context of religious uncertainties during the eighteenth and nineteenth centuries.[99]

Another issue to consider when reading prison history is that many of these writings tell stories of anonymous actors or, alternatively, use iconic names, such as Elizabeth Fry, John Howard or Edmond Du Cane, to highlight an era or particular perspectives. Indeed, there might be little record, if at all, of eighteenth and nineteenth century (and even later) prisoners' monographs; a fact that limits, to a great extent, prison history written from 'below'. However, there is a rich source of observations and personal reflections of people who were caught up in the trend of prison visiting, particularly during the late eighteenth and nineteenth centuries. Moreover, it appears that despite the contrasting historical analysis provided by the Whigs and Revisionists, they nevertheless have something in common: both appear to excessively accredit (negatively or positively) the input of those involved in the institutional management of prisons and prisoners. To some extent I agree with Ignatieff's 1981 'self-criticism', where he suggests that Revisionist histories provided 'distorting misconceptions' of the extent of state control and the 'monopoly over punitive regulation of behaviour', power relations, moral authority and social order and class subordination.[100] Indeed, I argue that an attentive historical analysis reveals that prison policy and the administration of prisons was largely uncertain, incoherent, inconsistent and less structured and systematic than was depicted by the two historical writing approaches.

Another significant consideration to make about histories of women's prisons and women prisoners is the critique by criminology writers suggesting that women have been invisible and ignored by the criminal justice system - a system predominantly created by men for men. However, despite the many reviews criticising the biased nature of the development of penal policy and practice, little evidence is brought to confirm that, indeed, women in prison were 'unforeseen' and 'somehow anomalous', as suggested by Priestly, for example.[101] Both his 1985 and 1999 editions rely heavily upon secondary data. In his two-page review on women prisoners, he notes that women 'were provided with separate quarters and female staff' and were 'protected to some extent by their sex from overly physical measures of repression'. He also points to the fact that babies could stay with their mother in a dedicated crèche until the age of one year. Following

---

[99] A good starting point to place religious enterprise in context is Englander, 1988.
[100] Ignatieff, 'State, Civil Society and Total Institutions', p.75.
[101] Priestley, p.69.

these remarks, however, there is a rather paradoxical statement that women were 'not otherwise dealt with all that differently (than men)'.[102] Similarly, Heidensohn's first and second editions (1985, 1996) reveal in an eight-page review on women's prison history a testimony of a prison matron in 1862 (which was recently discovered to have been written by a man) that 'women were allowed iron beds instead of planks, better uniforms and tea three times a week'.[103] However, similar to others, Heidensohn insists that 'during the nineteenth century women "enjoyed" the same regime as men in prison'.[104] Revisionist history and, more specifically, feminist prison histories have repeated mantras regarding power relations, women prisoners and female offenders with limited empirical support. In fact, a tenacious insistence on these claims is still maintained in the 5th edition of the Oxford Handbook of Criminology, in which Heidensohn repeats her inherently contradictory 1980s statement that: 'Since the start of incarceration as punishment, women have been subject to broadly the same prison system as men, but with distinctive variations introduced from time to time.'[105] This and similar statements appear to have acquired a 'common knowledge' status, so much so that no reference is provided to back it up.

However, research by Zedner, *Women, Crime, and Victorian England* (1994) has contributed new insight on the topic. First, Zedner's prison history is a more than 350-page dedication to the 'woman prisoner', thus filling the gap in prison historiography. The study is placed within the context of Victorian culture, and aspects of female criminality and related social perceptions are examined. However, most interestingly, Zedner's study is also concerned with the issue of prison policy and gender. Zedner suggests that 'historians […] have chosen to overlook the extent to which penal policy was differentiated by sex'. She goes on arguing that this 'has serious implications for the wider history of imprisonment in that it has led to a general portrayal of the prison as a place untouched by issues of gender'.[106] Moreover, unlike the authors of previous historical studies, Zedner uses a variety of primary sources to support her arguments. Inevitably, however, Zedner's work has also been subjected to some criticism. For example, Garland suggests that the study compromises its validity because it does not provide a comparative account of male and

---

[102] Ibid., p.69.
[103] Heidensohn, p.64.
[104] Ibid., p. 64.
[105] Heidensohn and Silvestri, p.353.
[106] Zedner, p.99-100.

female prisoners.[107] However, Garland's suggestion consists of a whole different study, with a different line of inquiry; why it is that the woman prisoner cannot own her own prison story? Wiener goes as far as arguing that Zedner's work might 'run the risk of distorting historical record' and that he 'would question whether the treatment of female offenders was quite so distinct from that of males as Zedner claims'.[108] In my view, these authors and others may have failed to acknowledge two issues: first, prison histories have not engaged much with identifying what the 'different' prison treatment imposed on the female prisoner might be expected to be —this should be investigated in a time-space context. Second, Wiener's comment above emphasises the misconception based on an overlap between 'different treatment' and 'bad treatment'; indeed, no prisoner escaped the claws of a degrading and sometimes deadly prison life, but this by no means implies that the treatment was imposed uniformly on both sexes.

*

Indeed, one of my main aims in writing a women's prison history has been to investigate the validity of the claim of 'women's invisibility' within prison policy, breaking away from the traditional male-oriented prison history framework. This historical investigation sheds light on the development of women's prisons and further supports Zedner's argument regarding the existence of a substantial level of sensibility towards the creation of a prison regime and policies that were thought to suit, albeit stereotypically, women prisoners.

The question to be asked, then, is which style of historiography I have adopted in my study. Rather than being categorised under either of the two main styles of prison historiography, I would like my historical writing to emulate those newer approaches that Marwick suggests have been affected by the opening of archives to the public (both on site and online), allowing the widening and deepening of critical examination of sources.[109] However, my study is also situated within a critical criminological context, thus investigating questions related to the experimental nature of the prison penalty, its state of 'crisis' and the validity of the discourse of prisoners'

---

[107] D. Garland, 'Women, Crime, and Victorian England. By L. Zedner (Oxford: Clarendon Press, 1991)', *British Journal of Criminology*, 33, 1, (1993) 113-115 (p.115).
[108] M.J. Wiener, 'Women, Crime and Victorian England by Lucia Zedner', *Victorian Studies*, 37, 1, (1993), 186-190 (p.189-190).
[109] See Marwick.

reformation. Therefore, the research also addresses penal perspectives, such as Carlen's 'carceral drawback', thereby responding to Howe's concerns regarding the need to further develop theorisation of imprisonment, particularly on the history of women's imprisonment.[110]

---

[110] Howe, p.157.

PART II

"REFORMING" THE PRISONER

This chapter focuses on the development of imprisonment as the main penalty from the late eighteenth century to the end of the nineteenth century. Historical sources of this period such as Parliamentary debates demonstrate that imprisonment as a main penalty was conceived as an experiment to abate a penal state of emergency. This shaped the foundation of prison policy. Personal writings, personal correspondence to the government and official reports clearly show that prison policies and prison discourses evolved out of 'spur of the moment' socio-political concerns. This, in turn, led imprisonment, as the main penalty, to be represented as being in a continuous state of crisis. It is for that reason that the legitimacy of this penalty has been routinely re-visited (or reinvented) to rationalise and justify its use. At the core of this discussion, and always considered to be one of the aims of imprisonment, is 'prisoners' reformation'. By examining policy and practice, this study reveals that 'reformation' is a concept formulated by socio-political discourse, but it has had little bearing in practice; hence, this aim of imprisonment is a myth.

The chapter begins by examining the slow shift in penal practice and the emerging new penal discourses. It first examines the extent to which the judiciary found it inconvenient to adhere to the strict framework of the death penalty policy; then, by drawing upon the punishment of female offenders, it considers the discretion applied by the judiciary to mitigate the lack of proportionality of this penalty. The chapter then addresses historical writings, such as Fielding's report on the state of robberies in the country, to assess some of the penal views typical of the mid-eighteenth century, namely, the understanding of the value of penal reformation. A brief evaluation of imprisonment as a secondary penalty follows, specifically focusing on gaols and houses of correction. This examination demonstrates that resources to sustain a reform of penal practice were still to be developed; and yet, penal policy saw the first experimental upgrade of prison as a penalty with the new arrangement of the labour houses through the Penitentiary Act 1779.

The chapter then turns to examine the development of the first penitentiary and its accompanying penal aims; in particular, the 'reform of the prisoner'. The discrepancy between the theoretical aspiration of this aim and its accomplishment in practice is examined. Next, Elizabeth Fry's prison reform is assessed in light of Pat Carlen's concept of 'carceral clawback', thus highlighting the first instance where, despite the drawbacks presented by the prison system, a justification for its use was nevertheless sought and found in the discourse of 'reformation'. The discussion then moves on to consider the systems of solitary and silent confinement as applied differently in the national (penitentiary) and local prisons in an attempt to further rationalise and justify the use of the prison penalty; here, the changing penal policy is assessed against its application to women's prisons. Finally, the last two sections of the chapter examine prison policy as shaped through the administration of the Directorate of Convict Prisons, and later the Prison Commission, and how these affected the administration of women's prisons, thereby addressing the nationalisation of the prison system and concluding with the period that prompted one of the most significant prison inquiries, held by the Gladstone Committee in 1895. Such a historical investigation will allow the examination of the 'reformation' agenda, assessing whether its implementation was indeed feasible in practice or whether it was merely a myth.

The Inconvenient Use of Capital Punishment

Prior to the introduction of imprisonment as a main penalty in the late eighteenth century, penance, fines, corporeal punishment, capital punishment and transportation covered the spectrum of the common penalties, and sometimes they took the form of the most disproportionate and atrocious executions.[111] Capital punishment has been the topic of a vast body of literature and remains a subject of debate and concern in twenty-first century society. However, to trace back the penal changes that led to imprisonment becoming a prime penalty, it is essential to briefly assess the events, social feelings and state of affairs that underlie these changes.

In the late eighteenth century, there was a sense of disapproval of what until then had been a legitimate social and moral penal practice. What was recognised as the 'Bloody Code' penal policy was now ill-suited to the rational and enlightened approach typical of this era which was responsible for the generation of legal concepts such as 'proportionality', 'individual

---

[111] See, for example, J.Q. Whitman, *Harsh Justice* (Oxford: University press, 2003).

justice', and 'fee individualism'.[112] Indeed, the statutes constituting the Bloody Code were named 'Bloody' for at least two reasons. First, the number of offences punishable by the death penalty was inconceivable (one Act could have generated hundreds of offences), but mainly, what was striking was the lack of proportionality in the punishment of lesser offences: capital punishment was similarly applied to, for example, the malicious shooting of a person (Waltham Black Act 1723), the theft of a sheep (Sheep Stealing Act 1741), and the stealing of a cotton cloth (the 1731 and 1745 Acts Against the Theft of Linen).[113] Moreover, the Code might have acquired its sanguineous reputation from being capriciously applied. For example, the case of Mary Jones stirred outrage in Parliament, when it was discovered that she was hanged for an offence that she did not (eventually) commit: she meant to steal a piece of linen from a shop counter but returned it when the shopkeeper saw her. She was nevertheless executed.[114]

Worse still was the inevitable label of the 'condemned'. Whitman reports that offenders and their families would be denounced in all possible aspects of social life, facing a life sentence of humiliation and the condition of social outcasts. A public 'putting on stage' would rank the offender and their relatives in a degrading status associated with the disgusting and horrific.[115] Those with 'convict status'[116] who would come to be perceived as a 'dangerous class'[116] were associated with ideas of threat and risk and therefore perceived as 'dirty' and 'polluted',[117] enhancing the need to preserve the integrity of the communal interests of safety.[118] This was particularly relevant in the case of women, for whom condemnation had notably devastating effects. Building up one's credentials was the only way to guarantee employment in domestic service; it established a respectable

---

[112] In that regard, see Norrie's discussion (A. Norrie, *Crime, Reason and History: A Critical Introduction to Criminal* Law, 2nd edn (Cambridge: Cambridge University Press: 2001), chapter 2.

[113] F. McLynn, *Crime and Punishment in the eighteen century England* (London: Routledge, 1989; repr. 2002), p. Xi.

[114] Reported by Cobbett in Parliamentary History of England, vol.9, 1777-78, cited by McLynn, p.125.

[115] Whitman, p.21.

[116] The concept would be further developed through the eighteenth century, where offenders in general were seen as a danger, especially morally, to society (L. Radzinowicz, *A History of English Criminal Law and it Administration from 1750*, Vol 1 [London: Stevens and Sons Ltd: 1948], p.401).

[117] Whitman, p.21.

[118] See also D.D. Raphael, *Moral Philosophy* (Oxford: University Press, 1994), p.68.

character, which, in turn, opened up the prospect for a future marriage.[119] The ruin of one's reputation, even by the mere suspicion of dishonest conduct, could mean the end of an honourable living and the fall into destitution. Isabella Stephenson, who was investigated for robbing her master in 1764, preferred committing suicide, knowing that her 'character' had been tarnished forever.[120]

Despite the wide application of the death sentence (this did not necessarily lead to actual execution), historical records demonstrate that Parliament and the judiciary had an ambiguous relationship with this penal policy. The Commonwealth period (1640s-1650s) was one of the first occasions in which dissatisfaction was voiced. Beattie argues that the proponents[121] of criminal reform presented a strong case for the mitigation of the death penalty for the crime of petty theft, arguing for a punishment that was proportionate to the gravity of the crime. Drawing upon the Holy Scriptures, these reformists saw the limits of moral applicability and pointed to the problem of diminishing the value of life by applying too harsh a punishment to property crimes. They suggested that the fatal consequence discouraged victims from prosecuting and encouraged the offender to kill the victim to avoid leaving a witness, thereby escaping prosecution. They also argued that it impelled jurors to acquit and it increased the practice of pardons.[122] The prospect for reform was almost tangible; however, in the years after the Restoration, the monarchy dismissed all propositions.[123]

The prospect of criminal reform did not occur again until 1750; however, in the meantime, it appears as though judges and juries ensured that, in practice, only a minority of offenders were ultimately executed. One of the problems faced by the judiciary in the application of capital punishment was that the statutes did not provide a mitigated or alternative punishment. However, the high level of discretion assigned to the judiciary allowed it to either commute the sentence to transportation or, in many other cases,

---

[119] In that regard, see historian Lucy Worsley's exposé in 'Housewives and Heroines: A 17th Century History for Girls', Lucy Worsley (presenter), Eleanor Scoones (director), BBC 4, May 2012.
[120] McLynn, p.125.
[121] Beattie considers that the Levellers, a political movement calling for 'popular sovereignty' and equality before the law, were involved in prompting and promoting new ideas for reform (J.M. Beattie, *Policing and Punishment in London, 1660-1750: Urban Crime and the Limits of Terror* [Oxford: Oxford University Press, Incorporated, 2001], p.280).
[122] Beattie, *Policing and Punishment,* p.280.
[123] Ibid., p.282.

approve an application for pardon.[124] Regarding this, research by Beattie provides invaluable statistical data specifically focusing on female criminality in the seventeenth and eighteenth centuries, further reinforcing the argument that women were not invisible in the criminal justice system, as they were in criminological writings. Beattie suggests that popular views were against sentencing women to death, in particular for theft (specifically in cases of domestic servants).[125] King's research further explores this by focusing on property offences tried in Essex up to 1830 (some of his research covers London too), demonstrating a complex but clear connection between gender and judges' discretion.[126] Significantly, King's findings indicate that for similar offences, men and women might have been sentenced differently, suggesting a far more lenient approach towards women.[127] However, King also clarifies that the limited historical sentencing records do not reveal much about why this might have been the case,[128] thus the wider context of the criminal justice system needs examination. No doubt, when it came to sentencing women, judges and juries faced a difficult dilemma. Indeed, according to King, female offenders were usually perceived as vulnerable and motivated by economic difficulties, having to provide for a number of children.[129] In many cases, the jury might have simply considered that it was costly and inconvenient - on the parish's behalf - to disintegrate the family by executing or severely punishing the mother; other times, sympathy and compassion for the wife with a 'dysfunctional' husband would lead the jury to opt for a lesser punishment for her unlawful means of providing for the family.[130] Similarly, in cases where prostitutes were prosecuted for robbing their clients, judges might have been more judgemental and less sympathetic towards their male 'victim'. For instance, when the court learned that the client of Margaret

---

[124] Ibid., p.290.
[125] J.M. Beattie, 'The criminality of women in Eighteenth Century England', *Journal of Social History*, 8, 4 (1975), 80-116 (p.92).
[126] P. King, *Crime, Justice, and Discretion in England 1740-1820* (Oxford: Oxford University Press, 2000).
[127] King, p.280.
[128] King, p.282.
[129] King, p.283.
[130] McLynn, p.125.

Faulkner spent three hours with her, the client's accusations of theft against her were dismissed and she was acquitted.[131]

Another concern faced by the judiciary when sentencing women was that women, until the 1690s, were not subject to the benefit of clergy, whose origins were in Medieval ecclesiastical practice. By claiming clergy, the offender escaped the death penalty and was instead awarded either transportation, imprisonment or any other corporal punishment. In the seventeenth century, any male offender could plead benefit of clergy by reading a verse from the Holy Scriptures. However, 'proliferate' and brighter criminals were able to recite the verse by heart, and it is not surprising that judges exercised some level of discretion in approving it. From 1623, women were also able to plead clergy, but only for petty theft below the value of ten shillings.[132] Thus, the introduction of transportation to the Americas in the 1650s, sometimes in the form of conditional pardon, was an appealing alternative.[133] This was achieved with the 1718 Transportation Act (recorded as the Piracy Act 1717 (4 Geo. I c.11)), by which hundreds of women were sentenced to transportation. The records indicate that from the 1670s until 1714, only approximately 30 women (none from 1700 to 1718) were sentenced to transportation. From 1718 to 1857 (the last year in which women were sentenced to transportation, destination Australia), approximately 10,254 women were sentenced to transportation by the Old Bailey. In addition, from 1700 to 1868, 35% of the total number of women found guilty in the Old Bailey were sentenced to transportation (although there is little data as to whether they were eventually transported), whereas only 5% were sentenced to capital punishment.[134]

Judges were eventually able to mitigate women's punishment further with the enactment of the 1691 Act (s.vi), which allowed 'Women convicted of Crimes for which Men have their Clergy, upon Prayer punished as Men'.[135]

---

[131] Beattie, 'The criminality of women', p.113, note 55.

[132] Beattie, *Policing and Punishment*, p.277. The benefit of clergy was completely abolished in 1827, following Sir Robert Peel's reforms (Criminal Law Act 1827 c.28 [7 & 8 Geo. 4]).

[133] Beattie, *Policing and Punishment*, p.293.

[134] Old Bailey proceedings, *search based upon the dates above*.

[135] J. Raithby ed., William and Mary, 1691: An Act to take away Clergy from some offenders and to bring other to Punishment [Chapter IX. Rot. Parl. pt. 1. nu. 7], Statues of the Realm: Volume 6: 1685-94, (1819), 311-312 British History Online, http://www.british-history.ac.uk/report.aspx?compid=46363, (accessed 13 Oct 2015); Beattie, *Policing and Punishment*, p.297.

Discretion in cases where no defence was raised, hence leading to an inevitable death sentence, might have been more complicated. For example, in the case of infanticide (in which the court could infer culpability for the death of the baby if proved that there was intention to conceal the body), it was not unusual for judges and juries to scrutinise all possible evidence to justify an acquittal.[136] In the case of Mary Martin's trial in 1759, the court found her not guilty despite evidence indicating that the baby had been dead for a week before it was found. Indeed, she was absolved of intention to conceal by presenting to the court baby linens (indicating her willingness to have the baby) and testimony by a midwife, who reported that there were no marks of violence on the baby.[137]

The judiciary's discretion is an important indicator of the general feeling and slowly evolving practice related to the death penalty. It is interesting to note that the yearly average of executions that took place in the City of London between the reign of Henry VII (beginning in 1509) and the end of the Commonwealth period (in 1659) was 180 (see Figure 1),[138] whereas from 1749 to 1799 the yearly average was only 34—almost half the number of the actual convictions for capital crimes in an average year (46%).[139] This is despite the sharp rise, from 1771 to 1787, in committals and executions indirectly caused by and during the American upheaval from the British Empire (1775-1783).[140]

---

[136] Beattie, 'The criminality of women', p.84.
[137] Quoted in Beattie, 'The criminality of women', p.111, note 15.
[138] Radzinowicz, A *History of English Criminal Law,* p.142. This data might just give an idea of the extent of the practice, but it should not be taken as an accurate reference because it is based on fragmented data and speculative calculations.
[139] Radzinowicz, A *History of English Criminal Law,* p.147.
[140] McLynn, p.260.

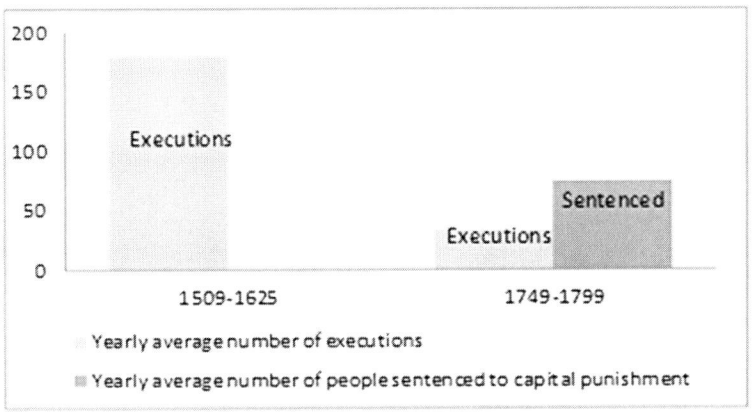

Figure 1: Yearly average of people sentenced to capital punishment and executed

During the Bloody Code years, from 1800 to 1810 (see Figure 2), the City of London and Middlesex recorded 939 capital sentences—157 of which were women[141]—but only 123 executions actually took place (both women and men), resulting in a yearly average of ten executions.

---

[141] *Old Bailey proceedings*, search based on related dates.

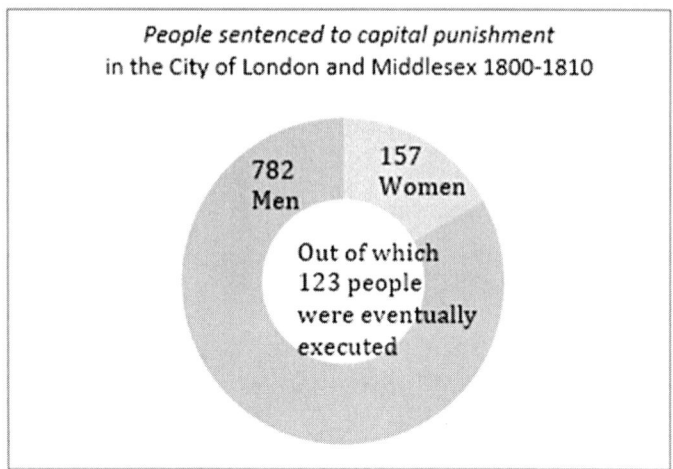

Figure 2: Sentences of capital punishment in the City of London and Middlesex, 1800-1810

The shift towards other forms of punishment is further emphasised by the increased use of these penalties as opposed to capital punishment. Radzinowicz indicated that in 1805, England and Wales recorded 595 people sentenced to transportation (see Figure 3). On a national level, 1,680 people were subject to some form of imprisonment and 158 people were either fined or whipped.[142]

---

[142] Radzinowicz, A *History of English Criminal Law,* p.160; *Old Bailey proceedings.*

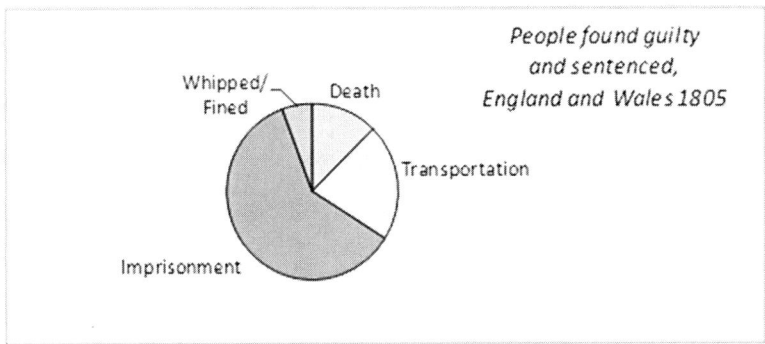

Figure 3: Found guilty and sentenced to one form of punishment, England and Wales in 1805

Indeed, records provided by the Old Bailey clearly indicate the shift in the use of punishment modes. Although people sentenced to capital punishment generally represented a smaller portion than those sentenced to transportation, from the 1750s both of these penalties were declining in use. Instead, imprisonment was slowly taking a central position among the core types of punishment (see Figure 4).[143]

---

[143] *Old Bailey proceedings* for the years indicated (people found guilty for any offence and sentenced to all punishments). The data in Figure 4 has as a total the following yearly averages of people found guilty and punished for each 50-year period: 284; 439; 1606; and 963.

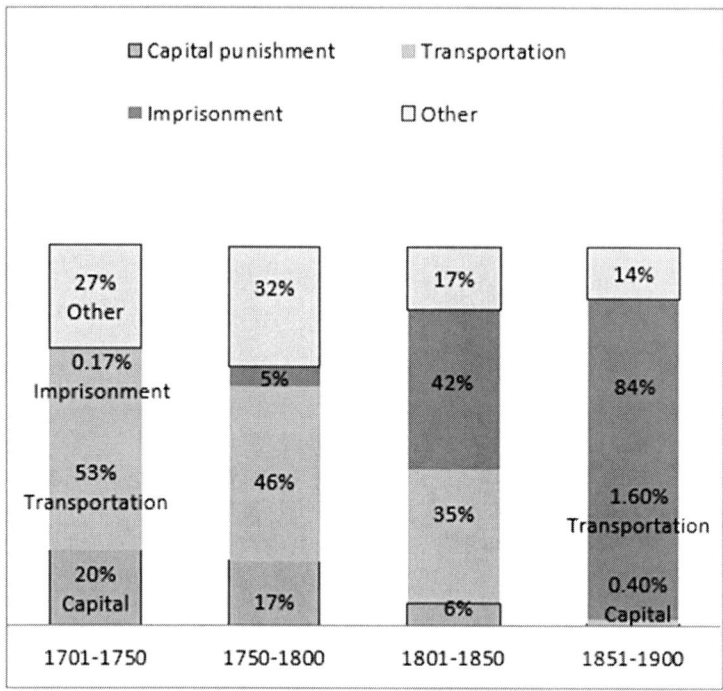

Figure 4: People found guilty and sentenced to one form of punishment in the Old Bailey

The Shaping of New Penal Discourses

It might be inaccurate to suggest that the capital punishment policy 'suddenly [...] collapsed' as suggested by Gatrell.[144] Drawing upon historical research, it is certainly arguable that 'there has been no greater nor more sudden revolution in English penal history than this retreat from hanging.'[145] If this was meant to be a revolution, it stretched over at least 80

---

[144] V. Gatrell, 'Execution and the English people', in *Key Readings in Criminology*, ed. by Tim Newburn, (Devon: Willan, 2009), pp.22-24 (p.23).
[145] Gatrell, p.23.

years,[146] defeating the requisite of being 'sudden'. In addition, the process was neither radical nor violent, and as explored earlier, the use of the penalty itself was mitigated by judiciary discretion; it was already applied less often to women offenders and was seldom thought to be a proportionate form of punishment.

Indeed, although capital punishment was challenged, albeit discreetly, in court and in many published writings, the reputation of the English legal system as the most liberal and advanced in Europe should not be underestimated when examining the slow evolution of penal reforms. According to Bentham, the government of England was 'the finest and most excellent of any of the world ever yet saw'.[147] Due to the pride generally felt by the English people for their institutions, Radzinowicz explains, Parliament was challenged to balance tradition with reform; thus, 'reform' was evaluated with suspicion. It is difficult to determine the extent to which the general public approved or disapproved of the capital punishment policy. However, according to Radzinowicz, the smooth passage of the statutes in both Houses of Parliament, and their prolongation, must have met with little public opposition-[148] at least until the 1750s.

However, the lack of effectiveness and consistency in the application of the death penalty was becoming the subject of extensive criticism. Despite the different moral standpoints, the writings across the century expressed similar concerns. For example, writings by early to mid-eighteenth century authors such as the anonymous author of the pamphlet *Hanging Not Punishment Enough,*[149] George Ollyffe's essay presented to Parliament *To Promote a Desirable Improvement and Blessing in the Nation,*[150] Reverend Martin Madam's *Thoughts on Executive Justice,*[151] and finally, William Paley's *Principles of Morals and Political Philosophy*-[152] commonly agreed that the penal law should be based upon the idea of deterrence and that punishment should be aimed at the prevention of crime; they explicitly

---

[146] Taking as a starting point for the process of reform Fielding's 1751 report, where its final point is Gatrell's indication as to the 1830s 'collapse'.

[147] Radzinowicz, A *History of English Criminal Law,* p.353.

[148] Ibid., pp.35-39.

[149] *Hanging, Not Punishment Enough, For Murderers, High-way Men, and House-Breakers*, (London: Warwick-Lane, 1701).

[150] G. Ollyfee, *An Essay Humbly offered, for an Act of Parliament to Prevent Capital Crimes, and the Loss of Many Lives: and to Promote a Desirable Improvement and Blessing in the Nation* (London: printed for J. Downing, 1731).

[151] M. Madam, Reverend, *Thoughts on Executive Justice* (London: Pall-Mall, 1787).

[152] Radzinowicz, A *History of English Criminal Law,* p.231-259.

argued for the legitimacy of capital punishment and considered it to be the most effective penalty in preventing crime. However, they also stressed that the penalty should be applied only as a last resort and to a limited number of offences.[153] Similarly, later in the century, writings by for example, Henry Fielding, William Eden and even Jeremy Bentham, introduced the novel concept of 'proportionality'; and although they did not explicitly and openly support the capital penalty, they did not call for its abolition either.

It could be argued that the challenges to capital punishment brought about a profound realisation: the recommendations for its proportional application, and hence its use as a last resort penalty, presupposed the need to reassess the management of the criminal justice system. This could be illustrated, for example, through Fielding's 1751 report on the state of robberies in the country.[154] It is interesting to note that Fielding was not opposed to capital punishment itself, but rather, as a justice of the peace and penal activist, he repudiated the way that it was carried out. Mainly, Fielding proposed that the executions should take place in private because they incited further crime and strong emotions among the public, which in turn glorified the executed.[155] However, his main concern, as it is the topic of his report, was with the crime of street gang robbery, the threat it posed on social order and ownership and the limitations of the criminal law in addressing it. According to Fielding's report, gang robbery was one of those offences in which the lack of evidence, limitations of criminal law, and a relatively high number of subsequent pardons, led to criminals being lightly, and hence disproportionately, punished. In other words, in these cases, due to the inconsistent and discretional application of the capital punishment, these offenders escaped executions or even the death sentence in the first place (despite being guilty of indictable offences).

Rather than recommending a more rigorous application of the death sentence, Fielding introduced a new approach to punishment, in which offenders could be given the chance to reintegrate into society after the 'completion' of the punishment. This permission to 'reintegrate' into or 're-

---

[153] For a comprehensive discussion on the different works, see Radzinowicz, A History of English Criminal Law, p.231-259.

[154] H. Fielding, An Enquiry Into the Causes of the Late Increase of Robbers, 2nd edn (London: A. Millar, 1751).

[155] Fielding, p.193. Radzinowicz interpreted Fielding's rather laconic discussion on the death penalty as evidence that 'he was in favour of a strict enforcement of all capital statute' and that it was 'obvious that Fielding was opposed to any curtailment of the scope of the capital punishment' (Radzinowicz, A History of English Criminal Law, pp.411, 413).

join' society became one of the typical characteristics of the modern prison penalty, but it is on the understanding of how this new alternative is meant to promote both individual and social justice as well as public interest that penal discourses have been shaped. Indeed, Fielding's report provides a thorough explanation of the thoughts underlying this new management of punishment, or rather, of offenders. Fielding was explicit in expressing his concern for some sort of a change of order in terms of social classes and their respective roles; the expressions 'luxury', 'morals' and 'evil' were used to emphasise this 'social disorder'.[156]

Fielding acknowledged that moving from one social order to another that is higher, and the 'emulation' of its respective habits was an issue faced at all levels of society; however, this issue had major implications when

> the very dregs of people, who aspiring still to a degree beyond that which belongs to them, and not being able by the fruits of honest labour to support the state which they affect, they disdain the wages to which their industry would entitle them; and abandoning themselves to idleness, the more simple and poor spirited betake themselves to a state of starving and beggary, while those of more art and courage becomes thieves, sharpers [sic], and robbers.[157]

According to Fielding, the 'lower order of people'[158] failed to cope with the 'excess' (or the need to obtain this excess); he suggested that the 'consequence must be ruin to many, who from being useful members of society will become a heavy burden or absolute nuisance to the public.'[159] Fielding's resolution was to emphasise education about the values of current acceptable 'morals' and 'habits'.[160]

This view was not fundamentally new; rather, it represented an approach that was already familiar, at least within socio-political practice. While Fielding replaced the word 'correction' with 'education', it is this concept of 'compliance' (or conformity and reformation) that penal discourses had in common throughout the seventeenth century and after. The consolidation of such a concept can be traced back to the Reformation of Manners

---

[156] Fielding, The Preface.
[157] Fielding, p.6-7.
[158] This is how he refers to the lower classes throughout his report.
[159] Fielding, p.16.
[160] Fielding carries out a philosophical argument in that regard in his preface and the first two chapters of his work.

campaign.[161] However, although Fielding was a member of that movement,[162] the second half of the eighteenth century was characterised by a much less controversial engagement than the one implemented from the 1690s to the 1730s, when this campaign was involved in an obsessive condemnation of immoral living.[163] In its initial formation the campaign was committed to 'assisting' justice by encouraging and bringing about prosecutions for petty offences and deviant behaviour. A sermon from 1727 instructed members about the

> duty of private persons to act subordinately to the magistrate and to render them capable of doing justice effectually in the way of information and testimony, as well as by assisting them in apprehending and conducting to due punishment all guilty persons […].[164]

Indeed, according to Shoemaker, over the span of 35 years ending in 1725, total committals to the Westminster house of correction increased by 86%, and similarly, over the span of 65 years ending the same year, total committals to the Middlesex house of correction increased by 165%.[165]

The campaign itself was supported by widespread printed propaganda that 'created a climate of feeling in which the establishment of prisons specifically designed to "correct" those guilty of petty offences might appear a useful contribution to social welfare'.[166] Inevitably, houses of correction came to be known as fulfilling the task of correcting those behaviours that offended social morals, namely, prostitution, adultery, bigamy, profane swearing, dice playing, drunkenness, slander and running

---

[161] More reading about this movement is available in *London Lives, 1690*-1800, T. Hitchcock et al., www.londonlives.org (version 1.1; last updated April 2012), Reformation of Manners Campaigns (reading list) http://www.londonlives.org/static/Reformation.jsp (accessed 19 Aug 2013) [hereinafter: *London Lives*].

[162] *London Lives*: Reformation of Manners Campaigns.

[163] Ibid.

[164] *Reformation necessary to prevent Our Ruin: A Sermon Preached to the Societies for Reformation of Manners, at St. Mary-le-Bow, on Wednesday, January 10th, 1727*, (London: Printed and Sold by Joseph Downing, in Bartholomew-Close, near West-Smithfield, 1728), p.6.

[165] R.B. Shoemaker, *Prosecution and Punishment: Petty Crime and the Law in London and Rural Middlesex, C. 1660-1725* (Cambridge: Cambridge University Press, 1991), p.166.

[166] J. Innes, 'Prisons for the poor', in *Labour, Law and Crime: An Historical Perspective*, ed. by F.G. Snyder and D. Hay (London: Tavistock Publications, 1987), pp. 42-122 (p.84); Shoemaker, p.166.

away from the master.[167] This aim of 'correction' is further emphasised in the 1727 sermon in which Lord Bishop of St. David argues against those who 'have most maliciously insinuated' that the purpose of work of the Reformation of Manners' members has been for financial gain; rather, 'it is hereby declared to the world, that such a charge upon these Societies is absolutely false' but it is 'Reformation which is intended'.[168]

The Question of Prison Upgrade

During this period interest in the principle of proportionality grew stronger and was accompanied by the need to realistically reassess the management of punishment. Views put forward by William Blackstone in his *Commentaries on the Laws of England*[169] and by William Eden's *Principles of Penal Law*[170] gave some attention to the matter.[171] For example, Blackstone briefly speculated that the secondary penalty of imprisonment might have the potential to take over from capital punishment. However, reports on this secondary penalty indicate that the resources available to sustain such a shift were yet to be developed. In practice, the secondary punishment of imprisonment came in the form of gaols and houses of correction— infamous places of detention that have been the object of debate of many historical and criminological writings.[172]

One of the first reports that openly brought the nature of gaols to wider attention was commissioned by the House of Commons in 1728, focusing on the Fleet and Marshalsea prisons.[173] The findings were not surprising in the least: they highlighted the keepers' gross management and the pitiful sanitary conditions in which the detainees were kept. In particular, the report contested the way of dealing with the sick and ill: not only were these individuals mixed with the healthy ones, but the ill were also poorly attended

---

[167] Innes, p.58.
[168] *Reformation necessary to prevent Our Ruin,* p.39.
[169] Blackstone, 1765.
[170] W. Eden, *Principles of Penal Law* (London: B. White and T. Cadell, 1771).
[171] For a discussion in that regard, see S. Devereaux, 'The making of the penitentiary Act', *The Historical Journal*, 42, 2, (1999), 405-433 (p. 411).
[172] See, for example, Innes; K. Grovier, *The Gaol: The Story of Newgate- London's Most Notorious Prison* (UK: John Murray, 2009); and Rusche and Kirchheimer, 2003.
[173] *A Report from the Committee appointed to enquire into the state of the Gaols of this Kingdom: relating to the Fleet Prison*, Great Britain Parliament House of Commons (London: R. Knaplock, 1729).

Without hope

to. For example, in the women's sick ward, one could see 'many miserable objects lying without beds on the floor, perishing with extreme want'.[174] In addition, one issue emphasised by the report was that the detainees paid for this 'lodging' but nevertheless were subject to hazardous living conditions. Indeed, the two cellmates of one Mary Trapps were denied transfer to another cell, despite Mary's escalating ill-health, 'and they were forced to lie with her, until she died'.[175]

Later reports recognised that gaols such as Newgate could be death sentences in themselves; indeed, another select committee noted that 'the allowance of food [...] is not sufficient properly to support life, without the assistance of friends, and casual charity'.[176] Every service incurred a fee; life in prison was expensive, and many detainees could not afford the cost of their release or the undoing of their shackling, let alone a bed, food or drink while imprisoned.[177] Only those who had money, or acquaintances kind enough to provide for them, could survive the short detention and avoid starvation, illness and death. Such was the case, a visitor to Newgate reported, for a detained woman who had to wear a metal cap until she was able to find someone who would pay the keeper for her head to be released.[178]

This was typical of the houses of correction too, but unlike the gaols, this mode of custody was part of a much more complex administration of punishment. In short, the houses of correction, or the 'Bridewell' (the 'hospital for the poor'), had been operating since 1553[179] as a welfare measure, allocating work rather than providing outdoor relief (i.e. benefits).[180] However, due to the aforementioned nature of the gaols, referring petty larceny offenders to the Bridewell hospital instead became a popular solution towards the end of the seventeenth century.[181] In addition,

---

[174] Ibid., p.4.

[175] Ibid., p. 3.

[176] A description made by a Select Committee of the House of Commons in 1814 quoted in J. Tobias, *Crime and police in England 1700-1900* (Dublin: Gill and Macmillan, 1979), p.155.

[177] Rusche and Kirchheimer, 2003 , p.62.

[178] Grovier, p.21.

[179] P. Hardman, 'The origins of imprisonment', *The Prison Service Journal*, 177 (2008), 16-22 (p.16). Only in 1865 did the houses of correction merge with the gaol to form the 'local prison' (Innes, p.43).

[180] Webb and Webb, p.13.

[181] Beattie, *Policing and Punishment,* pp.24, 26. Indeed, there is no indication of these procedures in the Old Bailey records, at least not before 1674, See *Old Bailey*

the Reformation of Manners movement, believing that offenders' morals were to be 'corrected' and 'reformed', brought about a surplus of prosecutions, making the use of the houses of correction inevitable. In fact, the understanding was that 'few or none are committed to the common gaol [...] but they come out worse than they went in. And few are committed to the House of Correction or Working House but they come out better'.[182]

It appears that magistrates found the houses of correction to be a better alternative for dealing with petty offenders, and especially women. Innes reports that women were committed to the houses of correction twice as frequently as men.[183] The penalty also stood, to some extent, as an unofficial substitute for the death penalty when discretion allowed. In fact, Beattie cites the examples of Mary Cooper, Suella Bellington and Ann Jones, whose offences (of a value beyond what would have been classified as petty)[184] should have been dealt with via a formal trial; they were instead diverted to the Bridewell court and sent to a short detention at one of the available houses of correction.[185]

Returning attention to the infamous conditions of these secondary punishments, Howard observed that as late as the 1770s, despite their committal to hard labour in the houses of correction (making them subject to some monetary remuneration, which was the core aim of the penalty), it appeared that prisoners could not sustain the costs of living. The reason for that was quite simple: very few houses of correction could provide any work, as most of them had no allowance for tools or materials.[186] Additionally, the great majority of the prisoners were malnourished or famished and in poor health; they were in no condition to be able to work in the first place.[187] This poor state of affairs was well known to the public, at least as reported by journals and magazines throughout the eighteenth century. In 1726, an article in the *London Journal* highlighted and condemned the abusive behaviour of the prisons' keepers (in both gaols and houses of correction), and it placed doubt on the 'corrective' effect of these

proceedings; also confirmed by Beattie, *Policing and Punishment,* p.27 including note 67.
[182] By Lord Coke, Justice of the Peace, quoted in Webb and Webb, p.14.
[183] Innes, p.85.
[184] For example, stealing pewter pots; stealing a gold ring and six shillings; and stealing cloths worth six shillings (Beattie, *Policing and Punishment,* p.29).
[185] Beattie, *Policing and Punishment,* pp.28-29.
[186] J. Howard, *The state of the prisons in England and Wales* (Warrington: William Eyres, 1777), p.8.
[187] Howard, p.12.

institutions.[188] The *Gentleman's Magazine* made it clear in 1757 that women detainees had no choice but to engage in prostitution to be able to eat.[189] In 1759, the same magazine reported the high mortality rate in the gaols and houses of correction,[190] and finally, an article from 1767 noted that 'the felons in this country lie worse than dogs or swine [...] The stench and nastiness are so nauseous [...] that no person enters there without the risk of his health and life'.[191]

Taking into consideration the state of these provisions, it is difficult to see how imprisonment could have provided the proportional punishment or 'correction' voiced by the Reformation of Manners campaign. In fact, making imprisonment the primary penalty was not the obvious option, as will be discussed shortly. Fielding reported in 1751 that the management and conditions of the houses of correction were not pertinent to any of their original or complementary penal aims, and resembled the old system depot gaols of exploitation and corruption. The houses of correction were 'no other than schools of vice, seminars of idleness, and common-shores of nastiness and disease'.[192] Subsequently, what was supposed to be 'correcting' in reality concealed harsh measures, such as extreme rationing of food and lack of water, corporal punishment, and no ventilation for fresh air. The lack of separation between men and women was the least of the prisoners' concerns: a house of corrections' record from 1711 indicates, for example, that 'one pregnant woman ate the hard flesh off her shoulder due to hunger'.[193] The gruesome state of affairs was described as follows by a shocked medical doctor during one of his visits:

> Vagrants and disorderly women of the very lowest and most wretched class of human beings, almost naked, with only a few filthy rags almost alive and in motion with vermin, their bodies rotting with bad distemper, and covered with itch, scorbutic and venereal ulcers.[194]

Setting Up the Experiment: Upgrading Imprisonment

Given the wretched conditions of the gaols and houses of correction, it is not surprising that both Fielding and Eden had a negative view of their

---

[188] *London Journal*, 19 March 1726, cited in Webb and Webb, p.21.
[189] *Gentleman's Magazine*, June 1757, cited in Webb and Webb, p.22.
[190] *Gentleman's Magazine*, January 1759, cited in Webb and Webb, p.20.
[191] *Gentleman's Magazine*, July 1767, cited in Webb and Webb, p.19.
[192] Fielding, p.96.
[193] Shoemaker, p.196.
[194] Dr William Smith in observation made in 1776, quoted by Webb and Webb, p.19.

value. Fielding considered the houses of correction to be a 'school of vice',[195] whereas Eden emphasised that imprisonment as a punishment was counterproductive, partly because it caused the deterioration of prisoners' morals, but mostly by 'being in its nature secluded from the eye of the people', it neutralised the deterrent effect.[196] Indeed, the preferred punishment, though sometimes difficult to implement, was transportation, and it continued to be until the mid-nineteenth century;[197] but although transportation was available for serious crimes, gaols and houses of correction were commonly used in petty crimes. For those who advocated penal reform, these places stood as a barrier to the illuminist (and to a great extent utilitarian) approach of social reform.

With this sense of uncertainty related to penal reform, the exposé of the state of the prisons presented to Parliament in 1777 by John Howard further emphasised the inappropriateness of currently available custodial resources. Incidentally, Howard was a member of the Reformation of Manners movement;[198] he supported custodial measures, but his interest in enhancing the general state of welfare was made clear by two Bills presented to the House of Commons in 1774: the first regulated the health and sanitary conditions of the prisoners,[199] and the second awarded relief to prisoners found not guilty so they could be immediately discharged.[200] His later contribution was a survey of 255 gaols, houses of correction and other facilities used for detention purposes, such as castles.[201] He noted that since his visits prior to 1774, some improvements had been made, but the conditions were nevertheless so degraded that when inside the prisons, he had to place a jar of vinegar under his nose to mitigate the stench.[202] According to Howard, women detainees had better care in London (at least they were not shackled), and generally, women debtors were better provided for than women felons and those who had committed misdemeanours.[203]

---

[195] Radzinowicz, A *History of English Criminal Law,* p.409, note.34.
[196] Eden, p.44.
[197] The *Old Bailey Proceedings* demonstrate that the year in which prisoners were last sentenced to transportation was 1857; also see S. Devereaux, 'In place of death: transportation, penal practice and the English state 1770-1830', in *Qualities of mercy: Justice, punishment and discretion,* ed. by C. Strange (UBC Press, 1996) pp.52-76.
[198] Webb and Webb, p.32.
[199] 14 Geo 3, C.59.
[200] Discharged Prisoners Act 1774 c. 20 (14 Geo 3).
[201] Howard, p.147-477.
[202] Howard, p.13.
[203] Howard, p.33.

Conditions were nevertheless unbearable: there was almost no separation between sexes, age, type of offence, or physical illness. Prisons seemed to accommodate not only the young children of a detained mother, but the whole family. Howard's recommendations were rather thorough, and they also provided a model-plan of a prison. The new prison design, although simple compared to future designs, was to include a dedicated ward for women felons and a separate section for women debtors; it designated a 'mother and baby' unit with proper beds and a fireplace with a chimney.[204] It is essential to note, however, that his recommendations did not intend to go beyond what was essential to keep good health and strength for work— Howard did not 'advocate for extravagant and profuse allowance to prisoners'.[205]

However, these specific thoughts and ideas on the need to better the custodial conditions of prisoners appeared to be the personal call of a handful of people. Moreover, Devereaux reveals that 'detention' in itself, as the potential main penalty, was not put forward as the immediate solution; rather, it was the principle of hard labour that was to constitute the apex of penal reform.[206] This is clearly expressed by the procedures that brought about the eventual passage of the Penitentiary Act in 1779.[207] In fact, both the 1776 Hulks Act (prison ships) and the 1779 Penitentiary Act were initially titled to express the core aim of these penalties: the first was originally phrased in terms of hard labour by way of cleaning the Thames shores,[208] whereas the 1779 Act was drafted as the 1778 Hard Labour Bill. Most importantly, however, Devereaux explains that to overcome opposition and to secure the passage of both Bills, Eden reassured Parliament that these were to be considered an

> experiment, more particularly to answer the spur of the occasion. When tranquillity was restored to America, the usual mode of transportation might be again adopted.[209]

---

[204] Fireplaces were sometimes available, but because the rooms had no windows, the smoke was released into the room (Howard, p.71).

[205] Howard, p.62.

[206] Devereaux, 'The making of the penitentiary Act', p.411.

[207] Transportation, etc. Act 1779 c. 74 (19 Geo. 3, c.74). The draft of the Act was the result of the preliminary work of William Eden and William Blackstone in the preceding years.

[208] Criminal Law Act 1776 c.43 (16 Geo.3).

[209] Eden quoted in Devereaux, 'The making of the penitentiary', p.411.

The 'experiment' presented to Parliament with the original proposal of the 1778 Hard Labour Bill was, in fact, well received in intellectual quarters, which welcomed the prospect of an abetment of transportation. Drawing upon a treatise on the subject by Jeremy Bentham, himself one of Eden's supporters, it appears that the new proposed penalty reflected an important socio-political discourse. Indeed, the 'labour houses', as they were termed in the Bill, materialised both economic and socio-moral objectives: on one hand, the profit gained by the prisoners' labour was meant to guarantee a self-sustaining system, thereby reducing public expenditure; on the other hand, the labour itself was thought to 'improve' the convicts' 'morals' by allowing them to develop a 'habit of steady and well-directed industry'.[210] According to Bentham's utilitarian and humanistic perspectives, the 'labour house' was an 'equal' penalty because unlike transportation, where only money could buy off the servitude, 'liberty', in the case of labour houses, was to be regained by all. In addition, the new penalty was national and, as such, visible to the public, thus satisfying the requirement of deterrence.[211] In that regard, Bentham further confirmed that the houses of correction were unfit for the purpose of labour, but he was convinced that the desired hard labour regime could be finalised in the new labour houses.[212]

It is important to note that these new Houses of Hard Labour (in total, there would have been at least eighteen)[213] were designated to accommodate offenders who had originally been sentenced to death: 'any person convicted of robbery or felony liable to death without benefit of clergy, can be subject to the King's mercy but upon condition of hard labour'.[214] The aim of the new policy was not to redefine (or reclassify) gaols and houses of correction; rather, the Houses of Hard Labour were to function as a specific type of custodial penalty.[215] The draft of the Bill clearly indicated that the core of the new custodial facilities was the hard labour 'so far as may be consistent with his or her health and ability'. This included a variety of activities such as treading in a wheel, drawing in a capstan for turning a mill, beating hemp, rasping logwood, chopping rags, sawing timber, working at forges, and smelting. However, as opposed to the modern

---

[210] J. Bentham, *A view on the Hard labour bill* (London: T. Payne, T. Cadell, P. Elmsley & E. Brooke, 1778), p.27.
[211] Bentham, p.3.
[212] Ibid., p.2.
[213] Devereaux, 'The making of the penitentiary Act', p.421
[214] *Draught of a Bill to punish by Imprisonment and Hard Labour*, Great Britain. Parliament, (London, 1790), p.24.
[215] Devereaux, 'The making of the penitentiary Act', p.421

criminological view concerning the lack of 'visibility' of women in the penal system (or rather, in penal historiography), the content of the Bill, in fact, placed attention on age and sex: it specified when regulations were applicable only to male detainees and devised a 'lighter' set of activities for the 'weaker' prisoners, such as making ropes, spinning yarn, knitting nets and similar.[216]

Clearly, Bentham was impressed by this future penalty; he noted that 'there is something singularly characteristic in the foresight and humanity displayed in this provision'.[217] Indeed, he seemed to consider the eventual 'return' of the convict to society once her sentence was completed to be a social achievement. However, the applicability of the future Act was problematic from the outset: Eden and Blackstone's plan proved to be too extravagant. It introduced an expensive system, with the hope that it could eventually sustain itself by drawing upon prisoners' labour. The applicability of labour might not in itself have been, necessarily and initially, the main drawback. Rather, it was the introduction of an undesired and controversial whole new system of regulations, responsibilities and obligations that had little precedent in the past.[218]

The final content of the Act passed in Parliament was not what Eden had intended, so that Blackstone determined 'never again [to] concern myself in a measure of this kind, unless it be taken up before Christmas; when Gentlemen's heads are cool and nothing else interferes with the business'.[219] First, it was anticipated that the principle of hard labour would not be popular; thus, Parliament was persuaded to pass the Act by renaming the Bill the Penitentiary Act.[220] Second, from a total of at least eighteen such new prisons to be built around the country, the Act reduced the provision to only two, emphasising, once again, that it was intended as an experiment and not as a replacement for transportation. Third, the Act removed the wording intended to differentiate these new prisons from the old gaols, houses of correction and any other form of custodial confinement available at that time (including workhouses), thus nationalising the expensive standard of this new regime. Finally, what was meant to mitigate the burden of costs carried by local governments struck the final blow to the

---

[216] *Draught of a Bill to punish by Imprisonment*, p.27.
[217] Bentham, p.66.
[218] Devereaux, 'The making of the penitentiary Act', pp.419, 422.
[219] Blackstone to Eden quoted in Devereaux, 'The making of the penitentiary Act', p.432.
[220] Ibid., p.429.

implementation of the Act: the provision that Parliament was to sustain the initial costs for the buildings and maintenance was by no means feasible.[221]

The issue of prison management was under continuous scrutiny, and was expressed in an increasing number of writings, observations and testimonies of various visitors to the prisons. One such observation was made by the Earl of Wedderburn in 1790; his suggestions were indicative and further fortified the socio-political aims developed around penal and prison reforms. The Earl argued that every prisoner should be employed, and this, he suggested, could be achieved by seclusion, total separation at night and solitary work.[222] Other observations, such as James Neild's, emphasised the ongoing state of crisis in the custodial facilities at the turn of the new century.[223] Neild assessed 611 custodial facilities across the country from 1800 to 1811. He found that of these, 53 prisons had no prisoners at all and 141 prisons accommodated less than ten prisoners. The only prison he considered to have decent facilities for women prisoners was Aylesbury in Buckinghamshire, which was operating as a hospital-type house of correction (Bridewell). Otherwise, he noted that the situation was 'as petty as described by Howard'. For example, in the Brecon South Wales gaol, he found two women: 'they were literally naked, without shoes or stockings, heavily loaded with double irons' who were eventually removed by the keeper as a personal favour to Neild.[224] In the notorious Clink prison,[225] he found three men and an ill woman confined together. Neild learned that the men had gathered enough money to buy straw to use as a mattress and donated some to the woman; the gaol-keeper lent her a blanket and let her spend the day in his accommodations, and so, she eventually recovered. Finally, in Tiverton Town Bridewell, Neild saw a woman whom he had met

---

[221] Ibid., pp.428, 430-1.
[222] A.R. Wedderburn, *Observation on the state of English prisons, and the means of improving them; communicated to the Rev Henry Zouch a Justice of the Peace* (London, 1793), pp.14, 17. Other contributions were made by V. Mainwaring, *Thoughts on the construction and management of prisons* (London, 1786); J. John, *Thoughts on the construction and policy of prisons, with hints for their improvement* (1785); and *Report of the sub-committee respecting the improvements which have been lately made in the prisons and houses of correction in England and Wales* (London, 1790).
[223] J. Neild, *State of the prisons in England, Scotland and Wales, Justice of the peace* (London: John Nichols and Son, 1812).
[224] Ibid., pp. ix-xiv, 1, 17, 21, 69.
[225] Borough Compter in Southwark, London.

in a previous visit to the prison three years earlier, still waiting to be transported.[226]

Straw for a bed

The Penitentiary Dream

Despite the compromised passage of the 1779 Act, adjustments to penal and prison policy were nevertheless taking place within the wider context of social reform typical of the time. This was a period when religious movements assiduously promoted charity and philanthropy; new philosophical and political views questioned the value of legislation and the administration of the economy; campaigns questioning the legitimacy of the criminal law were supported by Parliament; and finally, various social policy initiatives were engaged in amelioration of the infrastructure, such as the improvement of paving, lighting and sanitation.[227] Subsequently, Parliament seemed to be more receptive to the idea of a national penitentiary. The Commons debate in March 1811 openly supported the

---

[226] Neild, pp.57-58.
[227] S. McConville, *A history of English prison administration, 1750-1877*, Vol 1 (London: Routledge, 1981), pp.78-88.

option of having imprisonment as a main penalty; Sir Samuel Romilly
advised that the inquiry committee appointed to investigate such a prospect
should assess 'the comparative advantages of confinement in penitentiary
houses with imprisonment in the hulks (prison ships), and transportation to
New South Wales'. He went on to argue that 'the first of those punishments
might frequently be substituted, with benefit both to the culprit and the
public, for the two last'.[228] Interestingly, by that time, the term 'penitentiary'
had already been in use in penal practice. Versions of penitentiary-like
prisons had been gaining ground since shortly after 1779;[229] their small-
scale success was nevertheless taken as indicative of their ability to respond
to socio-political concerns for penal reform:

> For the last twenty years Penitentiary Houses had been erected and
> governed in conformity to the rules expressed in the first statute [...] (taking
> as an example) the utility of such an establishment in Gloucester; [and] in
> Southwell the usefulness of the institution had been such, that several
> persons who had been confined there were now living in credit, and atoning
> to society for their former crimes.[230]

The initiative for the construction of a national penitentiary was set by the
Holford Committee's findings: 'leave be given to bring in a Bill for the
erection of a Penitentiary House.'[231] However, Sir Romilly 'expressed his
regret that the scale recommended by the honourable member was so small,
as if it was intended only as a plan of experiment.'[232] In fact, to persuade
Parliament, the Committee's recommendation diverged to some degree
from the one formulated not long before by a previous committee chaired
by Bentham.[233] The Holford Committee's plan was to erect a limited
number of penitentiaries, designed for only a select number of prisoners.
Bentham's Panopticon, by contrast, was supposed to 'go national', thus
accommodating a huge number of detainees with the prospect of replacing
the hulks and transportation (a view supported by Sir Samuel Romilly).[234]
However, Parliament considered Bentham's plan too extravagant. Hence,
Holford reduced the jurisdiction of the penitentiary to just London and
Middlesex, limiting its reception to 200 men and 200 women.[235] Bentham's

---

[228] Penitentiary Houses, HC Deb 4 March 1811 vol 19 cc186-8 (cc187).
[229] McConville, *A history of English prison administration*, pp. 89, 98.
[230] Mr. Holford, HC Deb 21 January 1812 cc235-9 (c. 237).
[231] Ibid.
[232] Ibid., Sir Romilly (c. 239).
[233] Ibid., Sir Romilly (c. 238).
[234] Ibid., Sir Romilly (c. 239).
[235] Ibid., Mr. Holford (c. 237).

grand plan was further shrunk by reserving the penitentiary for the sole confinement of offenders sentenced to transportation, with the aim of sparing them from Newgate.[236]

Although the Holford Committee diverged from Bentham's earlier plan, it was nevertheless inspired by it, so much so that it 'snatched' Bentham's site in Tothill Field, which was bought specifically for the construction of the Panopticon.[237] Subsequently, the Penitentiary House Act's long title read as follows:

> An Act for the erection of a Penitentiary House for the confinement of offenders convicted within the City of London and County of Middlesex; and for making compensation to Jeremy Bentham, for the non-performance of an agreement [...].[238]

This was not the only gaffe; the absence of any consolidated management of the 'project' would, in the near future, foster cracks in the system (and in the foundation of the building).[239] The ten years of construction, starting in late 1812, saw an excess of spending, almost triple the prisoner capacity,[240] and a building that gave the impression, according to Mayhew and Binny, 'of a gigantic puzzle; and altogether the Millbank prison may be said to be one of the most successful realisations, on a large scale, of the ugly in architecture.'[241]

The new regime at the newly built (but not yet completed) Millbank penitentiary was tested upon 40 female convicts coming from Newgate on 25 June 1816, all of whom were sentenced to transportation or life imprisonment.[242] For a short while, Millbank appeared to successfully follow standardised techniques in the upkeep of the prisoners that led to reasonably improved custodial conditions, especially in terms of sanitation

---

[236] Ibid., Mr. Holford (c. 236-237).

[237] McConville, *A history of English prison administration*, p.135.

[238] Penitentiary House, etc. Act 1812 c.44 (52 Geo. 3).

[239] In that regard, see T.F. Buxton, *An inquiry, whether crime and misery are produced or prevented by our present system of prison discipline*, 6th edn (London: Black Horse Count 1818).

[240] McConville, *A history of English prison administration*, p.136.

[241] H. Mayhew and J. Binny, *The criminal prisons of London and scenes of prison life* (London: Griffin, 1862), p.234.

[242] 'New Penitentiary, Millbank', *The Times*, 27 June 1816, p.3.

and sleeping arrangements.[243] Indeed, Buxton's visit to the penitentiary about a year after its opening left him with positive impressions: the penitentiary had a chaplain and a surgeon, the prisoners were at work, and the place was 'remarkably clean, and free from offensive smells'. He saw women detainees engaged in cooking, washing, ironing, and various kinds of needle-work, reporting that 'their behaviour gave (him) a very favourable impression of the effects of employment, with religious instruction'.[244]

Labour was still considered to be the core of this penalty, where Millbank's governor confided that 'the grand secret was employment. Labour was the right hand of the police'; yet, Buxton found that, in fact, not all prisoners were employed. In his published report, Buxton hesitantly noted the dangers associated with prisoners' lack of employment, which could lead to 'an experiment of the effect of idleness';[245] this, he discovered, was a sensitive issue. Indeed, Buxton was obliged to make a formal apology to Millbank's authorities. The prison's governor asserted that there were no drawbacks in the system and prevention of its full implementation was only due to its being in the initial stages of operation. Buxton replied: 'I should not have felt warranted in offering advice, which I now see to be wholly needless.'[246] However, future developments indicate that Buxton's initial impression was more than merely accidental; rather, hard labour as a core aim of the modern prison penalty would be short-lived and the 'reform of the prisoner' discourse would accordingly accommodate this shift, while the reality of prison life would prove to be in dissonance with this latter aim.

If labour in prison was the ultimate aim of this newly devised penalty, prison management struggled to integrate what was considered to be the core purpose of punishment, i.e., deterrence, with the later theoretical development of the idea of 'offender's reformation'. Indeed, the Holford Committee clearly stated that 'prevention' and 'improvement of the mind' were the core objects to be pursued in terms of imprisonment.[247] However, McConville explains that the confusion in the pursuit of these two aims stemmed from the fact that these represented two different penal philosophies: the first

---

[243] The Times reported: "the cells were very comfortable, lofty with an arch and glazed window, furnished with an iron bedstead, table and stool, and warmed by flues placed in the passage" (quoted in G.W. Playfair, *The punitive obsession* (London: Victor Gollancz LTD, 1971), p.33).
[244] Buxton, p.107.
[245] Ibid., p.108.
[246] Ibid., p.112.
[247] The Holford Committee (1811-1812) quoted in McConville, *A history of English prison administration,* p.131.

combined rewarding labour and disciplinary sanction, whereas the other advocated the principles of seclusion and religious instruction.[248] Labour in itself appeared to be a problematic feature in this new context. In retrospect, the chair of the Committee, Mr Holford, recognised the limits of hard labour in the production of any profit, and it became clear that it could not cover prisoners' upkeep. Thus, 'labour' as the core and originally intended aim of prison policy became a loose feature of imprisonment, applicable, as later advised by Mr Holford, for the mere sake of exercise.[249]

With the erection of the Millbank national penitentiary, imprisonment was recognised and upgraded to function as the main penalty in the English penal system. The modern prison penalty was meant to replace capital punishment but also to mitigate the drawbacks of the widely preferred penalty of transportation. Inevitably, liberal, utilitarian and humanistic perspectives informed and shaped the understanding of the aims of modern imprisonment: labour was meant to be at the core of this penalty, functioning as a device to minimise public burden while the person was serving the sentence but also to allow an effective and law-abiding social integration once released. However, this new penalty was the object of contrasting aims, and the lack of clarity and expertise regarding the application of these within the context of imprisonment resulted in widespread poverty, reoffending, permanent illness and the death of detainees. More significantly, what was thought to be the core principle of imprisonment, i.e., reformation, was, in fact, almost impossible to attain. Indeed, the inspector of prisons, Mary Gordon, reported that

> once branded with the name, the girl's chances of a respected life or honest employment are often over. She is practically, to use a common phrase, 'ruined', and bankrupt of all character.[250]

'Carceral Clawback' and Elizabeth Fry

The above-described state of the 'new' prison penalty triggered a threefold socio-political position: First, imprisonment acquired a negative connotation; it was clear that the penalty was counterproductive to crime reduction. It was suggested that

---

[248] Ibid., p.160.
[249] G. P. Holford, *Thoughts on the criminal prisons of this country* (London, 1821), p.65.
[250] Gordon, p.99.

whilst society, in theory, appeared to be punishing individuals for past offences, they were in fact not only providing leisure and opportunity to learn, but even masters to teach the mode of committing more extensive and injurious crimes.[251]

Second, the squalid reality of imprisonment contributed substantially to the social gap and social segregation. The lack of basic hygiene and water supply to wash, the sleeping conditions on the bare floor or of more than three in a bed, the lack of heating and scant feeding with a poor diet which might be only bread and water, the small, crowded rooms and the lack of clean air, ventilation and light[252] reduced existence to the job of mere survival. Unsurprisingly, then, the general perception was, according to the social reformer Mary Carpenter, that 'these poor women, these female convicts, will then usually prove to belong to a perished class, which exist in our state as a something fearfully rotten and polluted [...]'.[253]

Therefore, a third- somewhat inexplicable- position developed with the need to further emphasise, in one way or another, that imprisonment's task was not only to deter others from committing crimes but also to 'reform' those apprehended.

At this point, Pat Carlen's concept of 'carceral clawback' can be used to explain prisons' historical durability, namely, 'the power of the prison constantly to deconstruct and successfully reconstruct the ideological constitutions for its own existence'.[254] According to Carlen, carceral clawback is also indirectly facilitated by those who advocate penal reform, where instead of questioning the legitimacy of imprisonment, they contribute to reshaping—albeit uncritically and unsuccessfully—'regimes designed to reduce both the pain and the damaging effects of imprisonment'.[255] Indeed, throughout the late eighteenth century and the beginning of the nineteenth century, the prison system saw a continuous reinvention of its purposes, aiming to mitigate its drawbacks and to suit governmental, professional, reformist and public views, discourses and

---

[251] G.E Fry, *Sketch of the origin and results of Ladies' Prison Associations, with hints for the formation of Local Associations* (London: A & J Arch and Hatchard and Son, 1827), p.3.
[252] For notes about the conditions of the various prisons he visited, see J.J. Gurney, *Notes on a visit made to some of the prisons in Scotland and the North of England in company with Elizabeth Fry* (London, 1819).
[253] M. Carpenter, *Our convicts*, Vol. 2 (London: Longman, 1864), p.208.
[254] Carlen, 'The Case of Women's Imprisonment', p.116.
[255] Ibid., p.116.

socio-political policies on the administration of social justice. Specifically relating it to the carceral clawback of the prisoners' reformation discourse, Kennedy refers to it as the 'welfare approach by imprisonment',[256] a term that emphasises the tendency to 'top up' the prison sentence with a variety of policy agendas such as rehabilitation programmes, education, employment, etc.—all aiming at justifying the use of imprisonment even for the pettiest of offences. The clawback concept illustrates the dynamic through which the prison system tightened its grip on the foundations of penal administration, despite being challenged regularly, as reflected in a comment made by the Pennsylvania Prison Society journal:

> Volume after volume, and pamphlets without number have been sent forth from British and Continental press, in addition to the reports and official manifestoes [...] We give the details of this brief sketch of prison discipline inquiries, at the risk of wearing out the patience of the well informed, by the repetition of familiar facts.[257]

As a result, imprisonment became so grounded in the social fabric that its legitimacy as a penalty was not challenged per se; rather, it was the prisons' physical conditions and their regimes that led to ceaseless efforts of prison 'reform'.

In fact, the earliest example of such a carceral clawback can be seen in the work of Elizabeth Fry. Elizabeth Fry's contribution to the development of social awareness during the first part of the nineteenth century was crucial— she was a pious noblewoman driven by strong Quaker[258] morals and social concerns about the ill and the needy. However, although she worked towards the abolition of the death penalty, for example, she also maintained the threefold socio-political view described earlier with regard to imprisonment (i.e. it is counterproductive; it produces a perished and dangerous class; but still, it should be geared towards reformation). The legitimacy of the prison penalty was not questioned; rather, the incorrect application of the punishment was at the core of her concern. Elizabeth Fry set in motion the first carceral clawback, in the sense that her prison

---

[256] H. Kennedy, *Eve was Framed: Women and British Justice* (London: Vintage, 2005, 1st edn 1992), p.85.
[257] *The Pennsylvania Journal of Prison Discipline and Philanthropy*, Vol 3, 1847-8 (Philadelphia: E.C. & J. Biddle, 1848), p.5.
[258] The Religious Society of Friends was founded in England in the seventeenth century. The Quakers are Christians, but they cannot be identified with the Catholic, Orthodox or Protestant denominations (see J. Marsh, *A Popular Life of George Fox: The First of the Quakers* [London: Charles Gilpin, 1847]).

engagement produced visible agreeable outcomes in relation to prisoners' reformation, which inevitably contributed positively to arguments supporting the prison penalty and its reformative aim. Indeed, the Quakers' views on charity meant that they focused their work on improving the person, and the environment and therefore the legitimacy of the prison *per se,* was overlooked. In other words, Elizabeth Fry and her company (e.g. Elizabeth Fry's brothers (The Gurneys) and husband), rationalised the use of imprisonment as a means to mitigate the 'despoiled characters' of the prisoners. The Quakers were able to afford such a charitable engagement where they integrated the values they endorsed, such as Puritanism, modesty and simplicity, with the wealth which was produced by their assiduous industriousness (e.g. the Gurney family had a successful banking business).[259] As stated by Hislop: 'Fry determined to give them [the prisoners] the habit of order, sobriety and industry, which the Quakers believed were the key to life whether you were a banker or a convict'.[260]

The prison environment that Elizabeth Fry was first confronted with is described by Grey in one of his visits to Newgate:

> Women who had committed petty offences found the company of women who were charged of murder. The women were then mixed all together, young and old; the young beginner with the old offender; the girl for the first offence, with the hardened and drunk prostitute; the tried with those under sentence of death; all were crowded together, in one promiscuous assemblage, noisy, idle, and profligate; clamorous at the greetings, soliciting money, and begging at the bars of the prison, with spoons attached to the ends of sticks.[261]

Elizabeth Fry learned that despite the occasional engagement in household chores such as cooking, washing, ironing, needle-work, knitting, sewing and spinning,[262] the majority of women were living in pitiful prison conditions. A combination of the 'corrupted environment' and deteriorating health conditions due to lack of proper food, clothing and ventilation[263] led the

---

[259] 'When Bankers were Good', Hislop, Ian (presented), Ford, Helena (director), BBC 2, 23 November 2011, 11.50pm.
[260] Ibid.
[261] B.H. Grey, *A letter to the common council and livery of the city of London: on the abuses existing in Newgate: showing the necessity of an immediate reform in the management of that prison,* 2nd edn (London, 1818), p.282.
[262] Buxton, p.114. In Millbank prison in 1818, women were paid £6 per annum for such chores.
[263] Fry, *Sketch of the origin and results of Ladies' Prison,* p.4.

women to spend most of their time drinking, playing cards, reading improper books or, as revealed by Buxton, exploring the mysteries of fortune telling.[264] In another of his observations, Buxton noted that 'two women were seen in the act of stripping a dead child, for the purpose of clothing a living one'.[265] Elizabeth Fry's resolution was to use personal influence to gently 'convert' the individual nature of the detainees:

> We may still hope that even the chance and unintentional interruption of their evil life, improved by kindness and pastoral ministration, would awaken their dormant sensibilities, and lead their thoughts to repentance.[266]

More specifically, Elizabeth Fry's plan was to change the inborn 'criminal character' of the women and to prevent them, while they were in prison, from growing worse,[267] targeting a 'moral reformation' or, in her words:

> To civilize and cultivate the minds of ignorant criminals. To rise, in any degree, the standard of their intellect or their state is a work which will not fail to produce beneficial results. Those who have been brought under a refining process of this description will not so readily, as before, yield themselves to the guidance of impetuous passion and brutal violence. They will become susceptible to superior motives; they will rise in the scale of being.[268]

The 'reformation' of the prisoner was to be combined with a reform of the prison regime, which included an emphasis on inspection, employment, instruction and classification.

However, Carlen poses an important question that should be asked even in light of Elizabeth Fry's magnanimous contribution: 'why do such absurd obfuscations about the possibilities of a benign prison persist and multiply?'[269] The answer lies in Carlen's own concept of 'clawback'. Indeed, Elizabeth Fry and reformers in general rationalised the use of

---

Most of the visits made to the different prisons around England reported similar conditions. However, Gurney recalls the visit made to York Castle (a county jail), where apart from insufficient light, the rooms and sleeping cells appeared to be comfortable, clean and ordered; the women were busily employed in washing for the debtors and seemed to be very decent (p.5).

[264] Buxton, p.126.

[265] Buxton, p.126.

[266] *The Pennsylvania Journal*, p.193.

[267] E.G. Fry and J.J. Gurney, *Report addressed to the Marquises Wellesley, Lord Lieutenant of Ireland* (London: A & J Arch, 1827), p.8.

[268] Fry and Gurney, p.17.

[269] Carlen, 'The Case of Women's Imprisonment', p.116.

imprisonment as a means to mitigate its own consequential effects or, to quote Mary Gordon, the 'ruin' of a girl.

In fact, the reform programme was launched with a series of rules and regulations—many of which mirrored the requirements set down in the Penitentiary House Act of 1812. First, a matron was put in charge of domestic arrangements, while monitors appointed from the group of women prisoners were to oversee the women's conduct. Male prison officers were forbidden access to the women's wards and were denied any sort of communication with them, to avoid any unwanted provoking effect on the prisoners. Female prisoners had to be placed only under the supervision of female officers because it was believed that 'one matron will be able to maintain far greater order amongst a number of female criminals than several male turnkeys. Her influence is less exciting and is at once safer and more powerful.'[270] These rules were further extended, whether implemented fully or partly (if at all), in the various custodial institutions across the country. For example, the 1822 booklet 'Rules, Orders and Regulations' for the county gaol and Bridewell in Fisherton Anger, replicated some of Elizabeth Fry's instructions. It stated that employment should be adopted 'as shall be best suited to his or her strength and ability; regard being had to age and sex'.[271] The booklet restates the importance of providing a matron for the management of the female ward. This emphasis appeared also in the 1835 'Rules and Regulations' booklet for the house of correction and gaol at Aylesbury. Indeed, the rules stressed that 'the male and female prisoners shall be confined in separate buildings [...] to prevent them from seeing or conversing or holding any intercourse with each other'.[272]

To support the carceral clawback argument in this period, it is essential to draw attention to the positive expressions of appreciation fostered by Elizabeth Fry's interventions. For example, an acquaintance noted that in one of his visits, 'instead of a scowl, leer, or ill suppressed laugh', he found women who were doing needle-work while listening to the readings of one of the Lady Visitors. He also 'observed upon their countenances an air of

---

[270] E.G. Fry, *Observation on the visiting, superintending and government of female prisoners* (London: A & J Arch, 1827), p.26.
[271] Rules, Orders and Regulations, for the Government of the County Gaol and Bridewell at Fisherton Anger, Salisbury: Brodie and Dowding, Easter 1822, p.10 (London National Archives [hereinafter: LNA] HO 20/1/59A)
[272] Rules and Regulation for the Government of the Gaol and House of Correction at Aylesbury, printed by the Court at Easter Quarter Session, 1835, p.5, (LNA HO 20/4/31)

self-respect and gravity, a sort of consciousness in their improved character.'[273] Furthermore, the Lord Mayor of London and the inspection committee of Aldermen 'resolved unanimously' to thank Elizabeth Fry and the Lady Visitors 'who have so kindly exerted themselves […] and that they be requested to continue those exertions, which have hitherto been attended with such good effect.'[274] Additionally, the following abstract from a letter sent to Elizabeth Fry in 1820 by one of the women prisoners, who had been detained in Newgate in 1817, exemplifies this appreciation:

> Honoured Madam, the duty I owe to you [...] compels me to take up my pen to return to you my most sincere thanks from the heavenly instruction I derived from you and the dear friends [...] that the world may see that your labour in Newgate has not been in vain in the Lord [...] and although we may never meet on earth again, I hope we shall all meet in the realms of bliss, never to part again.[275]

However, the attention was not always desirable. It is important to note that currently, hundreds of books can be found about Elizabeth Fry's life and her various charitable engagements; however, her work at the time was to some extent carried out in an 'underground' manner. In her collection of memoirs, she expressed her concern about publicity; once she was publicly exposed, her work was thoroughly scrutinised. Indeed, her daughter recounted that 'at that time [1818] Newgate had become almost a show': curious supporters and dissenters 'flocked to witness the extraordinary change that had passed over the scene'.[276] Moreover, according to her daughter, despite the enthusiastic collaboration of many of the prisoners, 'the officers of the prison, as well as the private friends of these ladies, treated the idea of introducing industry and order into Newgate, as visionary.'[277]

Within this context of support on one hand and belittlement on the other, the uncertainty of the aims of imprisonment was exposed; in fact, the foundations of Elizabeth Fry's work were never really secured. Interestingly, her memoir reviles a threat posed by a parallel movement of

---

[273] Elizabeth Fry's acquaintance visiting Newgate with her permission in 1817, quoted in K. Fry and R.E. Cresswell, ed., *Memoir of the life of Elizabeth Fry*, Vol. 1, 2 (London: J. Hatchard and son, 1848), p.268.

[274] Communication sent to Elizabeth Fry following an inspection by the above Committee in 1817, quoted in Fry and Cresswell, p.258.

[275] From Harriet S. letter to Elizabeth Fry quoted in Fry and Cresswell, p.263-4.

[276] Ibid., p.303.

[277] Ibid., p.258.

social reformists, specifically one person: Robert Owen.[278] Robert Owen of New Lanark, as he came to be known, was himself an activist, campaigning against children's employment and exploitation, promoting children's education and revising the Poor Law.[279] In fact, Robert Owen was inspired by Elizabeth Fry's work, and an overwhelmingly positive tone is clearly apparent in one of his first articles discussing her enterprise. Indeed, following a visit to Newgate, Robert Owen was struck by 'extraordinary instances of compassion'. He was particularly impressed by the women prisoners' admiration of Elizabeth Fry; he noted that they 'looked on her as human creatures might be imagined to look upon beings of a superior intelligence and beneficent nature'.[280] Robert Owen shared his astonishment that 'this change from the depth of misery to the state described' was achieved in only '*three months*'.[281] Despite this apparently marvellous publicity, Elizabeth Fry was aware that Robert Owen's ideology was fundamentally different from hers or, as she put it, he had been 'distinguished for his wild and theoretical views'.[282]

Undoubtedly, Elizabeth Fry's prison work brought about significant changes; however, it also emphasised the experimental state that the prison was operating under. Elizabeth Fry's success was an exception, fostered by the relatively small number of female detainees, whereas the male prison population did not experience much improvement from her methods. In his visit to Newgate, Robert Owen noted the sharp contrast between the female ward and the male ward, which 'was most revolting to common sense human feelings'; he thus urged the government to adopt Elizabeth Fry's methods all over the prisons' estate.[283] Regarding Elizabeth Fry's approach, he concluded by saying that:

> This principle, when it shall be well understood and rightly acted upon, will effect more for the substantial happiness of mankind than all the moral and

---

[278] Fry and Cresswell, p.282.

[279] Some of his major works: *A New View of Society: Essays on the Formation of Human Character* (London, 1813) and *The Revolution in the Mind and Practice of the Human Race* (London: Effingham Wilson, 1849).

[280] R. Owen, 'Hints, Plans and Proceedings of Benevolence', *The Literary panorama, 1806-1819*, 6, 36 (1817), 989-994, p.990.

[281] Italic in original. Owen R., 'Hints, Plans and Proceedings of Benevolence', p.991.

[282] Fry and Cresswell, p.282.

[283] Owen R., 'Hints, Plans and Proceedings of Benevolence', p.991.

religious system that have ever yet, at any period, or in any country, been forced upon the human mind.[284]

Robert Owen's vision of prison reform was shared and expressed by other prison activists, such as Reverend Sydney Smith. And here is what Elizabeth Fry's previously mentioned concern rested upon: Reverend Sydney Smith's standpoint was made clear in the influential political magazine *Edinburgh Review* in 1821: 'a return to prison should be contemplated with horror'.[285] It is of little surprise that Robert Owen's inspiring 'principle' turned out to be a twisted version of what Elizabeth Fry was in fact implementing, in her words, 'to civilize and cultivate the minds of ignorant criminals'.[286] This further emphasises the continuing state of confusion that the prison system was operating under, while also indicating a couple of additional issues: Reverend Sydney Smith voiced the view that Elizabeth Fry's approach was too holistic (to use a modern term) and did not seem to pay off. According to Harding et al., Reverend Smith 'rejected the idea that the first aim [of imprisonment] was to reform the criminal';[287] in particular, although 'he felt moral and religious instructions to be valuable', he 'rejected Fry's methods which extended to general education'. For Reverend Smith, prisons should function as an exercise in penitence, thus 'teaching' prisoners 'by sad experience to consider it as the greatest misfortune of their lives […].'[288] Also, it seems as if a financial drive rather than a socio-moral one was at the core of future changes; clearly, Elizabeth Fry's methods, which relied on private funds and volunteers, had to be re-evaluated, given the increasing (disproportionately male) prison population.

The Local and the National

Thus, frugality and penitence, the solutions put forward to cope with a growing prison population, led to the adoption of the notorious, and extensively documented, 'Separate System'. A short sketch of this development reveals that two custodial tools, the Philadelphia (Separate) system and the Auburn (Silent) system, were almost equally applied in the United States at the end of the 1820s. However, in the 1830s, the first system appeared to be more popular in England, as its 'philosophy' provided

---

[284] Owen R., 'Hints, Plans and Proceedings of Benevolence', p.992.
[285] Quoted in C. Harding et al., *Imprisonment in England and Wales: A Concise History* (London: Croom Helm, 1985), p.138.
[286] Fry and Gurney, p.17.
[287] Harding et al., p.137.
[288] Ibid., p.137-8.

answers to the unsuccessful implementation of prison-labour and the 'reformative' pursuit of the English custodial system, thus responding to the need for much desired 'prison reform'.[289] The Separate System was initially implemented in 1842 at Pentonville National Penitentiary, and as explained by Forsythe, this was to experiment, once again, with penal servitude.[290] The detainees were expected to live in absolute silence in solitary confinement both night and day for a period of 9 to 18 months; thereafter, they were either employed in public work or deported overseas.[291] The authority for this system, the Pennsylvania Society, emphasised that although

> it is very unnatural to isolate men and seclude them in separate cells; it is not more unkind, than to isolate an individual with the plague, and keep him under medical treatment, until the contagion shall have been removed, and the individual be fit to resume the duties of life.[292]

Indeed, the 'reform of the prisoner' remained a desirable aim of imprisonment, notwithstanding the consideration of new arguments. For example, it was suggested that the Separate System aimed at marrying the guilty with God in a state free of 'promiscuous' influence. In other words, the belief was that separation 'inevitably tends to arrest the progress of corruptness [...] day after day with no companion but his thoughts the convict is compelled to reflect and listen to the reproofs of conscience.'[293]

It is known that only the penitentiaries Pentonville, Millbank and Brixton, run by central government (thus national penitentiaries as opposed to local prisons), implemented the Separate System. However, even in these grand scale prisons, what was envisaged to be at the core of prisoners' reformation, i.e., moral penitence, prevention of corruption and public deterrence, instead led to further repression, excess of power and violent treatment – detention methods worse than those recorded at the beginning of the century. The religious idea that isolation would achieve penitence and reflection generated instead loneliness, idleness and madness. Susan Willis Fletcher, once a detainee, confessed after her release that

---

[289] See, for example, Harding et al., Chapter 4, and Forsythe, Chapters 2-3.
[290] Forsythe, p.25.
[291] Ibid., p.25.
[292] Reynolds, Rev R.V., *The outcasts of England* (Wakefield: John Stanfield, 1850), p.1, quoted in Priestley, p.37.
[293] *Report of William Crawford to Lord Duncannon on the American Prisons*, vol. XLVI, (1843), p.12, quoted in Forsythe, p.27.

cold, darkness, silence, and solitude [...] are not curative or reformatory, or humanizing [*sic*] influences. They disease the body, and depress, stupefy, and debase the mind. Their tendency is to fill it with gloom, hatred, and depression.[294]

Indeed, the standards of prison life fell below the official lower margin of 'minimum requirement of health' set in 1850 by a Royal Commission.[295]

Moreover, the implementation of the Separate System in the local prisons was either partial or it was not applied at all. For example, regarding solitary confinement, a report presented to Parliament in 1863 noted that 'it scarcely forms any part of the ordinary treatment of criminals, except as a punishment for prison offences, for which purpose it is found to be very effective'.[296] In fact, most of the local prisons operated according to the Silent System, which was economically affordable. However, like the national penitentiaries, the conditions in the local prisons were also gruesome. For example, an inspection conducted in Ilchester Gaol reported that many of the reforms brought about by Elizabeth Fry were present, yet the management of the gaol had major drawbacks: the inspection recorded the case of Mary Cuer, a prisoner who was still breast-feeding her baby when she was sent to the solitary confinement cell during the winter as a punishment for quarrelling with another female prisoner. The cell lacked heating, the diet provided consisted of bread and water, and she was not allowed to use the money granted by the parish for her maintenance; it was observed that 'her own milk having, under these privations, failed entirely, no mitigation to the suffering of the infant, could be derived from that source [the parish]'.[297]

---

[294] S.W. Fletcher, *Twelve months in an English prison* (Boston: Lee and Shepard, 1884), pp.403-404.

[295] Rusche and Kirchheimer, p.108.

[296] *Report on the Present State of Discipline in Gaols and Houses of Correction*, Select Committee of the House of Lords Minutes of evidence, Great Britain. Parliament. House of Lords (Dublin: Irish U.P., 1863), p. IV.

[297] *Report from the Commissioners appointed to inquire into the state of Ilchester Gaol*, The House of Commons, 8 February 1822, p.10 (LNA HO20/1/79).

Solitary confinement

Both the Separate System and the Silent System functioned as the 'new' justifications for the use of imprisonment; whichever approach was followed, it meant to reform the prisoner to become a remorseful and moral social being. Moreover, these two systems have had a considerable share in shaping socio-criminological discourses, particularly in relation to women prisoners. One of the main arguments, developed from an understanding of the roles of these two systems in the process of prisoners' reformation, established the perspective that women offenders' and women prisoners' penal treatment was affected by a social consensus about social conformity as well as feminine images of womanhood, albeit stereotypical.[298] Indeed, historical penal writings clearly indicate that female and male reformers alike shared this understanding of the feminine role upon which the eventual 'reformation' should be based. This reflection is important because it suggests that first, although based on stereotypical perceptions, reformers understood the need to implement prison regimes for women that were at least moderately different from those applied to men. In other words, this suggests that stereotypical ideas had a share in the shaping of discourses about women prisoners' reformation. Inevitably, however, because this approach was driven by stereotypical views, it was unlikely that the reformers would 'get it right'. In other words, what the reformers thought was suitable for women was not always experienced as the best option, as noted by the matron of Tothill Fields House of Correction. The matron explained that the Silent System was, in fact, not found to be the best alternative to the Separation System (as it was thought to be): due to women's natural sociability and their lower levels of self-discipline, the imposition of silence was not only difficult but also psychologically damaging.[299]

Women's-prison histories written about this period have suggested that women '"enjoyed" the same regime as men'.[300] However, the 'few sops to mitigate its [penal treatment's] harshness' referred to pejoratively by Heidensohn,[301] should not be underestimated. In fact, these 'few sops' were enough to provide the moral and socio-political justification needed to sentence women to prison even for the pettiest of offences, thus fortifying the clawback paradigm. Indeed, there is a need to understand how, in practice, this new penal policy (the Separate and the Silent) affected the management of women prisoners and how it fit within the 'reform of the

---

[298] See, for example, Zedner's discussion on that topic.
[299] Cited in Zedner, p.106.
[300] Heidensohn, p.66.
[301] Ibid.

prisoner' discourse. Criminologists have presented the perspective, as argued by, for example, Smith and Heidensohn,[302] that penal developments during this period (1840s-1860s) were shaped to address the male prison population; thus, 'women did not fit easily into the centralised, national system which aimed to standardise conditions in local prisons'.[303] Heidensohn went so far as to consider McConville's observation about the contrast between the management of male prisoners and female prisoners[304] as a 'lofty and detached comment' that 'misses the central issues of comparison and equality in penal system'— that is, as she insisted, 'the purpose of penal systems was clearly to address *male* delinquency and crime'.[305] Nevertheless, these accusations might be problematic, especially in light of Zedner's and McConville's suggestion that historical studies of women's prisons had overlooked the distinction between local prisons and national prisons (penitentiaries). More specifically, Zedner and McConville argue that examining local prisons and national prisons as if they represented the same thing and functioned for the same purpose has led to possible misconceptions regarding the development of women's prisons.[306]

In practice, the majority of the female prison population was accommodated in local prisons, which might explain why Smith and Heidensohn and many other scholars have considered the national penitentiaries to be a predominantly male-oriented environment. Moreover, the authority for the Separate System, the Pennsylvania Society, made clear in one of its first publications with reference to the English female prisoner that what was applied in Pentonville was not intended to likewise be implemented on women prisoners; rather, the Pennsylvania Society was in favour of 'hours of society and fellowship to sustain the spirit',[307] a view further supported in the House of Lords.[308] Interestingly, the 'reform of the prisoner' was not exhausted with the argument of deterrence, penitence and moral change; but in the case of women prisoners social integration post-prison was recognised as almost impossible. Therefore, the 'female version' of the

---

[302] Smith, 1962; Heidensohn, 1985.
[303] Heidensohn, p.65.
[304] McConville, *A history of English prison administration,* pp.425-428.
[305] Italic in origin. Heidensohn, p.65.
[306] See Zedner (1994) and McConville, *English Local Prisons 1860-1900: Next only to death* (London: Routledge, 1995).
[307] 'Female Penitentiaries', *The Pennsylvania Journal,* p.196.
[308] Whitworth Russell, evidence in HL select Committee on Goals and Houses of Correction (1835), cited in Zedner, p.116.

Separate System regime included their eventual removal to Fulham Refuge; most importantly, this removal was aimed at 'erasing the considerable stigma of being recognised as a female ex-convict'.[309] This perspective was plainly expressed by Fulham Refuge's governor; he hoped that people who might be intimidated by the idea of employing women ex-prisoners could 'be induced to take them from a benevolent institution such as a refuge'.[310]

The Directorate of Convict Prisons: Reformation by Discipline

The drawbacks of the prison system and prisons' and prisoners' reform through seclusion and hard labour were re-evaluated under a new Directorate of Convict Prisons which took on the task of managing the so-called penitentiaries. With Joshua Jebb's appointment as Chair of the Directorate, the ideas of 'reclaiming one's soul' and 'penitence' were giving way to a more systematic, military-like understanding of 'reformation'. Jebb argued that there was no sense, considering the short sentences, in dwelling upon an 'internal reformation'; rather, 'reform' should aim at preventing 'dissemination of vice' by facilitating labour.[311] In other words, the 'reform of the prisoner' responded to the need to 'produce prompt and entire obedience';[312] the link between military discipline and penal discipline became fundamental, as Jebb clearly emphasised in his first 1850 report on the convict prisons.[313]

The Directorate of Convict Prisons created a new tool for the administration of prisoners' reformation, namely, the Progressive Stage System.[314] This tool is still at the core of the twenty-first century English prison system, but its introduction in the mid-nineteenth century had the specific aim of replacing transportation with imprisonment. The rationale adopted was conceptualised in terms of 'proportionality'. Here, however, 'proportionality' is not to be understood as the utilitarian perspective of proportional-just-

---

[309] Zedner, p.171

[310] Revd J.H. Moran (1854), quoted in Zedner, p.182.

[311] Harding et al., p.155.

[312] A commentator of the time quoted in McConville, *A history of English prison administration*, p.180

[313] C.B. Jebb, *Report on the Discipline and Management of the Convict Prisons* (London: W. Clowes & Sons, 1851).

[314] See Jebb. This system was developed out of the Classification System already implemented during Elizabeth Fry's time.

human-retributive punishment; rather, 'proportionality' in this context meant supporting the justification for the use of the prison penalty even for those who until then could not escape a sentence of transportation. Hence, for those 'convict prisoners' who would normally be sentenced to transportation, the prison penalty had to be commensurate with the onus brought about by the penalty of transportation. As Jebb explained:

> If separate confinement be considered a privilege, or be disregarded, by an educated criminal, the labour of quarrying on the heights of Portland or Dartmoor (prisons) would wear a very forbidding aspect; and the further prospect of being compelled to engage and work for wages in a distant colony, under many restrictions, would be even more distasteful.[315]

Indeed, as suggested by Jebb, proportionality was achieved by first bringing to the fore the aim of penal deterrence and second, reformulating the understanding of 'reformation' by introducing the concept of 'discipline'. More specifically, reformation through discipline was meant to be achieved with an initial period of separate confinement, followed by a period of labour. The most compliant prisoners passed to the final stage, which guaranteed a 'ticket-of-leave', known as the 'licence'.[316]

However, the alternative to transportation, that is, the convict prison sentence, was not indiscriminately applied to women and men. In fact, Jebb's writings exemplify the common perception about the 'difference between the mental and physical conditions of the sexes.'[317] Jebb's report indicates that more than half of the male convicts at Portland were put in work such as quarrying and dressing stones for building, paving and breakwaters, whereas for female convicts, the authorities had to provide work that could be performed by the less physically able.[318] The job market was also taken into account: female prisoners should not compete for work with female seamstresses and washerwomen outside prison so they were employed in sedentary indoor labour such as rough sewing, knitting, cooking, baking, cleaning and laundering.[319]

---

[315] Jebb, p.48
[316] Ibid.
[317] *Reports of the Directors of Convict Prisons*, 1854, Brixton Prison (London: Spottiswoode, 1855), p.367.
[318] Jebb, p.30.
[319] Zedner, p.191-2.

Mary Carpenter's assessment of prisons for female convicts offers further emphasis of this point: she noted that 'the system and arrangements in them must necessarily differ from those for male convicts, for there is a very great difference between the inmates'.[320] Indeed, in the case of women prisoners, 'reformation by discipline' was informed by the understanding that imprisonment for women was recognised as a hindrance to social integration and the regaining of respectability for work and marriage purposes. Hence, the newly devised progressive system of reformation involved four months of separate confinement, as opposed to the 9 or 12 months served by the men.[321] This period was spent at Millbank, shaven-headed, working in their cells picking coir with an option to upgrade to needle-work.[322] This stage was considered the 'probationary class' (or the 'third class'); the progression to the 'second class' required the transfer of prisoners to another custodial facility. Although male convicts were transferred to the newly devised 'public works' prisons,[323] women were supposed to be relocated to Brixton.[324] There, the matron confirmed that the prison's rules would be applied in a flexible manner depending on the individual character of the prisoner and that 'without this individual treatment the attempt to reform them [the women prisoners] would be most superficial.'[325] The last stage for female convicts was their removal to Fulham Refuge.

Even under this new policy of 'convict prisons', as devised by Jebb, the system still revealed severe drawbacks. First, the transfer of prisoners from one prison to another for the purpose of progression proved to be unfeasible. Despite the comparably small number of women sentenced to penal servitude (thus sent to the convict prisons), Millbank, Brixton and Fulham Refuge became saturated and overcrowded; thus, the movement from one prison to the other was impractical.[326] This was not all. It was said that the Progressive Stage System displayed too much leniency, and the sentences were too short to produce any deterrent effect or worthwhile reformative outcome.[327] Moreover, there was little accountability across the prison estate; formal prison inspections were irregular and infrequent and thus

---

[320] Carpenter, vol 2, p.207.
[321] Zedner, p.179.
[322] Smith, pp.125-131.
[323] See Jebb.
[324] Report of the Surveyor-General (1853, p.64), quoted in Zedner, p.181.
[325] Emma Martin (1863), quoted in Zedner, p.187.
[326] Smith, p.94.
[327] Ibid., p.96.

unable to ensure good practices in general, something particularly needed in the local prisons.[328]

The attack on the prison system was further enhanced by the media; unsurprisingly, however, it drew public attention to the faults in the aims of imprisonment rather than being concerned with its actual existence. Of particular interest is an anonymous article published by the *Edinburgh Review* in 1863. Here, the author noted that 'the country is in the midst of one of its occasional panics about its convicts [...] the evil is very pressing, there is not a day to lose in dealing with it.'[329] However, the convicts themselves were the least of the author's concern. The article in fact criticised the prison administration for the 'ignorance [it] has been exhibit[ing]' and the 'nonsense' discussion around prison discipline. The author accused ministers and Parliament of shifting 'from one ground to another, and chang[ing] their minds' as to what the prison penalty sought to achieve.[330] Interestingly, the article's anonymous author reported that some people contested the legitimacy of the prison penalty (although there is no specific indication as to whom), and voiced a desire for the return of transportation.[331] However, the article's author, in fact, did not support this view; rather, the question of how to manage prisons to achieve the aim of reformation was at the core of the argument put forward by this anonymous critic. Views on prison policy still insisted on the centrality of prison reformation in one form or another; the above-mentioned anonymous author considered that 'reformation, to any extent whatever, requires that offenders should be dealt with individually'.[332]

Inevitably, political debate was also triggered, leading to the appointment of the Carnarvon Committee in 1863. The Committee lobbied for a firmer local prison policy, supporting the view that 'means employed for the reformation of offenders should always be accompanied by due and

---

[328] Harding et al., p.154.

[329] The article is not authored, but my investigation reveals that it has been attributed to Harriet Martineau, known as an English social theorist and Whig writer. The opening of the article cites six of the following publications as Martineau's object of criticism: The Prison Chaplain: A Memoir of the Rev. John Clay; Female Life in Prison: By a Prison Matron; and 4 official reports ('Reports of the Directors of Convict Prisons, England, 1861', *The Edinburgh Review,* 117.239 (1863), 241-268, p.242).

[330] 'Reports of the Directors of Convict Prisons, England, 1861', p.241-2.

[331] There is no clear indication of who supports the reinstatement of transportation.

[332] 'Reports of the Directors of Convict Prisons, England, 1861', p.263.

effective punishment'.[333] In other words, as advocated by Mary Carpenter in the case of women: 'there must exist (a) firm steady control [...] combined with a strict and vigilant discipline, administered with the most impartial justice'.[334] Subsequently, greater governmental accountability was sought with the new 1865 Prison Act.[335] However, the attempt to achieve consistency in the administration of all custodial facilities did not imply that views on the aims of imprisonment were unanimous.[336] Thoroughly documented by McConville, the years between the 1865 Act and the 1877 Act reveal a great degree of fracture in government regarding the issue of prison policy. On the one hand, some argued that discipline and uniformity were successfully achieved, whereas others lamented the ambiguous application of the system and the consequential betrayal of public trust.[337]

This resulted in the urgency to finalise prison legislation. Indeed, the Earl of Kimberly in a House of Lords debate spoke of 'a great army—an army making war on society, and it is necessary that society should for its own defence make war upon them'.[338] The 'great army' represented the criminal classes rather than the 'convicts' whose numbers were relatively small in comparison. The Earl of Kimberly cited the total of 115,646 known thieves and depredators, receivers of stolen goods, prostitutes, suspected persons, vagrants and tramps, to create the alarm needed to trigger social concern. He suggested that 'habitual offenders' (or recidivists) should be sentenced to imprisonment for life 'and should actually be confined for life'.[339] The overall agreement was that 'a sentimental feeling in favour of prisoners had prevailed in the public mind for some time before' and had forced Parliament and the government to act 'under the pressure of that sickly feeling'. It was argued that future legislation would have to target the issue with 'stern determination'.[340]

A solution was sought in the newly recognised scientific approach to criminality, as was happening in many other areas of life during that period. Indeed, a new empirical stance on matters of criminality was starting to gain support. The pathology of criminal behaviour was studied inside out and

---

[333] *Report on the Present State of Discipline in Gaols and Houses of Correction*, 1863, Minutes of evidence, p. xii
[334] Carpenter, vol.2, p.210.
[335] Prison Act 1865 c.126 (28 & 29 Vict.).
[336] McConville, *A history of English prison administration*, p.349.
[337] McConville, *English local prisons 1860-1900*, pp.146-148.
[338] HL Deb 26 February 1869, cc332-50 (c338).
[339] Ibid.
[340] Ibid., by Earl Grey, c348.

was supported by evidence drawn from biology, psychology and psychiatry. Forsythe explains that the use of statistics, measurements and records 'seemed to offer an objective validity and a general framework for understanding.'[341] However, Forsythe also suggests that this new 'understanding' and knowledge fostered 'deep pessimism': none of these new insights was able to offer 'hope of improvement in habitual criminal behaviour'.[342] In other words, if in the past, penal discourses entertained the idea that, for example, criminals subjected to Elizabeth Fry's methods could be reformed and thus expect future social integration, the 'new' 1860s prison discourses were constructed upon the scientific idea that criminals were 'constitutionally fixed' and thus 'could not be changed';[343] hence, social integration was excluded from the onset. This explains the somewhat unreasonable 'imprisonment for life' policy put forward by the Earl of Kimberly; indeed, how else could imprisonment be justified if it was scientifically proven that it served neither reformation nor deterrence?

The Prison Commission: Uniformity and Prevention

The Prison Act that followed in 1877[344] set two main goals: to establish a uniform imprisonment system under governmental authority and to alleviate public taxation for the maintenance of prisons.[345] In other words, the Act brought about the complete nationalisation of the administration of prisons, shifting the issue of custodial policy from local to central government. Subsequently, 53 prisons were closed, leaving fewer than 70 operating prisons (of which five were convict prisons) to cope with a yearly average of approximately 167,161 offenders on remand and convicts sent to prison.[346] Leading this new project was Edmond Du Cane, the chairman of the newly appointed Prison Commission. Du Cane's controversial aspirations

---

[341] Forsythe, p.182.
[342] Ibid., p.186.
[343] Ibid., p.187.
[344] Prison Act 1877 c.21 (40 & 41 Vic.).
[345]The local authorities agreed to let the government take control of the prison system after being promised relief of half a million pounds a year (B.E. Ruggles, *The English Prison System* [London: Macmillan & Co Ltd, 1921], p.69. See also McConville, *English local prisons*, p.192).
[346] Data taken from McConville suggests that 60 operating prisons were left (*English local prisons*, pp.200, 206-207). However, the second report of the newly appointed Prison Commission indicates that the number of prisons was reduced from 113 to 68 (*Second Report of The Commissioners of Prisons* [London: HMSO, 1879], p.2).

and views have been documented elsewhere,[347] but it is interesting to note that despite greater emphasis on the relationship between penal deterrence and imprisonment, particularly during this period, Du Cane nevertheless was able to revive and perhaps reinvigorate arguments supporting the aim of prisoners' reformation.

Du Cane was convinced the severe drawbacks in the prison system were not due to the system itself; rather, drawing upon the latest scientific perspectives, he recognised that some criminals were unable because of mental deficiency to absorb the intended benign influence of custody. The 'benign influence' of imprisonment referred to the aspect of 'reformation', although not without a hint of ambiguity. Du Cane argued that 'crime may very well be compared with physical disease', but it is not always possible to 'remove its causes'; thus, it has to be cured.[348] The aims of prison policy saw a revised agenda; in fact, Du Cane was able to reclaim the legality of and justification for the existence of the prison penalty. Instead of limiting the aims of imprisonment to the person of the detainee, Du Cane widened its scope by drawing on 'prevention'. His 'cure' was not necessarily to target the criminal, who might be unresponsive to it; rather, the deterrence of others was at the core of his approach. This is very well exemplified by Du Cane's citation of a judge addressing a prisoner: 'You are sentenced to be hanged, not because you stole the horse, but to prevent others from stealing horses'.[349] The application of uniformity across the prison estate meant to eliminate the partial implementation of the penalty, thereby intensifying the effect of deterrence.[350] However, although this new policy targeted 'prevention' by deterrence, Du Cane was convinced that his prison administration was also able to address reformation: he argued that once prisoners had gone through the first few months of hard labour, there would be an 'obvious reformatory effect' with the prospect of gradual progression and the acquisition of privileges within the prison.[351]

Du Cane expressed strong satisfaction with the prison system following the 1877 Act. In his publication, he highlighted improvements including the reduced expenditure borne by the prisons; the successful application of

---

[347] See McConville, *English Local Prisons.*
[348] Du Cane supports this argument by citing Dr Nicholson and Professor Bain's work from the Journal of Mental Science (E. Du Cane, *The Punishment and Prevention of Crime* [London: Macmillan and Co., 1885], p.2-3).
[349] Du Cane, p.2.
[350] Ibid., pp.73-74, 99.
[351] Ibid., p.77.

uniform treatment across the board; improved sanitation; a decrease in the death rate; a decrease in the number of prisoners committing suicide; a reduction in the use of corporal punishment; and the introduction of a greater variety of employment opportunities.[352] In addition, he argued that the changes meant the new prison administration would be able to contribute to a better understanding of the causes of crime, thus dismissing unfounded theories such as the one suggesting, for example, that crime prevailed during the winter season.[353] Most importantly, however, Du Cane indicated that there had been an exceptional decrease in the prison population since the enactment of the Act and that 'it certainly seems justifiable to infer from these figures that our penal reformatory system has been made effective'.[354] In a later article to *Murray's Magazine*, Du Cane further suggested that any apparent increase in criminality was simply proportional to the general increase in the population of England and Wales. In fact, he argued, 'our gaols are no longer "overflowing", but [...] are continually becoming less numerous and more empty.'[355] In addition, an anonymous account of prison life in 1878 by 'one who was there' described Holloway (male) local prison's cells as 'a model of cleanliness and neatness'; the cells each had three ventilation accesses (for cold air, hot air, and another for letting out consumed air), and the cells contained books, mainly religious but also scientific. The anonymous ex-prisoner recalled that the kitchen hall even had what was defined as a 'kettle'.[356]

However, despite Du Cane's personal satisfaction, the new system soon came under criticism. In the summer of 1878, the House of Commons expressed its concern regarding the new arrangements, as it seemed that, for example, 'the visits of the friends of prisoners have been much curtailed, and the diet of the prisoners much reduced by the cutting off of the coffee and cocoa formerly allowed'. The thin porridge and small bread at breakfast and tea time, Sunday's cold suet pudding, the absolute silence throughout the day, and a possible 24-hour lock up were all unacceptable practices for which the House requested clarification from the Secretary of State.[357]

---

[352] Ibid., pp.104-107.
[353] Ibid., p.108.
[354] Ibid., p.109.
[355] E. Du Cane, 'Crime and Criminals 1837-1887', *Murray's Magazine*, 2, 9, (1887), 289-299 (p.299).
[356] Anonymous, *Startling Disclosures! Six Months of hard labour in the City Prison, Holloway, by one who was there, and remand to Newgate* (London: Curtice & Co, 1878), p.43-44.
[357] HC Deb 25 July 1878 vol 242 cc216-8 (c217).

Moreover, Du Cane's new prison rules did not go unnoticed, and disagreement was made public. In a letter to the editor of *The Times*, Member of Parliament Mitchell Henry contested the rule of sleeping on a plank bed during the first month of the sentence. He argued that the lack of discretion when dealing with different categories of offenders implied that petty offenders sentenced to a month or less would 'pass the whole of that time in this kind of torture', whereas 'hardened offenders' sentenced to, for example, two years, would 'only [be] required to sleep for one month out of the 24 [months] on a plank bed'; the system lacked proportionality. Moreover, the Member of Parliament thought that the real shame was the extension of this rule to female prisoners. He stated that this was 'an act of barbarity which has drawn from Chief Baron Palles the declaration that until the rule is repealed he will not send women to prison except in cases of crimes of violence'.[358] Indeed, Mitchell Henry shared the concern about the need to treat women prisoners differently. Despite its basis in a stereotypical understanding of womanhood, in this case, his concern about the 'barbarous' use of the plank beds was to the benefit of the women prisoners.

Du Cane's period of prison management was criticised for being oppressive; the title of Playfair's book 'The Punitive Obsession' exemplifies his claim that in some aspects, prison management appeared to be even harsher than in the past.[359] The administration of the prison system during this period was perceived as driven by a 'mania for centralisation which possesses the Home Office and its army of many-titled commissioners'; this, it was argued, ruined England's reputation as a humane, civilized and Christian nation.[360] In fact, the Silent and the Separate systems were used as complementary methods where cellular confinement was implemented for the first 28 days of the sentence or for prison punishments. Playfair argues that the ethos of prisoners' reformation was overthrown by a uniform and exact system that dismissed any consideration of sex, age, culpability and mental responsibility.[361] According to Camp, the new Prison Commission generated a complex bureaucracy which, in turn, was unable to regulate the various establishments:

---

[358] M. Henry, 'The New Prison Rules and Plank Beds', *The Times*, Monday, Aug 12, (1878), 11, Letter to the Editor.
[359] Playfair, p.99.
[360] Henry, 'The New Prison Rules and Plank Beds'.
[361] Playfair, p.98.

The effect of the Prison Commissioners administration was to engender administrative efficiency, but to take no account of prisoners as individuals. Individuality was stifled and brutalising began.[362]

An assessment of this centralised prison system on the management of female convicts and local prison populations demonstrates that the aim of 'reformation' was visible in prison policy discourse rather than in the actual reality of prison life. Addressing convict prisons first, Smith notes 'the continual shifting round of the (female) convict population from prison to prison' before and during the Du Cane period.[363] More specifically, ten years before the introduction of the 1877 Act, four convict prisons— Millbank, Brixton, Parkhurst and Fulham Refuge—provided a total of 1,182 accommodations for women.[364] In 1869, female convicts were moved from Brixton and Parkhurst to Woking prison. With the enactment of the 1877 Act, a yearly average population of 1,199 female convicts had to be accommodated in the only three convict prisons available for women.[365] After 1886, Millbank no longer admitted women and Fulham also stopped receiving them after 1888, making Woking the only prison available for female convicts.[366] Finally, in 1896, Aylesbury prison became the only accommodation available for female convicts, possibly due to their small numbers: on an average day in 1897, only 202 women were accommodated in the prison, and the yearly average reception was less than 50.[367]

Interestingly, despite insisting on frugal and uniform prison policy, the need to allow for social integration, particularly in the case of female prisoners, was still at the core of the prisoners' reformation argument—hence, the availability of Fulham as a 'refuge' during Du Cane's chairmanship. Du Cane emphasised 'these "refuges" are not prisons either in appearance or in discipline—they are *homes*, and are intended to afford the advantages of a treatment approaching in its characteristics to that of home influence', and

---

[362] J.M.F Camp, *Holloway Prison- the place and the people* (London: David & Charles, 1974), p.43.
[363] Smith, p.125.
[364] Smith, p.125.
[365] *Report of the Directors of Convict Prisons for the year 1873* (London: Her Majesty's Stationery Office, 1874), p.xxi.
[366] Smith, p.129.
[367] Smith, p.130; and *Report of the Commissioners of Prisons and Directors of Convict Prisons for the year 1896-1897* (London: HMSO, 1897), pp.10, 43.

the Prison Commission advised that women should spend nine months there before release.[368]

However, Fulham Refuge would not last and soon enough it was reinstated as a 'prison'.[369] Forsythe notes that the general makeover of the system affected mood and morale; female prisoners' writings, in particular after the 1870s, 'without exception referred to the joyless, monotonous, severe oppression of prison life'.[370] Forsythe's research into women's prisons during this period reveals a marked change to 'a regime in which the normal mode of communication [...] was a detached, stilted, staccato set of commands rather than communication between human beings.'[371]

It is important to remember, however, that the great majority of women were sent to the 65 local prisons available around the country.[372] The records indicate that these local prisons might have had a daily average population of as few as one woman[373] and as many as 500 women at one time.[374] The second Prison Commission report for 1879 and Susan Willis Fletcher's memoirs *Twelve Months in an English Prison*[375] provide some valuable

---

[368] Italic in original. Du Cane, *The Punishment and Prevention of Crime*, p.170.

[369] Smith, pp.125, 129.

[370] B. Forsythe, 'Women prisoners and women penal officials 1840-1921', *British Journal of Criminology*, 33, 4 (1993), 525-540 (p.532).

[371] B. Forsythe, p. 533.

[372] Of all the local prisons, only about two did not have accommodation for women, and only Westminster gaol was a female-only prison. This data is correct for the year ending 31 March 1879 (*Second Report of The Commissioners of Prisons*, Part I, Appendix 2). Alternatively, as explained by Zedner, from the 1870s, habitual drunkards and feeble-minded persons were diverted to retreats and dedicated reformatories (pp.219, 231).

[373] The daily average number of women detained in Southwell gaol in 1879 was 1, whereas the yearly number recorded for 1879 was 18 (*Second Report of The Commissioners of Prisons*, Part I, Appendix 2 and Appendix 25).

[374] The Westminster female-only gaol accommodated the highest number of women; a daily average could reach 583, and in 1879, 8,402 women passed through this prison. The next local prison with a high number of women was Liverpool, with a daily average for 1879 of 418 women and 5,317 women passing through this prison in 1879 (*Second Report of The Commissioners of Prisons*, Part I, Appendix 2 and Appendix 25).

[375] Susan Willis Fletcher was an American woman who was devoted to Spiritualism; in fact, she and her husband worked as mediums (those who contact the dead). She was charged in the US and England 'of obtaining jewels and clothing of great value, by undue influence or false pretence' (p.1). She was found guilty in the Old Bailey

insight into the regime applied in these local prisons. First, it appears that the women were not subject to hard labour.[376] The only exception recorded was oakum picking, and only Lancaster gaol employed women in gum breaking and cotton picking. Otherwise, women prisoners were subject to the usual house-keeping employment. Indeed, Susan's memoirs confirm that the 'hard labour' she was sentenced to was 'rather a myth'.[377] She revealed that there was very little work picking oakum and assorting waste paper. The really hard work was in the laundry and kitchen. As far as she was concerned, she 'did a little knitting' because she liked it, 'but not an hour's hard labour during the twelve months'.[378]

As in the convict prisons, a system of progressive stages known as 'the mark system' was also applied in local prisons. In Westminster gaol (female-only) it was noted to be 'a great incentive for good conduct'.[379] However, Susan revealed that it was considered 'a position of trust' and was thus identified with the highest and most advantageous stage of the mark system, which entailed work outside the cell such as scrubbing or stone breaking.[380] The commissioners' report gives further information on the life of the women in the local prisons. For example, Westminster gaol provided a religious service once a day—Roman Catholic and Jewish ministers were summoned if needed. Additionally, the wording of the report might suggest that only 'uneducated' prisoners attended education classes, an hour a day. The commissioners were satisfied that the overall prisoners' health had improved (or at least it had not deteriorated),[381] and they noted that no woman across the local prison service was punished with corporeal punishment—the common forms of punishment used were 'punishment cells',[382] dietary punishment and loss of 'stage' and other privileges.

The commissioners found fault with women prisoners' behaviour in only five of the prisons inspected. For example, most of the prison offences committed in Knutsford prison 'by the female prisoners were chiefly confined to one or two particular bad characters', leading to a total of 54

---

and sentenced to 12 months of penal servitude. The book is her account of her experiences (Fletcher, 1884).

[376] *Second Report of The Commissioners of Prisons*, Part I, Appendix 25 and Part II.

[377] Fletcher, p.337.

[378] Ibid.

[379] *Second Report of The Commissioners of Prisons*, Part II, p.80.

[380] Fletcher, p.329-30.

[381] *Second Report of The Commissioners of Prisons*, Part II, p.80.

[382] The punishment cell was a 'padded cell' without any furniture (Fletcher, p.329).

punishments awarded in 1879.[383] Liverpool prison reported that the number of women punished for prison offences was a 'disproportionate' 15% of the total number of female prisoners.[384] However, Westminster prison recorded that 18% of the women were subject to this punishment, whereas Strangeways prison recorded an excessive 48%.[385] Finally, during 1879, Newcastle prison recorded a total of 659 prison punishments (male and female), of which only one was due to a violent offence, an assault committed 'by a female prisoner upon a matron'.[386] Otherwise, the commissioners commended the prisoners' behaviour. Susan Fletcher's memoirs confirm that prisoners' behaviour was reasonably good, but according to her, this was because the prisons functioned as unofficial alcohol rehabilitation centres. She noted that 'if these hundreds of poor women could only be sent to some country [...] where they could get no whiskey, they might be chaste wives, fond mothers, and good Christians'.[387]

These records also give insight into the food provided in prison. For example, the commissioners expressed satisfaction with the quality of the food—Aylesbury prison was reported to have 'excellent' food.[388] It appears that at the time of the inspections, bacon and beans were part of the menu. Although the commissioners recommended that these items be taken off prisoners' diet, Susan Fletcher was still served them during 1880-1881. Her impression of the prison food, however, was different from the one reported by the commissioners: according to her, the diet was of poor quality;[389] indeed, her ring, which 'fitted so tightly' when she had just arrived to prison 'came off very easily' after only a week in custody.[390]

As far as the Prison Commission was concerned, acting as an official monitor of prisoners' well-being, the system was entirely adequate. However, Susan Fletcher's memoirs reveal other aspects of prison life which suggest that the prison system was still far from having any understanding of prisoners' well-being, let alone an ethos supporting any of the aims of imprisonment. First, she described as 'filthy horrors of the reception': upon arrival at their newly allocated prison, 'all wash from one

---

[383] *Second Report of The Commissioners of Prisons*, Part II, p.36.
[384] Ibid., p.45.
[385] Ibid., pp. 80, 72.
[386] No specification of the type of punishment awarded. Ibid., p.51.
[387] Fletcher, p.331.
[388] *Second Report of The Commissioners of Prisons*, Part II, p.3.
[389] Fletcher, p.327.
[390] Ibid., p.321.

tank, and wipe on one towel, and the poor women, wild with grief, or crazy with delirium-tremens, are screaming in the reception-cells'.[391] Susan was eventually transferred to Westminster local prison. There, she spent 23 hours of the day alone in her cell in total silence. In that regard, she said:

> A saint might grow more saintly by such a discipline, perhaps; but even a saint's body could hardly get more healthy. Common men and women, social beings, with all their best instincts unsatisfied and blighted, must be made worse in every way by such unnatural conditions.[392]

A woman in a bed

[391] Ibid., p.320.
[392] Fletcher, p.329.

*

The examination of penal development, having women's prisons as its core focus, ends with the termination of Edmond Du Cane's chairmanship. Lionel Fox, one of the future Prison Commission chairmen, commented on Du Cane's period in these words:

> And so, in the English prison system, the lights that had been lit in Newgate by Elizabeth Fry, on Norfolk Island by Captain Maconochie, and at Portland by Colonel Jebb, went out: for twenty years our prisons presented the pattern of deterrence by severity of punishment, uniformly, rigidly, and efficiently applied. For death itself the system had substituted a living death.[393]

What followed was the setting up of the Gladstone Inquiry Committee in 1895.[394] The Committee noted the lack of any reforming advancement and social efficiency in the present system. It argued that 'prisoners have been treated too much as a hopeless or worthless element of the community.'[395] It suggested that

> the system should be made more elastic, more capable of being adapted to the special cases of individual prisoners; that prison discipline and treatment should be more effectually designed to maintain, stimulate or awaken the higher susceptibilities of prisoners, to develop their moral instincts [...] and whenever possible to turn them out better men and women, physically and mentally, than when they came in.[396]

This chapter focused on the development of imprisonment as the main penalty, arguing that this enterprise arose from the urgent need to replace capital punishment and transportation. Prisons, as a primary penalty, were set up as an experiment; this is supported by the events, words and discourses revealed in the historical records. The system evolved based on 'spur of the moment' socio-political concerns. The implication was that imprisonment as a main penalty continuously experienced limitations and drawbacks, as if it were in a constant state of crisis. Nevertheless, the legitimacy of this penalty was never challenged; rather, it was constantly reinvented to rationalise its applicability.

---

[393] L.W. Fox, *The English Prison and Borstal Systems* (London: Routledge & Kegan, 1952), p.51.
[394] This is further discussed in the next chapter.
[395] Ruggles-Brise, *The English Prison* System, p.75.
[396] Departmental Committee's Report on Prisons (1895), quoted in Playfair, p.158.

The aim of prisoners' reformation has played an important role in this task of rationalisation; in fact, this concept features at the core of every prison policy drafted since the 'birth of the prison'. However, the 'reform of the prisoner' is just a concept; it is a myth, so grounded in the social understanding of imprisonment that it has come to be taken at face value. Rather, the dramatic dissonance between theory and reality in relation to what type of reformation is accomplished in prison is at the core of the prison crisis. The following chapter develops this perspective by assessing how the Gladstone report affected a new understanding of imprisonment and the accompanying aim of reformation as well as the subsequent emergence of the borstal system and the later adult open prison.

A mother and baby in a prison yard

PART III

"TRAINING" THE PRISONER

In this chapter our attention shifts to the introduction of the borstal system in the late nineteenth century and the development of adult open prisons from the 1930s. These two custodial facilities provide insight into one of those few instances when penal policy demonstrated an understanding of the effects of imprisonment – namely prisoners' adaptation (or reformation) to institutional life. Select Committee reports, minutes of meetings, personal testaments and memoirs indicate that those involved in the borstal and open prison initiatives recognised that 'reforming' the prisoner to become a law-abiding citizen could not happen in an environment that aimed to limit the prisoner's liberties in the first place.

The discussion then turns to consider the inevitable link between prison reform and the mainstream orthodox closed prison. As the latter is counter-productive from the outset, any change or reform will be superficial and temporary, merely symbolising the socio-political view of the moment; this is further illustrated through the carceral clawback paradigm.

The chapter opens with an examination of the state of prisons in England, as described by the Gladstone report. The report's findings drew attention to the social and individual implications of the prison regime, suggesting that they undermined a healthy psycho-physical detention and a purposeful reintegration into social life. Hence, a new understanding of the 'reform of the prisoner' emerged, where the concept of 'training' acquired a core position in the discourse concerning the aims of imprisonment. The chapter moves on to consider this theory of training as it was first implemented through the borstal penal policy. Then, the discussion considers the development of this policy through the Criminal Justice Act 1948 and the constitution of the adult open prison. The second part of this chapter focuses on the materialisation of the first open prison for women, Askham Grange. The historical review aims at providing insight into what lay behind this, therefore the discussion traces pre-war and post-war proposals for reforms and the problems underpinning them.

The Gladstone Report: The Limitation to Prisoners' Reformation

The Gladstone inquiry, established by the departmental committee on prisons in 1895, was prompted by the uncertainty and lack of clarity in relation to the 'uniformity' principle endorsed by Edmond Du Cane and the Prison Commission.[397] In its first 20 years of operation the Prison Commission had brought about little practical amelioration in the conditions and effective administration of prisons. Therefore the committee's purpose was to ascertain whether the prison system could reflect modern developments: 'The time has come when the main principles and methods adopted by the Prison Acts should be seriously tested by the light of acquired experience and recent scientific research.'[398] Thus, the Gladstone committee provided a critical view of all possible features of prison life, and at the heart of the review was the prison routine. Importantly, although the committee considered that penal deterrence was an essential feature of prison administration, it was nevertheless sceptical about its implementation. It suggested that the chief failure of the Prison Act 1877 (which led to the centralisation of the prison system) was caused by an exaggerated application of uniformity and discipline.

Moreover, the fact that offenders sentenced to imprisonment were temporarily kept away from society, yet with the completion of their sentence, were permitted to re-join it, was considered by the Gladstone committee to be 'a growing strain on our civilisation.'[399] The 'strain' was not so much in relation to the social and moral acceptance of ex-prisoners; rather, at the core of the committee's concern was their mental state and moral degradation, worsened by the prison experience, which hindered released prisoners from achieving socially acceptable reintegration into an orderly, law-abiding society. Indeed, imprisonment was found to undermine what had become the established justification of the prison existence, that is, 'reformation'.

---

[397] The research was based on 56 interviews conducted with prison personnel and ex-prisoners; in addition, they visited seven convict prisons and sixteen local prisons (*Report (Minutes of Evidence) from the Departmental Committee on Prisons*, Chairman Gladstone H. J. (London: Parliamentary Papers. House of Commons, 1895) p.5 [hereinafter: Gladstone]).
[398] Gladstone, p.5.
[399] Ibid.

Although the Gladstone report assessed the whole of the prison estate, greater attention was paid to the younger prison population. Recognition of the effects the prison environment might have on prisoners was not confined to young offenders, but for reasons discussed below, it appeared that the justification for the use of imprisonment on the youth population had to be urgently reassessed. First, child[400] institutions, such as industrial and reformatory schools, had been in use since the second half of the nineteenth century. By 1870, England, Wales and Scotland had records of 7,000 young people lodging in these institutions. This number tripled by 1896, and the children could be allocated among different types of schools, all under private and charitable management.[401] However, the committee's main object of concern was not this age group; rather, they advised that people between 16 and 23 who were 'too old for commitment to reformatory schools, and too young to be classified with the ordinary grown-up criminal', should become a separate category; indeed, this age group comprised an average of 19,000 committals to custody at the beginning of the twentieth century.[402]

Interestingly, the 'problem' of adolescent offenders was not completely new, and it appears to have already been under constant scrutiny. In fact, the Gladstone report's suggestion was drawn from the experience of the Colony at Stretton, Warwickshire (set up in 1815), and the Farm School at Redhill, Surrey (set up in 1849).[403] Both were concerned with the effects of imprisonment on young people aged 16 to 21. The Stretton Colony had implemented an old statute that allowed the hiring of young people for agricultural work,[404] whereas the Redhill Farm School had been modelled on the successful French agricultural colony for young offenders in Mettray, established in 1839.[405] This issue was further discussed in the international prison congress held in Brussels five years after the Gladstone inquiry with a question about the adoption of the American State Reformatory System in Elmira. Although the Elmira system was ground breaking because it introduced the notion of the 'juvenile' as a person between the ages of 16 and 30, the records indicate that the congress attendees were frustrated by

---

[400] A child was classified by the Prison Act 1865 as 'juvenile' below the age of 16.
[401] *Report to the Secretary of State for the Home department of the Departmental Committee on Reformatory and Industrial Schools*, Chaired by Sir G. Lushington, Vol I (London: HMSO, 1896), p.7.
[402] Ruggles-Brise, *The English Prison System*, p.85.
[403] Fox, *The English Prison and Borstal*, p.330.
[404] Camp, p.63.
[405] Fox, *The English Prison and Borstal*, p.328.

the lack of clear evidence of the system's reformative success and how it differed from similar European projects.[406] Despite this general view, the English delegate to the congress, the future chair of the Prison Commission, Evelyn Ruggles-Brise, was impressed. Drawing on his visit to Elmira in 1897, he considered that

> the elaborate system of moral, physical, and industrial training of these prisoners, the enthusiasm which dominated the work, the elaborate machinery for supervision of parole, all these things, if stripped of their extravagances, satisfied me that a real, human effort was being made in these States for the rehabilitation of the youthful criminal.[407]

Ruggles-Brise recommended implementing this juvenile reformatory system, suggesting that it should be reserved for adolescents aged 16-21 and that longer custodial sentences should be applied in these cases. Ruggles-Brise's approach emphasised the need to acknowledge that the problem of criminality could be broken down into career phases; targeting the initial stages of this formation with 'long curative detention'[408] ensured the criminal career would not progress any further.

Garland notes that the scientific approach driving penal policy helped to rationalise concerns related to adolescent offenders.[409] For example, data from the 1920s provides valuable information about the background of these young offenders:[410] while the data refers to youths with 'bad homes' and various levels of intellectual abilities, the records also present a moderate percentage of 'intelligent and mentally fit' young offenders with reasonable

---

[406] Ruggles-Brise, *Prison Reform at Home and Abroad*, p.97.

[407] Ruggles-Brise, *The English Prison System*, p.91

[408] Question 2 of the Second Section of the Programme of the International Penitentiary Congress to be held in Brussels in 1900, p.14 (LNA, HO 45/10046 [A62024]).

[409] For a thorough review in that regard, see D. Garland, 'The criminal and his science', *The British journal of criminology*, 25, 2 (1985), 109-137.

[410] One research study was conducted by Dr. Baker at Pentonville prison on a sample of 2,185 adolescents; another unidentified research was conducted on a sample of 1,238 adolescents (both studies are reported by Ruggles-Brise, *The English Prison System*, p.86). More detailed information on Dr. Baker's research can be found in Question 2 of the Second Section of the Programme of the International Penitentiary Congress to be held in Brussels in 1900, p.7-10 (LNA, HO 45/10046[A62024]). Other small-scale data can be found in the First Statistics of the Experiment at HMP Bedford, Juvenile adults dated 29 June 1900 (LNA, HO 45/10046[A62024]) and in S.A. Moseley, *Truth about Borstal*, (London: Cecil Palmer, 1926), pp.36-39.

levels of education and good homes.[411] However, the most important indicator provided by the records is that the majority of this age group were proliferate offenders, especially for non-violent offences against property, such as larceny, and offences against the Vagrancy Act, such as gaming and frequenting. In fact, Ruggles-Brise wrote to the Secretary of State that

> the proposal is to deal systematically with the young ruffian, the hooligan of the London streets, the callous and precocious young criminal on whom the present system of treatment in prison makes no impression, and who graduates through a succession of short local sentences into a fixed career of habitual crime.[412]

The social concern triggered by the combination of uncontrolled youth and the inconvenience of proliferate petty property crime must have been more alarming than the masses of adult male offenders going through similar criminal procedures. Although the period's scientific research suggested that there was little that could be done to 'save' and 'reform' the adult criminal,[413] the case was different for adolescent offenders. First, the recognition that youths came out of prison as improved criminals was unanimously voiced; pleas to the government warned that 'they go out with the prison taint on them'.[414] In addition it was suggested, in line with the scientific trend of this period, that 'it is the duty of the state at least to try and effect a cure and not to class the offender off-hand and without experiment'.[415] Second, and perhaps most importantly, it was argued that the nature of the offences demonstrated the lack of a completed development from childhood into adulthood. Dr. Baker argued that 'it is charitable to conclude that they have not reached an age when ideas about personal responsibility and duty to society could be regarded as fully

---

[411] Youth with 'bad homes', the records suggest that many of them were not subject to any parental control due to their parents being drunk, criminally involved, ill or dead.

[412] From a communication to the Secretary of State Sir Digby by Ruggles-Brise dated 30 June 1900 (LNA, HO 45/10046[A62024]).

[413] See Garland, 'The criminal and his science'. This perspective of 'pessimism' was also emphasised in the previous chapter of this study.

[414] From a communication to the Secretary of State Sir Digby by Ruggles-Brise, 30 June 1900 (LNA, HO 45/10046[A62024])

[415] Ruggles-Brise, *The English Prison System*, p.87.

developed or mature',[416] and thus, adolescents should not be regarded as adults and should not be subject to the adult penal policy.

The debate culminated in the enactment of the borstal sentence. Although the borstal sentence was introduced by the 1908 Prevention of Crime Act, it was preceded by a few experiments at Bedford Prison and in a wing of a convict prison at Borstal (from which the borstal system took its name) in 1900 and 1902, respectively.[417] In the years preceding the Act, young offenders considered by the prison commissioners to be suitable for borstal conditions were transferred from prison to the borstals; because of their experimental nature, judges were not yet instructed on their existence, therefore members of the Borstal Association attended youth trials and if appropriate, advised the judge about the borstal alternative.[418] Significantly, the experiments and consequently the Act targeted a specific population of young offenders: youths 16-21 years of age; youths with previous convictions; and youths who were appearing before the court to be tried for an indictable offence.[419] In addition to these criteria, although it was at the discretion of the court to sentence to borstal, the judge was required to consider the prison commissioners' report regarding the

> suitability of the case for treatment in a Borstal Institution, and [he] shall be satisfied that the character, state of health, and mental condition of the offender, and the other circumstances of the case, are such that the offender is likely to profit by such instruction and discipline as aforesaid.[420]

Finally, to enable training and reformation, the borstal sentence was to last for a period varying from at least one year to at most three years.

In an attempt to protect society by preventing the psychological degradation of the prisoner while in prison, the core aim underlining these initiatives was to provide constructive life-coaching experience (to use a modern

---

[416] Dr. Baker's research quoted in Question 2 of the Second Section of the Programme of the International Penitentiary Congress to be held in Brussels in 1900, p.11 (LNA, HO 45/10046[A62024]).

[417] Fox, *The English Prison and Borstal,* p.332.

[418] As is evident from correspondence between the Borstal Association and the Prison Commission dated 26 Nov 1906, LNA, HO 45/10046[A62024].

[419] Prevention of Crime Act 1908, c. 59, (8 Edw.7) Part 1, Section 1. In 1914 the powers would also be extended to the Magistrate Court (Criminal Justice Administration Act 1914, c. 58, (4 & 5 Geo.5) Part 1, Section 1).

[420] Prevention of Crime Act 1908.

expression). Alexander Paterson, a prison commissioner responsible for these developments, especially during the 1920s, considered:

> If a prison is merely a cloakroom in which the enemy of society is duly deposited, till called for after a fixed period [...] then indeed the protection afforded is of a temporary nature, and it may well be that, after the security of a few months or years, society will be at the mercy of an enemy more bitter and implacable than before.[421]

Towards a Theory of Training

Moving back to consider the Gladstone report's recommendations, it is essential to note that another topic, prison work, was found to be of particular concern; the committee denounced its unproductive nature, which appeared to foster in the prisoner a state of 'mental vacuity'. Ideally, in the committee's opinion, prisoners should be occupied in the fresh air, working on the land outside the prison walls.[422] The committee had as its core interest not the 'Labour' of prisoners sentenced to Hard Labour; rather, it looked into the 'day to day' prison routine.[423] It was the futile nature of work such as a tread-wheel, carried out within the confinement of the prisoners' own cells, that was disputed by the Gladstone committee. Significantly, this recommendation emphasised the recognition of the actual effects of imprisonment, that is, 'institutionalisation' or, in other words, prisoners' 'reformation' (or adaptation) to institutional life. The value of prisoners' work was appreciated by the Gladstone report, but its view differed from the one endorsed by the Du Cane's Prison Commission: rather than implementing prison labour for the sole function of deterrence, it now recognised the 'reformative value of useful work'.[424]

The 'reformative value' stood for the un-learning of the prison 'taint'. Indeed, the Report of the Departmental Committee on Employment of Prisoners confirmed that: 'We cannot stress too strongly [...] that suitable employment is the most important factor in the physical and moral regeneration of the prisoner.'[425] It even concluded that prisons were

---

[421] A. Paterson, *Paterson on Prisons,* ed. by S.K. Ruck (London: Frederick Muller ltd, 1951), p.23.
[422] Gladstone, pp.18-19.
[423] Fox, *The English Prison and Borstal*, p.49.
[424] Ibid., p.178.
[425] 1933, Part I, p.64, quoted in Fox, *The English Prison and Borstal,* p.179.

responsible for corrupting prisoners' basic social instincts and suggested that

> after a long term of imprisonment, passive obedience and dependence upon authority have become habitual, and the prisoner finds himself, when he at last faces the tasks of normal life, without decision, without initiative, and lacking in self-control.[426]

It had become obvious that in its current operation, the prison had an adverse influence on the prisoner's mind and character: it 'crushed' her/his self-respect; it 'starved' her/his moral instincts; it deprived her/him of the 'opportunity to do a kindness or to receive it'.[427]

This view was further emphasised by the international prison congress in Budapest, held in 1910, which acknowledged the value of 'open air employment'.[428] Implicit pressure was put on the nations attending the congress, including England, to adopt new ways to reduce time spent in the cell and to provide physical activity outside the prison walls. Evidence from Hungary, Austria, Italy and France exemplified what was meant by the 'reformative value of useful work': it was suggested that open air employment improved both morale and conduct in custody, and most importantly, it helped to reduce diseases typical of cellular confinement while providing better sanitary conditions.[429]

In spite of these recommendations, the English prison service, scrutinised by the Labour Research Department inquiry in 1922, showed that only 1.68% of a total of almost 50,000 prisoners sent to prison in that year had been employed in gardens or other land-related work.[430] No legislation followed to enact the 'open air employment' recommendation, although prison commissioner Alexander Paterson actively worked towards it. Paterson objected to the conditions of 'captivity' under which men and

---

[426] Gladstone, p.573.

[427] Gladstone, p.8.

[428] Ruggles-Brise, *Prison Reform*, p.138.

[429] Ruggles-Brise, *Prison Reform*, p.138. Other countries presented 'open air employment' projects too, although of a somewhat controversial nature: the Greek young offenders' prisons under heavy military guard and in chains; the Russian convict labour camp in Siberia; and the prison on wheels in Sardinia (Ruggles-Brise, *Prison Reform*, p.140).

[430] Labour Research Department, *English Prisons To-Day: Being the Report of the Prison System Enquiry Committee,* ed. by F. Brockway and S.H. Hobhouse (London: Labour Research Department, 1922), p.115.

women were supposed to be 'trained for freedom'.[431] The incompatibility of the custodial environment and the 'outside' world was at the core of this discourse; indeed, Paterson considered how the lack of any similarities between the two affects the prisoner's mental state:

> In such an artificial surrounding it is difficult for men to develop or retain a normal social habit and attitude of mind. They may well become more hardened and anti-social, and return to the freedom that must come someday firmly pledged to prey rather than co-operate.[432]

The importance of this new wave of discourse concerning the reform of the prisoner lies in its recognition that imprisonment as a penalty did not simply worsen the criminal character of the detainees; the experience indeed had a reformative effect on the person, albeit not the one intended. 'Conformity' to the prison routine and regime was probably attained by most of the prisoners, but it came at the cost of losing those social skills that were supposed to contribute to effective social integration and the pursuit of a law-abiding life once released. Reinforcing the prisoner's sense of 'social citizenship' was at the core of this period's 'reformation' perspective. Paterson argued that 'the simplest way which should satisfy both common sense and idealism is to regard him [the criminal] as a fellow citizen who has, for one reason or another, become a liability to the State.'[433]

This perspective was, in fact, endorsed by the Prison Commission from the beginning of the twentieth century. Its new chair, Evelyn Ruggles-Brise, actively promoted the idea of training in open conditions, contributing to the policy related to the borstal system. An assessment of this new policy of 'training' reveals that at the core of Ruggles-Brise's argument was the rejection of the emblematic prison control and the inevitable effects it had on the prisoner's character. Led by the Gladstone report's recommendation that youths should be 'trained and work in agriculture' and 'tutored by high calibre staff who can exercise the best and healthiest kind of moral influence',[434] Ruggles-Brise foresaw that the borstals' task would not be 'to break him [the juvenile] into shape, but to stimulate some power within to regulate conduct aright'.[435] The project was further expanded, under Alexander Paterson's engagement in the 1930s, by fully implementing his

---

[431] Paterson, p.96.
[432] Ibid., p.24.
[433] Ibid., p.46.
[434] Gladstone, p.30.
[435] From the Borstal book: handbook guidance for Borstal staff, quoted in L.W. Fox, *The Modern English Prison* (London: Routledge & Sons Ltd, 1934), p.182.

credo 'training for freedom—in freedom' with the first open borstal in Lowdham Grange at Nottinghamshire.[436] The first 50 young offenders engaged to build Lowdham Grange were the most trustworthy youths recruited from other borstals. They were accompanied by a few officers and skilled tradesmen, who instructed them and assisted in the construction.[437] The land consisted of a large farm and 346 acres of level field, which was designed to accommodate a total of 312 boys and 75 officers.[438]

Within this liberal framework, the Prison Commission was able to propose the first 'open air employment' for adult prisoners. The project was led by the recognition that means of employment within the prison walls, particularly in highly populated prisons such as Wakefield, were scarce: 'the workshops are full, and it is impossible to employ the 500 men within the walls of the prison',[439] thus, many of the prisoners had to engage in old fashioned in-cell work.[440] Prompted by the Prison Commission's pressure for outdoor employment, the Departmental Committee on Prison Work, set up in 1933, recommended the purchase of land for use in agriculture and cultivation by prisoners.[441] Backed up by satisfactory supporting evidence of the successful working of Lowdham Grange,[442] concrete suggestions on suitable lands for this purpose were proposed.[443]

At first, New Hall Wood's 66.5 acres of woodland served as an 'open air employment' satellite for Wakefield prison. Every morning, beginning in March 1933, 15 prisoners and two officers would drive from Wakefield prison to the land, working on its clearance and cultivation, then drive back to the prison at the end of the working day. However, after two years of activity, its continuity was put at stake by a rise in the fuel price that increased the cost of driving every day. In late 1935, it was agreed that 50

---

[436] LNA, HO 45/16224.

[437] It was the first and only borstal built for that purpose; its construction continued until the late 1940s (Fox, *The English Prison and Borstal*, p.336).

[438] Surveyor of Prisons, June 1929 (LNA, HO 45/16224).

[439] Sir A. Paterson, minutes on employment at Wakefield prison, October 1932 (LNA, PCOM 9/156).

[440] Fox, *The English Prison and Borstal*, p.183.

[441] Departmental Committee on Employment of Prisoners, 1933, quoted in Fox, *The English Prison and Borstal*, pp.185-186.

[442] 'Experience [...] of camp conditions at the new borstal institution at Lowdham [...] have shown conclusively the great advantage of camp life over institutional life' (Minutes of the Under Secretary of State 15 February 1936 in LNA, HO 45/16456).

[443] Sir A. Paterson, minutes on employment at Wakefield prison, July 1931 (LNA, PCOM 9/156).

selected prisoners from Wakefield (this number would be increased to 100 when accommodation could be arranged) would live and sleep from Monday to Friday in New Hall Camp and be transported back to the 'closed' prison only for the weekend.[444]

New Hall Camp was declared a prison under the 1884 Prison Building Act in 1936[445] and was designated as an 'open prison' in 1949.[446] The enterprise was gaining approval, and it was considered that

> it is something of an innovation, for this country, to allow convicted prisoners to work on the land [...] Healthy outdoor life is good, not only for the body but also for the mind. There will be less prison taint, less of the mentality of the prisoner, about men who hear less of the key in the lock and the shutting of doors, and see less of the cell walls, the long corridor, the high walls.[447]

The Fundamentals of the Theory of Training

By the 1950s, penal policy was engaging with the concept of 'training', inspired by the penal objectives that by then were a common practice within the borstal system. The 'system of training' for adult prisoners set by the 1948 Criminal Justice Act will be discussed later in this chapter; first, however, it is essential to trace those objectives and aims that were at the core of the borstal policy.

The borstal penal aim is encapsulated in Ruggles-Brise's instructions to the governors of the male and female borstals that followed the 1908 Prevention of Crime Act:

> The system aims at an intellectual, physical and moral improvement and development of each inmate; [moreover] the key note of the system is, therefore, the 'individualization' of the inmate.[448]

---

[444] Harold Scott, Under Secretary of State, in a correspondence to the Prison Commission, November 1935 (LNA, PCOM 9/156).

[445] By John Simon, one of His Majesty's Principle Secretaries of State, Whitehall, 1936 (LNA, PCOM 9/156).

[446] LNA, HO 45/23223.

[447] One justice of the peace in correspondence dated 28 December 1935 (LNA, HO 45/16456).

[448] From the memorandum accompanying the Prevention of Crime Act 1908 (Ruggles-Brise, *The English Prison System*, pp. 244, 256).

Writings by Ruggles-Brise and Paterson emphasise the value of 'individualization' within the context of the borstal training, arguing that 'the object of the system [the borstal] was to arrest or check the evil habit by the "individualization" of the prisoner, mentally, morally, and physically.'[449] Indeed, views regarding the effects of individualised treatment had already been expressed before the emergence of the borstal sentence;[450] yet, through data related to the borstal training, it is possible to reconstruct the problematic relationship between individualisation, training for citizenship, and institutionalisation. The core analysis will draw upon an unpublished study on the effects of *Re-building Character in Delinquent Youth* conducted by Field during the 1930s. Field had unrestricted access to at least five borstals during a period of seven months. In addition, he annotated 85 detailed case studies of youths interviewed during this period.[451] Field argued that individualisation of treatment could be achieved by addressing the different and personal needs of a person while maintaining a positive connection to the system. The 'system' is what binds the individuals to a

> set of principles, rules, and methods, by which necessary arrangements for maintenance, training, and safeguard, are effected [...] in order to preserve a reasonable consistency, continuity, and balance in administration.[452]

The system is not necessarily antagonistic to individualisation; yet it might destroy it when it becomes 'mechanically uniform'.[453] The historical records indicate that the fragile relationship between individualisation and the system was maintained, in particular, through the practice of classification, the keeping of case records, and the system of progressive stages; these will be assessed consecutively below.

A core feature of the borstal system was 'classification'. It is important to note that youths sent to borstal were typically re-offenders below the age of 21; therefore classification was determined based on the ability of these offenders to comply with the purpose of the training, which embraced a variety of activities from physical exercise to a range of educational instructions. It also included, at a later stage of the consummation of the sentence, the designation of appropriate vocational training. In other words,

---

[449] Ruggles-Brise, *The English Prison System*, p.93.
[450] See previous chapter.
[451] H.E. Field, *Re-building Character in Delinquent Youth* (London: Institute of Education, 1933, unpublished PhD).
[452] Ibid., p.55.
[453] Ibid., p.56.

'classification' was intended to group the youths according to their physical and mental skills to maximise the effect of training. For instance, Portland borstal was planned for youths who had institutional experience (army, industrial school or prison), and as a consequence, their training was particularly strict. Feltham borstal accommodated the less physically and mentally fit youths who had been identified as being unable to pursue a demanding training programme such as the one followed in Rochester.[454] Classification of girls sentenced to borstal was affected by their small numbers; thus, all the girls were sent to Aylesbury, and the need to set up another institution did not arise.[455] Arguably, some level of classification aiming at promoting individualisation was possible due to their small numbers. However, in practice, Aylesbury's borstal-staff was left to address the issue of classification by themselves. It appears from Mary Size's memoirs that 'There were approximately fifty girls, who socially, mentally and educationally differed widely and presented a rather difficult problem. I interviewed them individually, gave them a simple test and then classified them.'[456]

The 'case records' were another typical feature of the borstal. Foucault saw the collection and maintenance of prisoners' records as a means to allow greater levels of 'control' and 'domination' over the 'correction' of the individual.[457] He argued that the information gathered was used to produce knowledge of practices in relation to an identifiable group (rather than to a single detainee) whose members had similar individual characteristics (such as character, type of offence, socio-economic status, sex, age, and health).[458] This 'examination' fostered the management of a group which was erroneously classified as homogeneous. This was indeed evident in the policy, implemented by the first Prison Commission[459] in 1877, which introduced a uniform treatment administration across the prison system; according to Camp: 'The effect of the Prison Commissioners was to engender administrative efficiency, but to take no account of prisoners as

---

[454] Field, p.108.
[455] Aylesbury reached a peak of 250 girls during World War II, but even so, the maximum containment capacity of the institution was not reached (Fox, *The English Prison and Borstal*, p.361). Only in 1946 was East Sutton Park in Kent opened as an additional borstal for girls.
[456] M. Size, *Prisons I Have Known* (London: George Allen & Unwin Ltd, 1957), p.37.
[457] Foucault, p.191.
[458] Ibid., p.190.
[459] In that regard, see Part I of this study.

individuals'.[460] Arguably, however, the borstal's meticulous documentation of the youths' behaviour, character, progress or regression in their training achievements[461] was not used in the way exemplified by the panoptical perspective identified by Foucault. Rather, the borstal system of documentation facilitated

> the arrangements and methods by which the distinctive personal needs of each subject are ascertained and satisfied, and by which adaptation is effected between the individual and the given system.[462]

In other words, the knowledge gathered was not necessarily (or at least not only) used to compose a communal set of rules to be applied to the individuals as a group; rather, the aim was to use that knowledge to facilitate every individual's personal training process. The borstal system of documentation was essential for promoting greater levels of freedom and higher degrees of trust, resulting in greater benefits. One of the ways of achieving this was through regular interviews, as noted by Ruggles-Brise:

> Those doing well encouraged; those doing badly cautioned, and made clearly to understand that they will not be allowed the privilege of the higher grades until the institution board is completely satisfied that they are doing their best in every way to profit by the opportunities afforded.[463]

As Paterson further explained:

> It becomes necessary to study the individual lad, to discover his trend and his possibilities, and to inflict him with some idea of life which will germinate and produce a character, controlling desire and shaping conduct to something more glorious than mere satisfaction or acquisition.[464]

Case records were of great importance to the 'progressive stage system', the last typical feature of the borstal. Inevitably, young prisoners had to be periodically assessed for their promotion (or regression) in a system whose last stage envisaged less supervision and greater levels of liberty. The goal of the progressive stage system was the promotion of the deserving youths, towards the final stage of their sentence, to positions of leadership and unsupervised freedom. This final target was fundamental to the borstal policy and involved preparing the youths for a useful and law-abiding life

---

[460] Camp, p.43.
[461] As indicated by Field, p.154.
[462] Field, p.55.
[463] Ruggles-Brise, *The English Prison System*, p.256.
[464] Paterson, p.97.

once released, providing them with opportunities for empowerment, trust and self-growth.

However, although the three borstal features discussed above were all geared towards the maintenance of individualised treatment, having at the top of the agenda the abatement of institutionalisation, the dynamic of this enterprise should not be taken at face value. In fact, an assessment of the evidence provided by Field suggests that the initial stages of the borstal penalty might have contributed to the development of institutionalisation rather than to its elimination. To clarify that, it is possible to draw on Goffman's and Foucault's discussions on the 'total'[465] and 'complete'[466] institutions: within this context, the process of institutionalisation materialises the desire to 'correct' the detainee into a 'shape' that conforms to an idea of what is acceptable in that particular time and place. However, to do so, the total institution has to 'break it [the detainee] down and rearrange it'.[467] In other words, not only do the total institution's characteristics and environment bring about an 'untraining'[468] from known social skills but they also have an adverse effect on the personality of the detainee or, as described by Goffman, lead to the 'mortification of the self':[469]

> After a long term of imprisonment, passive obedience and dependence upon authority have become habitual, and the prisoner finds himself, when he at last faces the tasks of normal life, without decision, without initiative, and lacking in self-control.[470]

Indeed, the borstal individualised 'training' appeared to be a feature enjoyed by those who had reached the advanced grades within this process of promotion, whereas the newcomers were subject to a dull regime of activities, mainly cleaning and physical training, in addition to higher degrees of discipline and punishment and greater levels of restraint and limited physical movement. One of Field's case studies may illustrate the initial process of institutionalisation:

> During the first few months the lad appeared to be almost a-moral, and lacking in sense of responsibility regarding the future. In response to one

---

[465] Goffman, 1961.
[466] Foucault, chapter 4.
[467] Ibid., p.138.
[468] Goffman, p.23
[469] Ibid., p.24.
[470] Labour Research Department, p. 573.

year of training he has slowly become orderly and steady at work. Desire to earn remission and dislike of punishment has served as incentive to control some of his irresponsible ways. Under constant supervision he is cleaner and more orderly in habits [...].[471]

Significantly, the myth of the 'prisoners' reformation' perspective is also illustrated through the borstal enterprise. As with the adult prison system, there was an incompatibility between what was desired, on one hand, and what happened in practice, on the other hand. Indeed, statements by Paterson and the Official Handbook on Borstals can be considered typical expressions contributing to the shaping of this myth. For example, Paterson stressed that 'if the institution is to train lads for freedom, it cannot train them in an atmosphere of captivity and repression';[472] the Official Handbook on Borstals instructed that it '[...] is to regard him [the lad] as a living organism, having its secret of life and motive-power within [...]',[473] or that 'the aim should rather be [...] to eliminate from the regime whatever was merely negative and repressive, and to emphasise or introduce whatever might be positive and constructive.'[474]

It is worth taking a closer look at the relationship between penal policy and the borstal sentence. Although borstal advocates rejected physical control and its impact on prisoners' personality, they recognised that borstal training had to be 'compatible with compulsory detention'.[475] In other words, anything that might have fostered individualised treatment or any other novel system of training had to be in line with the demands of security, control and containment typical of imprisonment, which, inevitably, were also at the core of the process of institutionalisation. Though borstal was a sentence in its own right drawing upon values of citizenship and social integration, it was nevertheless dependent upon mainstream penal-prison policy and affected by drawbacks in the prison system. Any attempt to bring about reform in the custodial system is futile from its outset because the system itself is not challenged, but the 'reform' is shaped and dependent upon the existing framework; indeed, the borstal sentence lasted for less

---

[471] Field, Appendix II, case study A11, p.237.

[472] Paterson, p.96.

[473] *The Principles of the Borstal System*, Prison Commission, Home Office, 1932, quoted in M. Fry, 'The Borstal System', in *Penal Reform in England*, ed. by L. Radzinowicz and J.W. Turner, 2nd edn (London: Macmillan and Co., 1946), pp. 127-151 (p.157).

[474] *Prisons and borstals*, Home Office (London: HMSO, 1945), p.10.

[475] Fox, *The English Prison and Borstal*, pp.355-7.

than 80 years and was not without controversy.[476] Carlen's concept of carceral clawback also makes us aware that the rationale behind the use of imprisonment was justified under the specific socio-political concerns of the time. The Prison Commission provided the sought-after justification for imprisoning young offenders, while also responding to social concerns regarding crime, the youth offender, and punishment.

Plans for Reform: Pre-War

The above discussion reveals the problematic issues underlining the borstal system as seen in retrospect; in fact, however, the borstal was a successful 'clawback', because not only was there a social justification for its use, but it also provided principles to be adopted by the adult prison management and, in particular, the female prison population. It was believed that 'in view of the success achieved at Lowdham [open borstal] possibly, a further experiment might be tried in building a prison for women on cottage lines.'[477] However, a meeting held in 1934 on the subject of female prisoners reveals that the prison commissioners were concerned about the feasibility of such a project: in their view, the classification of men prisoners created homogeneous manageable groups, but 'when you come to women prisoners and try to classify them you break the mass up into individuals.'[478] Furthermore, though the male prison population was increasing, the female one remained relatively steady after the war (always below 1,000);[479] it was financially inconvenient for the Prison Commission to invest in such a small and varied population. The prison system already found it hard to cope with the geographical distribution of women offenders. Because of the large number of male offenders, there was a reasonable distribution of male local prisons around the country, whereas the availability of women's local prisons was much more limited: Holloway prison in London and a few

---

[476] Abolished by the Criminal Justice Act 1982.
[477] Miss Kelly E.H from HMP Winchester in the Prison Commission minutes 1934 (LNA, PCOM 9/192).
[478] Alexander Paterson's reply to Miss E.H Kelly from HMP Winchester and Mrs. Dewar Robertson J.P. from HMP Holloway in the Prison Commission minutes 1934 (LNA, PCOM 9/192).
[479] *People in prison England and Wales*, Home Office (London: HMSO, 1969), p.111.

wings in male prisons around the country which were gradually closing down, clearing space for the increasing male population.[480]

The number of women prisoners appeared to be a key issue in assessing the prison system's capacity to provide appropriate treatment. It appears that across the system, female prisons found it difficult to accommodate provision for physical exercise, work, and other benefits such as wages and eating in association.[481] For example, the Prison Commission was aware that 'while the Governor and his keen staff [at Holloway prison] do everything possible [...] it will easily be understood how impossible it is to provide training suitable to their capacity or incapacity, for about a hundred different types of women.'[482] Moreover, both reports on *Persistent Offenders* (1932) and the *Employment of Prisoners* (1933) expressed the opinion that neither Holloway nor the additional six women's wings in the male prisons were of sufficient standard. In particular, the report on persistent offenders condemned the 'fortress type' building, suggesting that it could have an adverse effect on prisoners' susceptibility to reoffending, whereas the report on employment of prisoners suggested that the 'fastnesses of Holloway' should be replaced with 'houses [on the outskirts of London] sufficiently small and un-institution-like.'[483] Holloway castle, which had represented the ultimate prison design in the 1840s and 1850s,[484] was now an impediment to the success of prisoners' reformation.

---

[480] Miss Kelly E.H,Prison Commission minutes 1934 (LNA, PCOM 9/192). The availability of local prisons for women was similar in the following years. As for 1945, Holloway prison was still the only local prison available with five additional male prisons that provided separated wings for women: Birmingham, Cardiff, Durham, Exeter and Manchester. Aylesbury was a convict prison for the Star Class only (*Prisons and borstals*, pp.47-48).

[481] Miss E.H Kelly, Prison Commission minutes 1934 (LNA, PCOM 9/192).

[482] Miss E.H Kelly, Prison Commission minutes 1934 (LNA, PCOM 9/192).

[483] Both the reports were quoted in the Prison Commission minutes 1934 (LNA, PCOM 9/192).

[484] P. Rock, *Reconstructing a women's prison- The Holloway redevelopment project 1968-88* (Oxford: Clarendon Press, 1996), pp.16, 21; J.A.F. Watson, 'The Prison System', in *Penal Reform in England*, ed. in L. Radzinowicz and J.W. Turner, 2nd edn (London: Macmillan and Co., 1946), pp.152-169, (p.169).

Holloway

Some suggestions were put forward for improving the situation, including small-scale refurbishment and even a proposition for completely new accommodations.[485] Nevertheless, the 1934 meeting's minutes reveal a worrisome argument; to provide better treatment, the number of women prisoners should be greater: 'The trouble is that there are not enough women criminals! [sic].'[486] It may be that this view was fuelled by the idea that exactly the same 'system of training' as in the Lowdham Grange open borstal and New Hall Camp male prison should be applied to women,[487] instead of considering a more flexible, tailored approach that would correspond to women prisoners' custodial conditions and needs. It was only after the war that the Prison Commission changed this perspective.[488]

The plans for building a new prison for women to replace Holloway became tangible in 1938 with the appointment of Sir Samuel Hoare as Home Secretary. Incidentally, Sir Samuel Hoare was the great nephew of Elizabeth Fry, and like her, he was particularly interested in the reform of prison administration. As nicely put by Captain Heilgers in a House of Commons debate regarding the Criminal Justice Bill: 'May I say to the Home Secretary that in view of the almost unanimously favourable reception of this Bill I feel certain that when history comes to be written his name will go down with the name of his ancestor Elizabeth Fry among the great prison reformers.'[489] Further support for prison reform was expressed through the 1938 Criminal Justice Bill, where in the second reading, the House of Commons voiced the view that it would 'want more places like New Hall Camp at Wakefield [...] the great feature about [it] is that there are no real boundaries.'[490] Subsequently, news headlines such as 'Better Prisons and Fewer Prisoners',[491] 'Famous Gaols to be Pulled Down',[492] and 'Camp Gaols For Women',[493] praised the governmental plan.[494] The 'prison

---

[485] Prison Commission minutes 1934 (LNA, PCOM 9/192).
[486] Mrs. J.P. Earengey, from HMP Holloway in the Prison Commission minutes 1934 (LNA, PCOM 9/192).
[487] Prison Commission minutes 1934 (LNA, PCOM 9/192).
[488] Memorandum by the prison commissioners on their proposals for the development of the prison system for adults during the immediate post war years, 1944, LNA, PCOM 9/1386.
[489] HC Deb 29 November 1938, cc321.
[490] By Mr. Muff, HC Deb 29 November 1938, cc311.
[491] *Evening News*, 28 July 1938 (LNA, PCOM 9/139).
[492] *News Chronicle*, 28 July 1938 (LNA, PCOM 9/139)
[493] *Daily Mirror*, 26 July 1938 (LNA, PCOM 9/139).
[494] The 'prison plan' was presented to the House of Commons on the 27 July 1938 (Home Office Administration, HC Deb 27 July 1938 vol 338 cc3140-251).

reform' to be implemented included the eradication of fortress-like prisons and the construction of modern prison accommodations. 'Modernisation' of the prison system was to be based upon the idea of borstals and camps. Drawing on the examples of the Lowdham Grange open borstal and New Hall Camp, reformers believed that the combination of smaller accommodations (house units) and an outdoor working routine (ideally in agriculture and gardening) were beneficial to the prisoners' wellbeing. Sir Samuel Hoare explained that 'The kind of prison I have in mind is something entirely different from Holloway, something much more in the nature of a camp in the country...'.[495] The 'housing programme', as it was defined, was intended to be cost effective because of its gradual application; it consisted of a new purpose-built women's prison, and Holloway was to be modernised and would eventually accommodate all the male prisoners currently housed in Pentonville prison.[496]

Inevitably, the new construction plan aired a couple of popular concerns: lenient punishment and public expenditure. Despite the successful experiences of Lowdham Grange and New Hall Camp, a new custodial facility had to be re-justified on the grounds of effective and financially feasible penal policy. It is essential to remember that the launch of Lowdham Grange was justified under a wide socio-penal policy concerning youth offenders and although New Hall Camp targeted adult prisoners, it was first initiated as an emergency plan to tackle prison work. Thus, the argument put forward to legitimise this new enterprise (hence the carceral clawback paradigm) was motioned by the Home Secretary Sir Samuel Hoare as follows. First, with the use of statistics, Hoare was able to demonstrate a decline of 77% in prison receptions from 1907 to 1937. The statistics also indicated that 79.9% of the total number of first offenders released from prison throughout this period had not reoffended. Finally, the data suggested that public security would not be jeopardised because the number of 'irredeemable' habitual offenders, 170 men and 70 women, was very small.[497] The 'picture' presented to the House of Commons and the public was aimed at emphasising the great success of penal policies since the beginning of the century; in turn, this 'success' suggested that the

---

[495] Quoted in the *Daily Express*, 28 July 1938 (LNA, PCOM 9/139).
[496] London County Council was considering designating the site of Pentonville for a housing scheme for North-East London (HC Deb 27 July 1938, col3160).
[497] Sir S. Hoare (HC Deb 27 July 1938, cc3152). Media support was evident in their unquestioning citation of these statistics and further boosting public confidence in the penal success (*Evening News* 28 July 1938 'Better prisons and fewer prisoners'; Birmingham Post 29 July 1938 'Prison Reform' (LNA, PCOM 9/139).

reforms presented could only lead to further success. Indeed, as the *Evening News* declared in the summer of 1938: 'The chief justification of model penal methods in Britain lies in one simple fact [...]: in 1927, 47,049 men and women were admitted to prisons, whereas twenty years ago the figure was 211,519.'[498] In reality, there might have been at least two reasons that could have explained such a drastic decline in prison receptions. Brockway and Hobhouse argue that the outbreak of World War One led to an 81% decline in prison receptions in only five years; thereafter, the average remained below 50,000 prisoner receptions per year. The significant reduction could also be due to changes in recorded figures: from 1914, the usual Prison Returns were replaced by Court Returns.[499]

Justification for reform was also sought in public sentiment. This was expressed by the various news reports: 'restore criminals to society as self-respecting creatures' and 'the taxpayer has no occasion to grumble about having to put his hand in the pocket [...] Nobody currently would call in question the psychological influence [...] upon women's self-respect'.[500] However, it was also made clear that the reform would not affect just punishment; indeed, the Home Secretary, in his speech in the House of Commons, made it clear that reform had little to do with 'a sentimental feeling of benevolence', arguing that it was the outcome of expert opinions[501] regarding the 'successful way of keeping down crime and of preventing people who get into prison from coming back'.[502]

Sir Samuel Hoare had an important share in the promotion of these prison plans; yet, historical records, although scarce, reveal that in charge of these plans was the newly appointed assistant prison commissioner, Miss Lillian Barker.[503] Insight on Lillian Barker's approach is limited, but her most memorable statements have been quoted in a number of monographs and memoirs, where the full quotation is given by Lillian Barker's niece, Elizabeth Gore:

---

[498] *Evening News* 28 July 1938 'Better Prisons and Fewer Prisoners' (LNA, PCOM 9/139).
[499] Labour Research Department, pp.27-33.
[500] *Daily Mirror* 29 July 1938; Birmingham Post 29 July 1938 (LNA, PCOM 9/139).
[501] By 'experts', Sir Hoare refers to 'the people who know most about these things'. Yet he only cites two sources to support this view, one being an ex-prisoner's memoir and the second being a report by a prison governor. There is no disclosure of the titles of these sources (HC Deb 27 July 1938, cc3159).
[502] HC Deb 27 July 1938, vol 338, cc3140-251 (c3158).
[503] Camp, p.99.

Instead of parking women in prison I should like to imprison them in a park. It should be possible for them to live not in the atmosphere of huge stone buildings, but of trees and grass [...].[504]

Subsequently, the plan was approved by the Treasury,[505] and locations at Heathrow in London[506] and at Stanwell in Middlesex were considered for purchase by the Prison Commission.[507]

Nevertheless, all these plans were abruptly stopped by the war.

Post-War: New Plans and the Lease of Askham Grange

The above-discussed reforms never took place due to the outbreak of World War Two; yet Sir Samuel Hoare's efforts were not completely fruitless. The debate regarding women prisoners' custodial facilities was raised again in 1944. In a Prison Commission document addressing the issue of prison reform for the period after the war, the commissioners proposed a clear operational outline.[508] Most importantly, they recognised drawbacks in the pre-war reform proposals. First, the report highlighted the need for 'radically different' treatment and training for women prisoners. The Commission argued that a system specifically designed for women prisoners rendered the 'problem' of having a small number of women in prison redundant, and that the small number was in fact an advantage. The key solution was to deal locally with remanded prisoners and those with short sentences (below six months), whereas for longer prison sentences, women would be allocated to one of the two small prisons which would be designed for that purpose.[509] Interestingly, the commissioners rejected the

---

[504] E. Gore, *The Better Fight: The Story of Dame Lillian Baker* (London: Bles, 1964), p.235.

[505] Figures from the draft Financial Memorandum for the Criminal Justice Bill 1938 demonstrates that a capital budget of £200,000 and an annual maintenance budget of £50,000 was to be allocated for prisons and borstals (from a Home Office Correspondence dated 14 November 1938, LNA, HO 45/177768).

[506] Today, the site is the airport runway (Camp, p.100).

[507] Prison Commission minutes 1944: Memorandum by the prison commissioners on their proposals for the development of the prison system for adult during the immediate post war years (LNA, PCOM 9/1386).

[508] Prison Commissioners' minutes 1944: Memorandum by the prison commissioners on their proposals for the development of the prison system for adults during the immediate post war years (LNA, PCOM 9/1386).

[509] An additional prison was planned for women prisoners classified as 'persistent offenders' (Prison Commissioners' minutes 1944, LNA, PCOM 9/1386).

'camp' idea as generally being inappropriate for women. The construction plan to be adopted was still along the lines of the minimum-security home-cottage style; suggesting that it should not be far from a city or town, as proximity would facilitate a healthy interaction with the community and a realistic living environment; the commissioners noted that 'we cannot expect them to live in a convent'.[510]

The aspiration to find adequate accommodation for women prisoners 'in the country within easy reach of a city or town, where it would be possible to obtain land for cultivation and facilities for raising poultry and pigs, as well as flowers, vegetables and fruit'[511] was materialised with the lease of the Victorian mansion of Askham Grange. The 10 acres of property was about to be relinquished by the war office after functioning as a military hospital during World War Two. Previously, the property had belonged to the wealthy Fairbairn family since its construction in 1886. The lady of the house donated it to the Red Cross during World War One to function as a convalescent house for wounded soldiers while her husband and son were serving in the war. From 1939, the house was taken over by the war office after first being offered again to the Red Cross, who declined it because of practical inconveniences.[512] The historical records indicate, however, that the Prison Commission was not the only bidder for the land, as the West Riding local education department found the property attractive for the establishment of a special school for children with disabilities. The Ministry of Education wrote in despair to the Prison Commission, imploring them to abandon their bid on the purchase: 'if, by any chance, it would be possible for you to get hold of some other place [...]'.[513] However, in 1946, the mansion house and surrounding land was successfully leased to the Prison Commission, where 'from the Home Office point of view, the need for the establishment of a training prison for women is urgent; the opportunity of obtaining any place as suitable as Askham Grange is unlikely to occur'.[514] Shortly after, the Prison Commission was informed that 'the Treasury have

---

[510] Prison Commissioners' minutes 1944 (LNA, PCOM 9/1386).

[511] Prison report 1947 quoted in B. Lewis and H. Crew, *The Story of a House, Askham Grange Women's Open Prison* (Yorkshire: Yorkshire Art Circus and HMP Askham Grange, 1997), p.45.

[512] Lewis and Crew, pp.22-23

[513] From correspondence by the Medical Branch of the Ministry of Education to the Prison Commission, 1946 (LNA, HO 45/23223).

[514] Home Secretary's communication to the West Riding Education Department, 1946 (LNA, HO 45/23223).

now agreed that the commissioners should take over the above property, in accordance with the terms of the Ministry of Works'.[515]

The pressure exercised by the prison commissioners for the acquisition of Askham Grange was not only due to the rare chance of finding available estates to be used as prisons; they were also driven by the opportunity to appoint the recently retired Mary Size to the position of prison governor.[516] Mary Size, 39 years in service, a former governor and deputy governor in Aylesbury prison and borstal and in Holloway prison, was the only person judged by the prison commissioners to have the experience and outlook needed for the new prison.[517] She accepted the post, yet records indicate that the appointment had little approval from the wider prison officers' community. For example, the *Daily Mirror* reported the following in autumn 1946:

> Protest against Miss Mary Size's appointment as governor of Yorkshire's new prison without bars for women—because she retired in 1942—was made by the Prison Officers' Association at a Prison Commissioners' London meeting yesterday.[518]

In retrospect, Mary Size proved to be a remarkable governor for the launch of Askham Grange as the first open prison for women. However, the Prison Officers' Association's protest was not completely without foundation. The post-war years saw many highly trained prison officers with little prospect of professional development.[519] This was further undermined by the Prison Commission's initiative to open up high ranking positions to external

---

[515] Communication from Under Secretary of State to the Prison Commission, Minutes Prison Commission book, 1947 (LNA, PCOM 9/1989).

[516] See the communication to the West Riding Education Department from the Home Secretary in 1946 on the decision taken with regard to Askham Grange (LNA, HO 45/23223)

[517] 'They are (the Prison Commissioners), however, in something of difficulty about the Governorship. There is at present in the Service no woman Governor or Housemistress who in their view would be suitable for starting a new establishment on entirely new lines such as they proposed [...] They have, however, ascertained that Miss Mary Size who [...] resigned on medical grounds early in the war, is now fully recovered and would be willing if approached, for a year or two at any rate, to come back in an un-established capacity for work such as this.' (from the Prison Commissioners minutes August 1946, LNA, PCOM 9/1989)

[518] *The Daily Mirror* 22 November 1946 (LNA, PCOM 9/1989).

[519] Prison Officers' Association minutes on 'The appointment of prison governors' 1948 (LNA, HO 45/21911).

recruitment.[520] Thus, being retired, Mary Size's appointment took away this opportunity from younger female colleagues. Indeed, *The Daily Herald* reported that: 'Women prison officers are objecting to the appointment of Miss Mary Size: "We consider there are women in the service capable of taking over the job" said the Association Secretary.'[521]

Although the actual operation of Askham Grange under the governorship of Mary Size will be discussed in the next chapter, it is important to review here how this new enterprise was received by the community and the media. First, it is essential to note that Askham Grange mansion was (and still is) situated at the heart of the two small Saxon villages of Askham Bryan and Askham Richard, in a central location (just next door to the local pub), which could not be missed by the neighbours. However, the initiative was not condemned by local residents. Their view supported the discourse of prisoners' reformation by way of training, as was advocated for the younger prison population. Indeed, one resident of Askham Bryan considered that 'if they are moved to these delightful surroundings they should have a much better chance of rehabilitation', and the village vicar stated that he 'can't see how there can be any objection to a plan which is obviously aimed at helping unfortunate girls'.[522] However, once the first prisoners were released from Askham Grange in the early 1950s, their views were reported by the media, which, in turn, fostered a somewhat stereotypical perception of the system. Headlines such as 'Life is Marvellous at our prison', 'They earn diplomas in gaol' and 'Lipstick used in no bar prison'[523] contributed to an ambiguous fascination with Askham Grange's penal regime. Undoubtedly, it did not provide a clear indication of what was really going on 'inside', but rather helped to create the misconception of the open prison as a holiday camp.[524] Joan Henry, who spent some of her sentence in Askham Grange during the 1950s, expressed a similar concern:

---

[520] From the 'Star Industrial Correspondent' 1 January 1948: 'Discontent has arisen among 3,600 prison workers because the Prison Commission are advertising vacancies for governors of Borstal Institution and prisons...' (LNA, HO45/21911).
[521] *The Daily Herald* 21 November 1946 (LNA, PCOM 9/1989).
[522] Mrs. J. M. Lees and the vicar of the village quoted in the Newcastle Journal, November 1946 (LNA, PCOM 9/1989)
[523] Daily Mirror 7 Jan 1948; Daily Dispatch 18 May 1949; The Newcastle Journal 18 May 1949 (LNA, PCOM 9/1989)
[524] For example, as reported by the Daily Mirror: 'My husband sent me a full set of make-up. It's just like a holiday camp—and there's no queuing to be done. Food is marvellous. And her husband said: She never looked better and is really happy' (7 Jan 1948, LNA, PCOM 9/1989).

On one occasion representatives of the BBC had been over Askham and were mentioning it in a broadcast talk on prisons. We were allowed to come down to listen to it [...] They certainly made Askham Grange sound like a rest home. From the commentary, you would have thought that our time was spent going to the pictures [...] certainly we had privileges which were greatly appreciated, but we worked extremely hard to earn them, and we all felt aggrieved that this aspect of our lives had been virtually ignored.[525]

Arguably, to the satisfaction of the anxious taxpayer, a balance was achieved with news articles that reported a less supportive account such as the one provided by another prisoner: 'I soon found that we were given so much work to do that there was no time to enjoy the delightful grounds, even in our exercise times'.[526]

The Training for Freedom

The 12th International Penal and Penitentiary Congress in The Hague, Netherlands, in 1950 debated the following question: 'Should not some of the methods developed in the treatment of young offenders be extended to the treatment of adults?'[527] The resolution was positive, and it appeared that the congress attendees agreed that

> because a young man or woman is legally an adult [above the age of 21], it does not mean that he or she must be condemned to a form of imprisonment which is shorn of all chances for education, training and reformation.[528]

However, by that time the English penal system had a recognised official framework:

> In pursuance of the Prison Rules 1949(a), I hereby approve of the setting aside of the prisons specified in the Schedule hereto for the treatment in open conditions of prisoners who have been sentenced either to imprisonment or to corrective training.[529]

---

[525] J. Henry, *Who lie in Gaol* (London: Victor Gollancz LTD, 1952), p.143.

[526] B. Minns, 'Girls have to Work Hard in Bar-Less Prison; too much Gardening and Evening Classes—says No 1 Prisoner', 20 July 1948 (name of newspaper unidentified) PCOM 9/1989.

[527] Resolutions of the XII International Penal and Penitentiary Congress quoted in Fox, *The English Prison and Borstal*, Appendix F, p.443.

[528] Fox, *The English Prison and Borstal*, Appendix F, p.443.

[529] One of His Majesty's Principal Secretaries of State, minutes 2 September 1949 (LNA HO 45/23223).

On this occasion, eight open custodial facilities were officially allocated to function as 'open prisons.' Among these was New Hall Camp, the first open prison, operating since the early 1930s, and Askham Grange, the first and only open prison for women. Instructions were further provided by the 1948 Criminal Justice Act on the 'system of training' to be applied to the adult prison population. More specifically, the Act created a somewhat complex system of sentencing, of allocation of prisoners, and of their assessment and their later relocation to 'specialised' prisons. Put simply, the system envisaged that male prisoners would be sent from court to a local prison and then transferred to an Allocation Centre for a risk assessment of their character and skills. Women, on the other hand, were to be assessed in a local prison (usually in a women's wing in a male prison, or alternatively in the female-only Holloway prison).[530] After their assessment, male prisoners would be sent to either a Closed Regional Training prison or to a Corrective Training prison if maximum security was needed. It was expected that a prisoner could be sent to an Open Regional Training prison either from the Allocation Centre or from a Closed Regional Training prison.[531] Although the choice was wide for male prisoners, the only specialised prisons for women were the 'training prisons' Holloway and Aylesbury and the 'open prison' Askham Grange.[532]

Within the first year of the open prisons' operation, the 1947 report by the Prison Commission provided some convincing information regarding the new prisons. For example, the Commission recorded that 89% of the prisoners released from New Hall Camp from 1937 to 1944 had not reconvicted. They were particularly positive about the work of Askham Grange, suggesting that 'it is at least most noticeable that the women benefit greatly in health by it.'[533] Similarly, the 1950 report on Prisons and Borstals was reassuring against any doubt regarding the credibility of these by stating that 'the open prison is therefore beyond the stage of experiment.'[534] Indeed, the report emphasised that 'training [...] in self-respect and a sense of personal responsibility, can be carried much further in the more normal and humane atmosphere of a camp or a country house than in the repressive conditions of a walled prison.'[535] In an attempt to introduce clarity with

---

[530] Fox, *The English Prison and Borstal*, pp.313, 433.
[531] *Prisons and borstals*, p. 40.
[532] Fox, *The English Prison and Borstal*, p.433.
[533] *Report on the Commissioners of Prisons for the year 1947, Report of the Commissioners of Prisons*, Home Office (London: HMSO, 1947-55), p.38.
[534] *Prisons and Borstals,* p.20.
[535] Ibid., p.21.

regard to imprisonment's aims and to 'sweep away the remnants' of what was referred to as 'Victorian Melodrama',[536] the 1950 *Statement of Policy* said that priority should be given to 'the social rehabilitation of the prisoner, so that after his release he will encounter the fewest possible obstacles'[537].

The 'system of training' for adult prisoners set up by the 1948 Criminal Justice Act drew upon the penal objectives that were then common practice within the borstal system. The 1950 *Statement of Policy* explained that the 'system of training' was developed 'from five basic ideas'.[538] These ideas, all identifiable in the borstal system, were as follows: the prison's regime should be constructive; prisons other than the local prison should be designated for training purposes; the 'training prisons' could be of a low security nature or, when possible, in open conditions; there should be a certain level of community engagement while the prisoner was in prison in the form of work or any other voluntary involvement; and finally, the prisoners should be supported through the process of release and shortly thereafter to guarantee effective social integration.[539]

*

Interestingly, despite this significant socio-political framework of prison reform, imprisonment itself was not challenged; rather, the new system was set up to mitigate what the 1950 report recognised as the 'de-formative effects of imprisonment'.[540] In other words, within the context set by the Act, adult prisoners would eventually move to a training prison, but only after they had spent the required amount of time in a local prison. Hence, this new system of training was built upon the same decadent system that it was intended to mitigate. The policy of the system of training was not challenging the framework of imprisonment; rather, it looked at how to 'fix' the damage caused by it. This is the fundamental problem that will condemn the system of training in the future to come. However, this is not all. Not only was the mainstream prison system not challenged, it was maintained that it constituted a pillar of the penal system. In fact, the 12th International Penal and Penitentiary Congress at The Hague, 1950, debated whether

---

[536] Secretary of State for the Home Department, Sir Samuel Hoare, Criminal Justice Bill, HC Deb 29 November 1938 vol 342 cc267-377, cc282.

[537] *Prisons and borstals: Statement of policy and practice in the administration of the prisons and Borstal institution in England and Wales*, (London: H.M.S.O, 1950), pp.10-11.

[538] *Prisons and borstals*, p.11

[539] Ibid.

[540] The 1950 report (*Prisons and Borstals,* p.21).

'open institutions [can] take the place of the traditional prison'. The answer given was unanimously in the negative, the reason being that there will always be prisoners who will be considered unsuitable for such conditions.[541]

This chapter focused on the development of two exceptional custodial systems antagonistic to the mainstream orthodox closed prison. The analysis reveals a new wave of thought in policy and socio-political discourses in relation to the understanding of prisoners' reformation; it uncovers the attempt to 'take' the 'reformation' of the prisoner outside the prison's walls. The borstal and the open prison were set up to 'untrain' the prisoners from the acquired prison culture while retraining them to regain those social skills lost through the process of imprisonment. However, 'reforms' to the prison system must be understood as contingent on the foundation of the orthodox closed prison; this is because the change is applied within the context of an already established and grounded method. Thus, the mainstream prison, being in a permanent state of crisis, implies that any attempt for prison reform would be at risk. The next chapter develops this understanding of the role of the open prison within the context of the mainstream prison system, using the women's open prison Askham Grange as a case study.

---

[541] Resolutions of the XII International Penal and Penitentiary Congress quoted in Fox, *The English Prison and Borstal*, Appendix F, p.439.

PART IV

UNDERSTANDING OPEN PRISONS:
THE FIRST WOMEN'S OPEN PRISON HMP
ASKHAM GRANGE[542]

In her research on Soviet Russia's prisons conducted in 1931, Lenka Von Koerber describes two agricultural prison colonies as 'Prisons with Open Doors',[543] emphasising the rather flexible but controversial nature of this type of prison. Indeed, an open prison can be described as

> a custodial facility with no locked gates or wired fences demarcating the prison territory, and thus the levels of security (as for detention purposes) are minimal. A suitable example is Askham Grange open prison for women in Yorkshire. The entrance to the prison's estate, at the far edge of an extensive garden, is open to the village road; and apart from an iron garden-gate (which stays open at least during the day) and a Prison Service sign, nothing keeps one from stepping in and out of the estate. Inevitably, this system is only suitable for low-risk prisoners, who pose few security concerns or threats to themselves (as for self harm), on other prisoners and staff (as for assault and violent behaviour), or on the community (as for public safety concerns).[544]

This chapter focuses on the regime of the open prison, using as a case study HMP Askham Grange open prison for women in Yorkshire. The argument addressed in the previous chapter is developed here by assessing the dynamic of the penal policy of 'prisoners' training for freedom' outside the

---

[542] To clarify, I have used a variety of official statistics throughout this chapter. However, statistics specifically regarding Askham Grange have been considered up to 2008, when the prison's management was united with the management of New Hall female closed prison. Although the study does not cover the period after 2008, when possible, I have quoted the most recent statistics, at the time of writing, published by the Ministry of Justice and related organisations regarding the prison service's general state of affairs.

[543] *Soviet Russia Fights Crime* (London: Routledge, 1934) pp.179-194.

[544] From my field-note reflections prepared for this study (2007-8); these characteristics will be further discussed throughout this chapter.

prison walls. The concept of 'training', rather than 'reformation', was understood by socio-penal discourses of the 1930s-1950s as the process through which prisoners should be retrained for those social skills lost through the process of prison institutionalisation – adaptation to prison life. However, the drawbacks of the mainstream prison system and its constant state of crisis have gravely affected and undermined the policy of prisoners' progression through the prison system (from a closed to an open prison). Although the open prison was devised to fulfil the training component of the open conditions agenda, its success has been dependent on the (in)effective operation of the closed prison; this dysfunctional dynamic has been overlooked by penal policy. The interrelation between closed and open prisons also raises questions about the totality of the open prison; thus, to what extent is the open prison suited to the abatement of institutionalisation? Drawing upon characteristics of the Total Institution as identified by, for example, Goffman and Sykes, and testing them against open prison policy and practice, the open prison is indeed a Total Institution. However, due to the intrinsic characteristics and ethos of the open prison, totality is mitigated, and institutionalisation is largely abated.

The chapter begins by examining how prison policy concerning prisoners' progression from closed to open prison conditions was affected by the 1948 Criminal Justice Act and the 1966 Mountbatten report. It then examines issues stemming from the problematic implementation of the policy of prisoners' progression, addressing concerns such as waiting lists for prisoners' transfer to open conditions, the limitations brought about by prisoners' distance from their home residence and the subsequent over- or under-categorisation of prisoners. More specifically, the chapter then addresses aspects related to security categorisation and the risk assessment required for transfer to open conditions; the analysis draws upon data produced through the interviews I conducted for this study as well as Prison-rules; this unveils a discrepancy between risk assessment policy and its implementation in practice. The chapter then addresses the role of Askham Grange in the abatement of institutionalisation; here, the characteristics of Total Institutions and the effects of institutionalisation will be addressed by specifically examining the deprivation of liberty, the deprivation of autonomy and prisoners' culture. The last section of the chapter examines prisoners' adaptation to open conditions.

The Open Prison: Surviving Under the Shadow of the Orthodox Closed Prison

The first three women transferred to Askham Grange arrived on 9 January 1947, less than six days after Governor Mary Size arrived on the premises, which were not yet fully habitable.[545] It is likely that the women were transferred from Aylesbury which, according to Fox, apart from being a borstal for girls, also functioned as a women's prison for the long sentenced Star class[546]—those who were to be targeted for open prison accommodation. Askham Grange's ethos was soon revealed to the three prisoners, as described in Mary Size's memoirs:

> Another woman placed a chair for me by the fire. I sat down and talked with them for a little while, and then wished them 'Good-night' and closed the door as I left. I had walked some distance along the corridor leading to my bedroom when I heard the patter of feet. Looking round, I saw one of the women who exclaimed excitedly: 'Madam, you have forgotten to lock us in.' I returned to the dormitory with her and pointed out to the three women that they would not be locked in their room at any time, day or night. 'I trust you absolutely and I feel sure you will never betray that trust,' I told them. Back came the assurance. 'We will never let you down, Madam, whatever happens.'[547]

Governor Mary Size's memoirs *Prisons I Have Known* (1957) and the more recent *The Story of a House* (1997), produced in collaboration with HMP Askham Grange and Helena Kennedy, provide rather optimistic and idealistic accounts emphasising the holistic nature of this prison. And this might have been so. However, apart from researching the (hi)story of Askham Grange as a women's open prison, the interest of this study also lies in the assessment of the historical events and prison policy affecting the open prison; these events reveal several questions about the intrinsic nature of the open prison and the important but overlooked and detrimental relationship it has had with the mainstream orthodox closed prison. Indeed, it is this relationship, based upon the persistent drawbacks and crises typical of the mainstream prison, that, in turn, has led the open prison enterprise to acquire a marginal role in the process of prisoners' 'reformation'.

---

[545] Size, p.144.

[546] Fox, *The English Prison and Borstal,* p.435. See also Part I of this study, *The Myth of Reformation.* At the time of writing, Aylesbury is a Young Offender Institution for prisoners with long sentences.

[547] Size, p.146.

The problematic relationship between the mainstream orthodox prison and the open prison was set by the legislative provision that, in fact, gave life to HM Open Prison – the 1948 Criminal Justice Act.[548] The Act reinforced the concept of 'prisoners' training', implemented until then by the borstal system, which was perceived as establishing 'in them [convicted prisoners] the will to lead a good and useful life on discharge, and to fit them to do so'.[549] More specifically, the last stage of training - the transfer to an open prison - reflected the relatively new discourse related to prisoners' reformation: the abatement of the 'deformative effects of imprisonment'.[550] In other words, moving prisoners from highly secure and restrictive regimes to custodial facilities that allowed for greater levels of liberty would help 'untrain' them from the typical institutional habits gained through their imprisonment. Hence, the prospect was that almost all prisoners would go through this process (apart from those deemed 'unsuitable' to be accommodated in open conditions).[551]

However, the strategic complexity of the penal system and the unrealistic logistics set by the 1948 Act had greatly jeopardised the implementation of the progressive system of training. First, the 1948 Criminal Justice Act had also introduced two new penalties: Corrective Training and Preventive Detention (s.21). It appears that these penalties brought about a disproportionate increase in the number of offenders sent to prison. Indeed, it was reported to the House of Lords in 1952 that the prison service faced an urgent need for 3,232 additional beds.[552] It is essential to note that when the Act came into force, the prison service was able to comply with the Act's new policy requirements in relation to prison receptions, the number of prisons and the number of prison officers available. The total yearly reception of prisoners for 1949 was even lower than the preceding year's, standing at 48,493 people; the total daily average population recorded was

---

[548] c.58 (11 and 12 Geo.6).
[549] *Prisons and borstals*, p.11.
[550] Ibid., p.22.
[551] Ibid., p.22. See also 'Classification and Allocation pre-Black' diagram in D. Price, 'The Origins and Durability of Security Categorisation: A Study in Penological Pragmatism *or* Spies, Dickie and Prison Security, *British Society of Criminology Conference Selected Proceedings*, vol.3 (1999; published 2000), p.8.
[552] Conditions of Prison, HL Deb 18 November 1952, cc318-72, (c321). In that regard, see also J.C. Spencer's examination 'The Use of Corrective Training in the Treatment of the Persistent Offender in England', *Journal of Criminal Law and Criminology*, 44, 1 (1953), 40-44.

19,879.[553] However, by 1952, the number of yearly receptions had swollen to 52,805, and the daily average population had reached 23,670.[554] In his assessment of the system conducted in 1953, Spencer noted that 'the difficulties caused by overcrowding were hardly anticipated by prison administration'.[555] By 1959, prison receptions had increased by 52% and average daily population by 11%.[556] Inevitably, the prison service collapsed due to a lack of resources; the few open prisons available were only able to accommodate a limited number of prisoners, and thus, the mainstream prison estate became saturated with the excess: too many prisoners, not enough prisons and too few prison officers. Concerns were voiced:

> In such conditions, individualised treatment is bound to suffer; continuity of staff cannot be maintained, and the mere volume of work and the need for frequent transfers to relieve overcrowding impedes classification and the planning of a treatment programme suited to the needs of the individual offenders.[557]

While the open prison continued to be part of the prison system, its restricted use was finally settled just after 1966, following the Mountbatten report's recommendations.[558] The report was a response to several escapes in previous years; hence, it was concerned with the security measurements applied by the prisons. The Mountbatten report brought about an abrupt overturning of the system of training: in fact, the Corrective Training sentence was abolished by the 1967 Criminal Justice Act. The most insightful aspect of this new situation has been presented by Price. He indicates that the new security categorisation did not alter, at least initially, the existing system of Stars and Ordinaries.[559] The new arrangement of an A to D system of classifications of prisoners (categories) did not require a restructuring of the prison service's estate; on the contrary, the new

---

[553] *Report of the Commissioners of Prisons for the year 1950*, Home Office (London: HMSO, 1947-55), pp.11, 13.
[554] *Report of the Commissioners of Prisons for the year 1953* (1947-55), pp.6, 8-9.
[555] Spencer, p. 43.
[556] *Report of the Commissioners of Prisons for the year 1960*, Home Office (London: HMSO, 1956-62), pp.2-3.
[557] *Report of the Commissioners of Prisons for the year 1961* (1956-62), p.5.
[558] *Report on the Inquiry into Prisons Escapes and Security*, Admiral of the Fleet, the Earl Mountbatten of Burma, Great Britain, Home Office (London: HMSO, 1967).
[559] Star prisoners were those who faced imprisonment for the first time, whereas the Ordinaries were those who had been subject to the prison penalty more than once.

categories fit comfortably and overlapped with the existing practice.[560] However, the effect it had on the prison regime was rather dramatic. Price's analysis demonstrates that the main goal of the prison service shifted, although gradually, from the idea of treatment and training to security and containment.[561] Inevitably, categorisation and transfer to open conditions became the object of assiduous scrutiny.

On the face of it, open prisons were still highly regarded nationally and internationally, at least until the end of the 1960s. In fact, despite the doubts expressed by the House of Lords in 1952 regarding the workability of the system of training against the increase in prison population, the Lords still expressed their wish to see greater use of the open prison. For example, Viscount Simon thought that

> there is a great hope in the idea that a man who has the fate before him of remaining locked up in prison year after year, before the time comes for his release, should he be able to live in a freer atmosphere and learn again to become a citizen.[562]

In addition, Lord Chorley agreed that the Prison Commission's plan 'to open up a series of new prisons of this type in different parts of the country, is very much along the right lines'.[563] Indeed, up to the mid-1960s, the Prison Commission was still entertaining the idea of open prisons: 'Ministers had asked for the population of open prisons to be brought up to 5,000. The Board agreed to recommend that the present restrictions relating to crimes of violence should be relaxed.'[564] Similarly, the first UN Congress on the Prevention of Crime and Treatment of Offenders in 1955[565] plainly disregarded security in respect of the benefits of training:

> While in the open institution the risk of escape and the danger that the inmate may make improper use of his contacts with the outside world are admittedly greater than in other types of penal institutions, these

---

[560] Price, p.7.
[561] Ibid., pp.2-3.
[562] HL Deb 18 November 1952, cc318-72 (c326).
[563] Ibid., cc338-339.
[564] Prison Commission minutes, May 1963 (LNA, PCOM 14/10).
[565] *First UN Congress on the Prevention of Crime and Treatment of Offenders*, Geneva, Switzerland 22 Aug – 3 Sep 1955, http://www.asc41.com/UN_Congress/1st%20UN%20Congress%20on%20the%20 Prevention%20of%20Crime/first_congress.htm (accessed 01 Sep 2013).

disadvantages are amply outweighed [by its] advantages, which make the open institution superior to the other types of institutions.[566]

The Congress further recognised that 'open prison development was one of the most important steps in modern penological reform' and that it presented 'a successful application of the principle of individualisation of treatment with a view to social re-adjustment'.[567] Even the Mountbatten report expressed high regard for the open prison system in its 1966 assessment. Although the report focused its investigation on closed prisons, the committee gathered some informal evidence on open prisons. Indeed, Earl Mountbatten highlighted that the 'open establishment [...] is a policy which I warmly support' and

> nothing which I say subsequently in my report is intended to suggest a reversal of the trend to award treatment in open conditions. On the contrary, it is my impression [...] that many more prisoners now in closed conditions could be transferred to open conditions without danger to the public.[568]

However, in line with the Mountbatten report's recommendations, it followed that any decision regarding prisoners' welfare and the prison regime had to be tested against and function with the aspect of security.[569] Indeed, from 1965 onwards, the Prison Commission's meetings' minutes show a particular concern for aspects of prison security, something that had rarely been discussed in previous years.[570] From 1967, the minutes indicate increased engagement with the idea of categorisation as proposed by the Mountbatten report,[571] and from the 1970s, the open prison was given less and less attention, if any, by the Home Office and Government. Minutes by the Prison Board and Home Office prison statistics stopped reporting its progress and achievements. In 1977, the Home Office clarified that prison's aim

---

[566] *Open Institutions- Recommendations adopted by Section II*, Plenty Meeting, First United National Congress on the Prevention of Crime and the Treatment of Offenders, Geneva, 22 August to 3 September 1955, http://www.asc41.com/UN_Congress/1st%20UN%20Congress%20on%20the%20 Prevention%20of%20Crime/009%20ACONF.6.L.2%20Open%20Institutions.pdf (accessed 01 Sep 2013), p.4.
[567] *Open Institutions- Recommendations adopted*, p.5.
[568] *Report on the Inquiry into Prisons Escapes and Security*, p.55.
[569] Price, p.7.
[570] See Prison Commission minutes covering the years 1948 - 1970 (LNA, PCOM 14/9, 14/10 and 14/11).
[571] Prison Commission minutes 1967 (PCOM 14/11).

is to accept and contain, as long as necessary, those whom the courts send to them; and although men are sent to prison for a number of different reasons, they are not sent for treatment or for training in the first place.[572]

Thus, the open prison was surviving under the shadow of the orthodox closed prison. Moreover, around this time, a new discussion emerged involving community-based penalties.[573] This created a potent dichotomy between The Prison and The Alternative to Prison, which further dimmed the existence and relevance of the open prison.[574]

Both the increase in the prison population and the new security restrictions brought about by the new system of categorisation mainly related to the male prison population; and yet, the female prison estate was directly affected too. First, it is important to note that the female prison population had, in fact, been decreasing since 1945: from a peak of 7,381 yearly receptions and a daily average of 1,528 female prisoners, the numbers decreased by 33% and 19%, respectively, the following year. Through the 1950s, the yearly reception of women remained relatively steady, whereas daily average population trends were on the decrease until 1970, but since then, the female prison population has experienced a constant increase.[575] Second, the Mountbatten system of categorisation was never applied to the female prison estate. Although the old system of Stars and Ordinaries was eventually abandoned, the categorisation of women prisoners was established based on the apparently simple distinction between closed and open prison, without the sub categorisation available in male prisons.

---

[572] *Report on the work of the Prison Department for the year 1976-1977*, Great Britain. Prison Department, (London: HMSO, 1964-1986), p.10.

[573] The introduction of non-custodial penalties followed the recommendations developed by Baroness Wootton in 1969 (*Community Service Orders: a first decade of promise,* Howard League for Penal Reform, K. Pease [London: National Institute of Justice, 1981]).

[574] The emergence of community-related penalties and their effects on the penal system will not be discussed here.

[575] *Prison Population Statistics*, House of Commons Library, G. Berman (version: 22 December 2010; 7 November 2011), p.6.

A glimpse of freedom

The Prisoners' Progression Policy: Limitations

Although the female prison population estate was not faced by overcrowding while also not being subject to the new system of categorisation, the relationship between the system of progressive training and security categorisation presented a problematic dynamic. In other words, the discourse of prisoners' reformation shifted away from the 'prisoners' training' perspective and the importance it placed on diminishing institutionalisation while enhancing social integration; yet, policy in that regard was not changed, and prisoners were still expected to go through the process of progressive stages, notwithstanding the lack of commitment to cater for such a provision. The issues underlining this dynamic can be seen in the story of the imprisonment of Vicky Pryce in 2013. Headlines such as the *Sun*'s 'Vicky's cushy new jail: Pryce moved to soft prison after FOUR days [*sic*]'[576] instructed the public to reflect on the unjust practice whereby the prisoner was transferred to open conditions 'after just four nights inside tough Holloway Prison'.[577] However, it is a comment made in the *Mirror News* that reveals the real drawback of the system:

> The families of prisoners at Holloway Prison, North London, reacted angrily to the news yesterday. One couple visiting their daughter said: "It's a disgrace as there are girls in there who have been waiting for months and then she comes along and jumps the queue."[578]

The core of interest of the above report is the existence of a 'queue' for the transfer to open conditions. The 'queue' for transfer is evidence that the system of progression from a closed prison to an open prison is being implemented. However, despite having a waiting list, in practice, prisoners might never be transferred to an open prison, the main reason being the small number of spaces available across the country. Further exemplifying the existence of the progression policy, but lack of engagement with it, is

---

[576] Vicky Pryce was convicted in March 2013 of preventing the course of justice and was sentenced to eight months in prison (P. Rhodri, 'Vicky's cushy new jail: Pryce moved to soft prison after FOUR days', 17 March 2013, *The Sun*, http://www.thesun.co.uk/sol/homepage/news/4845651/Disgraced-Vicky-Pryce-is-moved-to-softer-open-prison-in-countryside-after-just-FOUR-days-in-Holloway.html (accessed 20 Aug 2013)).
[577] Ibid.
[578] J. Penrose and A. Wellman, 'Vicky Pryce moved to Cushy open prison just three days after she was jailed', *Mirror News*, 17 March 2013, http://www.mirror.co.uk/news/uk-news/vicky-pryce-moved-cushy-open-1769457 (accessed 20 Aug 2013).

the changing of the security categorisation of HMP Drake Hall in 2000 from a women's open prison to a 'semi-open prison',[579] thus reducing the total number of available beds in open prisons from approximately 500 across the country to less than 250.[580] In 2009, however, Drake Hall was again redesigned, this time to function as a closed prison.[581] The press release sent out by Women in Prison (WIP) expressed the charity's anger 'about the quiet abolition of semi-open prison for women', arguing that 'this action was taken without consultation or notification and without any apparent consideration of the impact that this will have on women.'[582]

The small number of accommodations in open conditions becomes an additional concern when considering the geographical location of these prisons as opposed to prisoners' home residences. Despite policy advice to categorise and transfer immediately to open conditions women sentenced to less than 12 months imprisonment,[583] there might be a problem in allocating prisoners to a prison that is a reasonable distance from their relatives' home. In general, prisoners will be accepted from court by a local prison within the court 'catchment area'. The higher the number of local prisons in the court's catchment area, the greater the chance that the prisoner will be imprisoned in proximity to her domicile. Of a total of approximately 136 prisons in the country, courts in England and Wales have approximately 47 local prisons, to which they can send remanded or convicted prisoners (bearing constant changes). At the time of writing, of the 47 prisons, nine are local female closed prisons (see Figure 5), with an estimated average

---

[579] The 'semi-open' prison was developed in 2001 to accommodate women who could be categorised at lower levels of security but were not suitable for transfer to an *ad hoc* open prison (*National Offender Management Service Annual Report 2011-12: Costs per place and costs per prisoner*, NOMS, Ministry of Justice (25 October 2012) https://www.gov.uk/government/uploads/system/uploads/attachment_data/file/218 336/prison-costs-summary-11-12.pdf (accessed 29 Aug 2013).

[580] Carlen and Worrall, p.36.

[581] *Drake Hall Prison Information*, HM Prison Service, Public Sector Prisons, Justive.gov.uk (last updated Aug 2013), http://www.justice.gov.uk/contacts/prison-finder/drake-hall (accessed 29 Aug 2013). At the time of writing, there are no semi-open prisons for women in England and Wales.

[582] *The End of Semi-Open Prison for Women- Preventing Family Contact*, Women in Prison (registered Charity No.1118727, http://www.womeninprison.org.uk/news_show.php?id=31 (accessed 29 Aug 2013).

[583] PSI 39/2011, s.4.2.

Figure 5: Distribution of women's prisons in England, 2013[584]

distribution of operational capacity[585] of approximately 336 places in the North East, 460 places in the North West, 446 places in Yorkshire and

---

[584] Prison finder, HM Prison Service (data and prisons' facade). The prison facade used to represent the closed prisons is HMP wormwood Scrubs male closed prison. This is one of the most inspiring and ironic prison facades, designed by Edmond Du Cane in 1875 and showing the portraits of Elizabeth Fry and John Howard. The two mansion houses are Askham Grange and East Sutton Park. The template map has been taken from d-maps.com designed by Daniel Delet.
[585] Operational Capacity stands for the maximum number of prisoners that can be legally held in a certain prison.

Humberside, 310 places in the East Midlands, 362 places in the South West, and 1,665 places in Greater London.[586]

The above statistics imply that there might not be enough prison places available in a court catchment area; or that the only prison in the court catchment area might be far too distant from the prisoner's home residence. This is even more dramatic with transfer to an open prison. HMP Askham Grange in Yorkshire and Humberside and HMP East Sutton Park in Kent and Sussex allow a total of only 200 places for a North and South distribution (see Figure 5). For example, the 2008 Inspectorate's report for Askham Grange noted that 63.3% of the total prison population was located over 50 miles (c.80 km) away from home.[587] The need to maintain a reasonable distance from home was addressed by the Prison Service Order (PSO) 4800 'Women Prisoners', issued in 2008. According to these instructions, priority will generally be based on a prisoner's request and cases will be evaluated on an individual basis. As a matter of principle, the PSO urges transferring women prisoners close to their release date and closer to their home.[588] Although the objective behind these instructions is to facilitate and reinstate prisoners' interaction and communication (especially with regard to visits) with their families, it also means that women who have spent months in an open prison and are then transferred back to their local closed prison will again have to face the pains of the closed prison regime.

Another concern which may affect a transfer to an open prison is highlighted by Carlen and Worrall. Female prisoners, for whom there is a narrower range of applicable prison regimes, may be either 'over or under categorised' – more frequently the former.[589] 'Over-categorisation' implies that female prisoners may be assessed as presenting a high security risk, so they will be denied the opportunity to be transferred to open conditions (unless this status changes after a follow-up risk assessment). However, evidence has demonstrated that women generally pose a low level of risk to the public. Statistics ending June 2012 indicate that 81% of women given an immediate prison sentence had committed non-violent offences, such as handling

---

[586] Data taken from the Prison finder, HM Prison Service, Public Sector Prisons, Justive.gov.uk (last updated Aug 2013), http://www.justice.gov.uk/contacts/prison-finder (accessed 29 Aug 2013).
[587] *Report on an announced inspection of HMP Askham Grange*, 2008, p.78.
[588] PSO 4800, Issue E, p.14.
[589] Carlen and Worrall, p.36.

stolen goods, and 26% had no previous convictions;[590] yet a rough calculation reveals that less than 7% of the total female prison yearly population were accommodated in the two open prisons available.[591] This concern was further voiced by a European Commission research study on women prisoners and social integration. Regarding 'measures to aid gradual transition' from prison to the community, the research findings concluded that

> regarding a very powerful 'transitional' measure—daily work/training activities organised outside the prison with return for the night—we may conclude that its application is very limited, despite the enabling legislation.[592]

Security Categorisation: Incompatible Risk Assessment

Risk assessment of prisoners and their categorisation has become the core feature of the prison service security agenda since the changes brought about following the Mountbatten report in 1966. On the face of it, the careful selection of prisoners to be accommodated in open prisons was also an intrinsic feature of this custodial facility: due to its 'open' nature, it could only host those prepared to not abscond and be subject to purposeful training. The Prison Commission's minutes for 1944 reveal an estimation of 32% of the total number of women in prisons in that year who were

---

[590] *Women Offenders: After the Corston Report*, Second Report of Session 2013-14, House of Commons Justice Committee, Vol. I, (London: The Stationery Office Limited, 2013), http://www.publications.parliament.uk/pa/cm201314/cmselect/cmjust/92/92.pdf (accessed 28 Aug 2013), p.8; the report also provides a comparison with male prisoner statistics.

[591] A calculation was made based on a yearly average of the total female prison population and a yearly average of the female prison population in Askham Grange and East Sutton Park for the year ending June 2012. Data were taken from *Prison Population Figures*, Statistics, Ministry Of Justice, GOV.UK, version 2.0, Crown Copyright, https://www.gov.uk/government/publications/prison-population-figures (accessed 31 Aug 2013).

[592] Pat Carlen and Anne Worrall were partners to the research project providing evidence from the UK (*Women, Integration and Prison. An Analysis of the Processes of Sociolabour Integration of Women Prisoners in Europe,* Mip Project, European Commission, September 2005, http://ec.europa.eu/research/social-sciences/pdf/mip_en.pdf (accessed 31 Aug 2013), p.12.

potentially able to be transferred to open conditions.[593] The prisoners initially identified as suitable for that purpose were the Star prisoners and Ordinaries prisoners with a character 'below persistent offender'.[594] Both these categories of prisoners were already familiar with the justice system: whereas the Star class was reserved for offenders sent to prison for the first time (but not necessarily first offenders, having been subject in the past to fines, probation order or approved schools),[595] the Ordinary prisoners were those with a track record of more than one prison sentence.

However, despite the original plan set by the Prison Commission, during Askham Grange's first year of operation, only Star prisoners were transferred to its premises from the available closed prisons.[596] In fact, although 190 Star prisoners were identified as suitable for the purpose (and an additional 180 Ordinary prisoners),[597] Mary Size's first annual report for the prison indicates that only 82 prisoners went through Askham Grange during 1947, while the daily average number of prisoners could not have exceeded 60, as this was the number of available beds.[598] Indeed, Mary Size reported that at that time, Askham Grange welcomed mainly women serving their first prison sentence who were between the ages of 21 and 55.[599] The criteria for the transfer required, in the first place, that the women were not identified as having 'hardened' criminal tendencies; although, as revealed by Mary Size, many of them were not first-time offenders.[600] Nor did Askham Grange take women with 'infectious disease' or those who were mentally or physically unfit; the 1947 annual prison report indicates that six women had to be moved back from Askham Grange to a closed prison because of the need for 'mental observation', 'treatment of venereal disease', and 'pregnancy'. Two other women were transferred from Askham Grange due to breach of trust, which encompassed refusal to co-operate, stealing money and intending to escape.[601]

---

[593] Prison Commissioners' minutes 1944: Memorandum by the prison commissioners on their proposals for the development of the prison system for adults during the immediate post war years, p.12 (LNA, PCOM 9/1386).
[594] Prison Commissioners minutes 1944, p.11 (LNA, PCOM 9/1386), p.12.
[595] Size, p.155.
[596] Ibid., p.155.
[597] Prison Commissioners' minutes 1944, p.11 (LNA, PCOM 9/1386).
[598] *Annual Report for 1947 HM Prison Askham Grange, York*, Mary Size.
[599] Size, p.155.
[600] Size, p.155.
[601] *Annual Report for 1947 HM Prison Askham Grange.*

Inevitably, however, the selection process for prisoners deemed suitable for open conditions has been affected by the 1966 security changes. Risk assessment and security categorisation of prisoners has developed through the years, but it has been consolidated by the Prison Service Instruction (PSI) 39/2011 'Categorisation and re-categorisation of women prisoners'; this is further supplemented by the protocol 'Women's Prison Allocation Strategy'[602] in accordance with the 'National Security Framework' guidance.[603] The process of categorisation for open conditions raises the following two issues for consideration: the first, discussed below, is the security risk that the prisoner may pose in a less restricted environment; the second aspect, which will be addressed later, is the level of adaptability of prisoners to open conditions. The first, 'security categorisation', is meant to set a threshold for a security risk assessment; this should indicate nil threat in the case of absconding.[604] The threat, as indicated by the National Security Framework, can be raised by any concern related to child protection and protection from harassment (under the 1997 Act). As well as concerns for the safety and integrity of the people working and living in the prison, including the children coming to visit their mothers and the infants in the Mother and Baby Unit.[605]

The chart below summarises the percentage of offences committed by women in Askham Grange as a variant of the total population in Askham Grange during the periods 1947, 1978, 1996 and 2008. It clearly demonstrates that in its 60 years of operation, Askham Grange has hosted prisoners with a varied range of offences, including murder and manslaughter - annotated under violence against the person.

---

[602] *Women's Prison Allocation Strategy,* Women & Young People's Group, HM Prison Service, E. Reed and H. Dichinson, February 2008.

[603] *Categorisation & Assessment*, National Security Framework, page 5 of 15, available online http://a1538.g.akamai.net/7/1538/13355/v001/homeoffice.download.akamai.com/13355/Doc/1016/10160005.pdf (accessed 01 Sep 2013).

[604] I am using the term 'abscond' rather than 'escape', as it applies better to an open prison. The distinction between the two terms is well explained in the Scottish Prison Service website's FAQs: 'What is the difference between an 'Escape' and an 'Abscond'? The definition of Escape is "where a prisoner breaches a perimeter security barrier or evades a secure escort". Everything else would be classed as either an "Abscond" or "Fail to return".' http://www.sps.gov.uk/faq.aspx#FAQno16 (accessed 01 Sep 2013).

[605] *Women's Prison Allocation Strategy*, p.49.

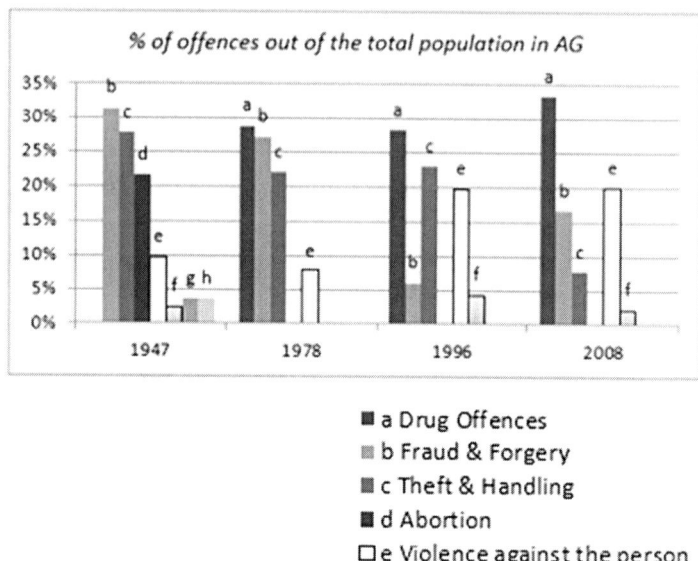

Figure 6: Percentage of offences based on the total population in Askham Grange[606]

In general, the policy for categorisation urges that women sentenced to less than 12 months of imprisonment should be considered for categorisation for open conditions as soon as possible.[607] In addition, categorisation for open conditions could take place for any other length of sentence of less than three years, although the actual transfer will not happen if the length of the time left to serve is more than two years, as this is the maximum length of time that a prisoner can spend in open conditions.[608] The following elements will also be considered when assessing a prisoner's security categorisation for open conditions: the prisoner has not been convicted for anything related

---

[606] *Statistics on Women and the Criminal Justice system,* Immediate custodial sentences population into prison establishments, 2007, Ministry of Justice, The Institute for Criminal Policy Research, School of Law, King's College, London, January 2009, p.47; *Statistics on Women and the Criminal Justice system,* Home Office, 1999, http://webarchive.nationalarchives.gov.uk/20100920143552/rds.homeoffice.gov.uk /rds/pdfs/s95women.pdf (accessed 02 Sep 2013) chapter 7, p.28; *Annual Report for 1947 HM Prison Askham Grange;* Lewis and Crew, p.32.
[607] PSI 39/2011, s.4.2.
[608] PSI 39/2011, s.5.5.

to actual or threatened violence or harm, offences of a sexual nature, drug dealing or importation (nor in any previous conviction); the prisoner does not have a record of being associated with serious criminals; and finally, the prisoner has not been diagnosed with serious mental health problems.[609] Therefore, drawing upon the statistical data provided by the Bromley briefings, it could be speculated that excluding those who experience mental health related issues, only 22% of the women in the data sample could be found suitable for open conditions.[610] Furthermore, by analogy this 22% stands for approximately 865 women from the total female prison population,[611] from which, due to the limited availability of accommodation in the two open prisons, only 200 women could potentially be moved to open conditions. Following the same reasoning, the Bromley briefings indicate that at least half of the women have a history of drug misuse or related conviction;[612] this might lead to possible exclusion from open conditions categorisation. However, applying these statistical data to the whole of the female prison population means that of those 1,886 women who do not pose a security risk from a drug misuse point of view, only 200 could potentially progress to an open prison. Security categorisation and risk assessment become even more complicated when considering the likelihood of a prisoner meeting more than one criterion that might exclude her from progressing to an open prison.

However, the prisoner progression policy's practical inconsistency and the unfeasibility of its implementation also plays a role in risk assessment procedures. First, although the general rule is that women charged with sexual offences and arson will be less likely to be transferred to open conditions, Askham Grange's deputy governor, interviewed for this study, suggested that 'in general, also these offences will be looked at'. The deputy governor further clarified that women transferred to an open prison may have committed 'any offence, as far as there has been done enough work during the sentence to address the risk - including homicide.' This is

---

[609] PSI 39/2011, Part 2, Security Category.

[610] For a research sample of 500 women (E. Plugge et al. [2006] The Health of Women in Prison, Oxford: Department of Public Health, University of Oxford, p.479, cited in Bromley Briefings Prison Factfile [Autumn 2014] Prison Reform Trust, http://www.prisonreformtrust.org.uk/Portals/0/Documents/Bromley%20Briefings/Factfile%20Autumn%202014.pdf [accessed 06 Jan 2015], pp.35-37).

[611] Based on the figures provided by the Bromley Briefing for Autumn 2014 (that is 3,929 women in prison).

[612] The Bromley Briefing indicates 52% of the women surveyed (p.37).

particularly evident in the case of substance misuse. Indeed, PSI 39/2011 on 'Categorisation' instructs that drug users 'present the bigger risk of abscond', and thus, it is advised that neither drug users nor prisoners undergoing a detoxification programme should be allocated to an open prison; yet, Figure 6 indicates that women with drug-related offences make up the majority accommodated in Askham Grange. This is no surprise, and there is a need to take into consideration that drug-related offences have increasingly represented one of the highest percentages of offences committed by women.[613] In fact, those interviewed for this study, who have been working in Askham Grange for several years, were able to identify this shift in the prison's population. For example, the head of healthcare noted that 'we get to Askham now people with problems that might be difficult to settle here: drugs, anger, bullying—sometimes they abscond and will be shifted back to a closed prison'. Indeed, Askham Grange has found itself accommodating prisoners who have not completely 'sorted out' their drug or alcohol misuse; hence, these women are incompatible with the risk assessment criteria mentioned previously.

Accommodating prisoners in open conditions despite their incompatible risk assessment might have considerable implications. Indeed, having prisoners who are not suited to coping with an open regime might undermine other prisoners' and prison personnel's safety (from being exposed to drug use and trafficking), impair prison integrity (by abusing trust and taking advantage of the low levels of security) and threaten public security (by way of absconding and trafficking with the outside). Arguably, however, the above considerations might appear redundant when assessing the state of affairs at Askham Grange. First, the inspectorate report published in 2004 showed that only 7% of the prisoners[614] reported having drug problems when they arrived at Askham Grange, as opposed to 70% of the total female prison population who were identified as requiring some level of detoxification when entering prison.[615] In addition, the report

---

[613] *Prison Population Statistics,* Berman, 22 December 2010; and *Prison Population,* 24 June 2011, Ministry of Justice, http://www.justice.gov.uk/publications/statistics-and-data/prisons-and-probation/prison-population-figures/index.htm (accessed 02 Sep 2013).

[614] That is, 7% of 90 prisoners who responded to the inspectorate survey (the population of Askham Grange at the time was 127) *Report on an Announced Inspection of HMP/YOI Askham* Grange, 15-19 March 2004, HM Chief Inspector of Prisons Anne Owers, June 2004, p.45.

[615] Cabinet Office Social Exclusion Task Force, Short Study on Women Offenders (London: Cabinet Office, 2009) quoted in Bromley Briefing Prison Factfile, 2011, p.49.

observed that 'Askham Grange could not be described as drug-free but it was not flooded with drugs either. Some women continued to use but we found no evidence of dealing or bullying'.[616] And yet, although it appears that, in the case of Askham Grange, discreet personal use of drugs does not necessarily disrupt the delicate dynamic between prisoners, prison staff and the community, it nevertheless might have implications on a vertical level, that is, the relationship between prisoners and prison security.[617]

Prisoners' Adaptation

An examination of the understated relationship between the open prison and the orthodox mainstream closed prison uncovers a complex recognition: being risk assessed as suitable for open conditions still does not guarantee that the prisoner herself will want or be able to cope with the 'open' environment. This reality is problematic because it suggests that the prisoner, sometimes by her own choice, would prefer to live in the artificial, depressing and largely degrading regime of the local closed prison. Indeed, this aspect was identified early in the life of Askham Grange, where the 1953 Prison Commission report noted that when prisoners are transferred to open conditions

> some become depressed because they have fewer visits; some prefer the privacy of the closed prison to the gregarious life of a small open community; and some resent the harder work and greater range of activities made possible in such a community.[618]

Little, if any, research has dealt with the above concern, an incomplete research study by Mawby[619] sheds some light on this issue. First, the research suggests that women arrive at the open prison with high expectations. From 'stories' heard back in the closed prison, the women transferred to an open prison expect to find something different—anything else but a prison: 'Beautiful house, beautiful grounds, good food, lots of

---

[616] Bromley Briefing Prison Factfile, p.49. This was also highlighted by the Askham Grange IMB report for the year 2009-2010, p.13.

[617] This will be discussed in the section 'under-categorisation in a zero tolerance environment'.

[618] *Report of the Commissioners of Prisons for the year 1953*, p.37.

[619] Part of this study was published in Crime & Delinquency 1982, 28, 1, 24-39, under the title 'Women in Prison: A British Study'. Although it was suggested that the full study will be published in the future, no record of it was found. I have contacted Professor R.I. Mawby (senior), and he confirmed that the manuscript was rejected by the publisher, and thus, the findings were never brought to light.

privileges [*sic*], swimming pool, fashion shows, day outings, you name it!'[620] However, according to Mawby, it appears that the freedom and the fresh air clash with what is still part of any prison regime: restrictions and rules, which in the context of an 'open' environment, seem to be harsher than expected. Thus, unsurprisingly, Mawby found this to foster alienation and feelings of vulnerability. Another trigger for vulnerability highlighted by Carlen was lack of familiarity with the country environment: 'women from inner London are often desolate and disorientated when located in an unfamiliar rural setting [...] and many request to be transferred back to Holloway'.[621] Indeed, the Women's Prison Allocation Strategy[622] has recognised some prisoners' inability to cope with prison life in general and the relaxed environment of the open prison in particular. Thus, it is advisable that these prisoners be located in a closed prison, which may give a more orderly and structured (cellular accommodations and more supervised routine) sense of living.

The above discussion further demonstrates how the orthodox prison's powerful dominance affects any other penal measure, and particularly the open prison. First, there is the possibility that those women who struggle to adapt to greater levels of liberty may have underlying issues related to their own personal background. Arguably, it is not that they prefer the depressing and limiting environment of Holloway Prison, for example, or its urban setting; rather, the controlled environment and the highly institutionalising routine and regime may become a 'safe' alternative to life prior-imprisonment; the stripping of responsibilities may, in fact, be soothing. This is a troubling realisation for at least two reasons: firstly, prisoners might become 'stuck' and even 'attached' to the prison environment; indeed, Martin suggests that 'giving up' its own 'mundane' responsibilities 'is the first step towards institutionalization'.[623] Secondly, this situation also provides the needed justification for the existence of the mainstream closed prison; thus, carceral clawback in this context perhaps furnishes the simplest justification for prison, that is, mere containment.

Issues concerning prisoners' adaptability to open conditions are not always related to the prisoner's inability to cope with an open environment, but as

---

[620] Mawby, p.31.
[621] Carlen and Worrall, p.55.
[622] Chapter 3, Section 7, p.9
[623] Martin (1955) quoted in M.J. McNown and R. Rhodes, 'Institutionalization: A Theory of Human Behaviour and the Social Environment', *Advance in Social Work*, 8, 1 (2007), 219-236 (p.21).

specified in the 'suitability assessment' instructions,[624] it may well be that other hindrances will limit prisoners' progression to the open prison. One such concern, mentioned earlier, is the accommodation of prisoners in prisons that are excessively far away from their family and relatives – this should not be underestimated. In fact, distance from home may determine the successful safeguarding or otherwise breaking down of family bonds, which, in itself, may have major implications for the life of the prisoner during imprisonment and after release.[625] More specifically, although in recent years the prison service has been recognising the legitimacy of 'dads' in prisons,[626] unsurprisingly, women prisoners have more frequently been perceived as the primary caregivers of their children and family. In fact, the focus here is not so much on whether the prisoner is a 'parent', but rather the extent to which the prisoner was the main home 'caretaker' before entering prison. Statistics cited by Baroness Corston in her 2007 review and reconfirmed by the Prison Reform Trust's 2010 and 2011 reports[627] highlight the important position of women prisoners in relation to their household. For example, 34% of women in prison are single parents; 80% of the women who had a partner before entering prison lost their partner's support. In fact, only 9% of the children are cared for by their father while their mother is in prison.[628]

The dismembering of the nuclear family has affected women prisoners' urge to keep caring for their loved ones mainly through phone calls and visits.

---

[624] PSI 39/2011, Part 4, Recommendation and Decision.

[625] See, for example, research by Hardesty et al. Also, an ESRC research study by the University of Birmingham on the issue of prison visitation and reoffending was under way at the time of writing.

[626] For example, at the time of writing, many of the male prisons in partnerships with prisoner-related charities (such as the Prisoners Advice and Care Trust) arrange family visit schemes that emphasise recreation with father-prisoners and their children; also, occasional funds are available to produce story-telling recording by father-prisoners to their children.

[627] The version used here is dated September 2010; however a more recent version is available on the net: Women in Prison, Prison Reform Trust, March 2012 http://www.prisonreformtrust.org.uk/Portals/0/Documents/Women's%20briefing% 20March12.pdf (accessed 01 Sep 2013); and the Bromley Briefings Prison Factfile, Prison Reform Trust, June 2011, http://www.prisonreformtrust.org.uk/Portals/0/Documents/Fact%20File%20June% 202011%20web.pdf (accessed 01 Sep 2013).

[628] *The Corston Report*, Baroness Jean Corston, Home Office, 2007, http://www.justice.gov.uk/publications/docs/corston-report-march-2007.pdf (accessed 31 Aug 2013), pp.20-12.

Indeed, the 'caretaker' dilemma was better put by an Askham Grange prisoner to Baroness Corston while visiting in the prison:

> The reason why the majority of men are more relaxed while in prison is that men always have females whether it is their mother, sister, aunt or girlfriend to take care of their needs [while] women have greater ties to the household and when they are taken away, the operation within the home becomes disrupted which leads to greater confusion and dysfunction.[629]

The need to caretake for the family while in prison becomes even more problematic, and perhaps frustrating, when the prison does not impose physical barriers.[630] The prison personnel interviewed for this study suggested that many of the women who absconded from Askham Grange did so to sort out a family problem; not really intending to 'leave' the prison, they returned to it voluntarily. None of my interviewees thought it to be a concern in terms of security related logistics. In fact, across the female prison estate, women's escapes and absconds had not even reached two dozen, whereas the number of male prisoners who have escaped is in the hundreds.[631] Women prisoners absconding from an open prison is not the core concern here; rather, it is the limited resources available to implement a policy that, at least in theory, requires prisoners' progression to a less restrictive environment—an environment that, in principle, could allow better communication and contact with the prisoners' families.

Under-categorisation in a Zero-Tolerance Environment

It is fair to say that the relationship between prisoners and the open prison environment is characterised by low levels of security, and thus, low levels of containment, based upon trust but also upon prisoners' readiness to cope with such an environment. Indeed, the PSI 39/2011 clearly states that the open prison is not prepared, or rather, it does not have the resources to address incompatible prisoners:

---

[629] *The Corston Report*, p.21.
[630] The last published research found on the topic of absconds from open prison dates back to 1975 by Banks et al. Their findings, although limited to only one year, suggests that only a small portion of open prisons' prisoners absconded (about 3%). An assessment of their research should also take into account the fact that the research was commissioned by the Home Office and to what extent policy during these years might have affected the outcome of the findings (see C. Banks et al., *Absconding from Open Prisons*, (London: Home Office Research, 1975).
[631] Carlen and Worrall, p.36.

When considering a prisoner for categorisation to open conditions, governors must bear in mind whether the low physical security and low staff [...] are sufficient to reasonably manage any risk presented by the prisoner.[632]

At the heart of the open prison system is the idea that prisoners who have been found suitable for open conditions are willing, in their own personal interests, to collaborate and comply with the relaxed milieu of this unconventional custodial environment. Thus, the open prison has less desire, and fewer means, than a closed prison to exercise control and restraint by limiting prisoners' physical movement and personal liberties. In fact, the deputy governor interviewed for this study confirmed that the number of prison officers in relation to the number of prisoners in Askham Grange is very small. Consequently, although the prison officers might be adequately trained to address security threatening behaviour such as assault, abuse, bullying or any incompliance with the prison regime, the small number of prison officers allows little margin for manoeuvre in case of unexpected disturbances. The deputy governor further suggested that frequently 'staff will work higher than their grade'; for example, she clarified that 'at night we only have an officer and three support officers who are in charge of the prison.' In addition, the male officer interviewed for this study explained that approximately 22 prison officers were employed at Askham Grange, but only a daily minimum of seven officers is required (against an average of 100 prisoners) for smooth operation of the prison; in fact, this would usually be the number of officers available in a normal day.

'You probably can see it doesn't look like a prison, does it?', the male officer interviewed for this study asked me. However, although this appeared to be a rhetorical question, and despite having worked in male and female closed prisons and spending the past 12 years in Askham Grange, the officer also expressed some concern in relation to the officers-prisoners ratio. He explained that

[as an officer,] when you are in a closed condition, you have much more control, and there are more staff around (and other physical restrictions)' [while] 'in open conditions there are more people [prisoners] looking at you (in the eating hall for example), and generally the officers are quite isolated most of the time.

---

[632] PSI 39/2011, Annex B, Part 3, n.16.

The officer had further mixed feelings. He observed that, based upon his personal work experience, there is greater understated pressure on the shoulders of staff and officers in an open prison because they are inevitably much more approachable than in a closed prison. He also recognised, however, that prisoner-staff communication is much more 'open' in an open prison; hence, prisoners more freely discuss their problems with staff, and staff are easily able to access the resources needed to provide support.

However, at the core of this discussion is the problematic dynamic of having 'under-categorised'[633] prisoners in a custodial facility aimed at enhancing, rather than restricting, prisoners' liberties. It is important to consider that unlike most closed prisons, Askham Grange does not have a designated segregation unit (or as some prisons call it Care and Separation Unit) to use as a disciplinary tool (as a punishment for prison offences) or security measure (for their own safety) where prisoners can be held in single cells for the period adjudicated. In 2004, Askham Grange had the provision of '3 rooms for holding in secure conditions',[634] whereas the 2008 inspection reported that 'no designated segregation or special accommodation' was available at that time.[635] Indeed, under the heading 'Discipline' the 2008 inspectors were pleased to record that

> women were largely well behaved, well motivated and valued their place at the prison. There were few adjudications [...] and punishments were reasonable. There was no segregation of women and no recent use of force.[636]

Moreover, since 2008, the prison has converted the secure rooms into a 'quiet-space' (the bedsit),[637] allowing women to have some short-term space for private time. However, these limited arrangements for disciplinary purposes (as in cases of absconding or any other prison offence) imply that first, in line with the low security regime, the prison would expect a priori zero levels of disturbance, but when disturbances do occur, the prison must exercise (because of lack of resources) a zero-tolerance approach by transferring the prisoner straight back to a closed prison. Such an

---

[633] Carlen defines under-categorised prisoners as those who are categorised as suitable for lower levels of security, despite having one or more risk factors incompatible by policy with these lower levels of security (such as drug use or mental health concerns).

[634] Inspectorate report Askham Grange, 2004, p.93.

[635] Inspectorate report Askham Grange, 2008, p.53

[636] Ibid., p.52

[637] IMB report 2008-2009 Askham Grange, p.8.

inconvenience emphasises the counter-productivity of a prison policy that still endorses prisoners' progression but does not cater for its adequate implementation.

The Question of Totality of the Open Prison

'Hotel killers' was the headline given by the *Mail Online* to the story reporting the employment of three women in a Travelodge in York in 2011; they were serving a prison life sentence (ranging from 12 to 16 years) for being involved in murder cases.[638] The women were Askham Grange prisoners, and such publicity certainly does not contribute to the understanding of what the open prison stands for. Indeed, despite NACRO's[639] news release aiming at supporting the initiative, comments made by readers demonstrate that 'the reform of the prisoner' and 'prisoners' progression' perspectives might feature in political, academic and reformist-activist discourses, but they do not necessarily feature in the popular perception concerning punishment. For example, some readers expressed their view that 'life should mean life', 'criminals are given jobs willy nilly', and 'the country is becoming more insane by the minute'. One reader thought that the Travelodge could be a 'good location for another re run of PSYCHO [*sic*]'.[640]

Those familiar with Askham Grange's regime, both staff and prisoners, know that its aim goes beyond mere detention. Indeed, the ethos of the open prison is better described by its first prison governor, Mary Size:

> Our aim was to improve mentally, physically, and morally every woman and girl who came into our care, and return her to society without loss of self-respect or any undue feelings of bitterness, so that she might become an asset instead of a liability to the state, and take her place as a normal and useful citizen.[641]

To what extent is the open prison in general and Askham Grange in particular able to implement in practice what has been, within the context of the mainstream prison system, merely a myth—that is, 'prisoners'

---

[638] Hotel killers: Three female convicted murderers given jobs at same Travelodge, Mail Online, 18 January 2011, http://www.dailymail.co.uk/news/article-13478 39/Travelodge-killers-3-female-convicted-murderers-jobs-hotel.html (accessed 18 Aug 2013).
[639] NACRO, 2013, http://www.nacro.org.uk/ (accessed 18 Aug 2013).
[640] *Mail Online*, Hotel Killers, readers' comments.
[641] Size, p.189.

reformation'? It was argued in the first chapter of this study that reformation as an aim of imprisonment was developed as a socio-political discourse, but its actual implementation on the ground has been rather adverse. The discourse of prisoners' reformation expressed the need to help prisoners outgrow their criminal tendencies and become law-abiding citizens; the first chapter's historical analysis demonstrates that this was far too ambitious a project. This study also argues that prisoners do indeed go through a process of reformation, but it is conformity to institutional routine rather than to law-abiding life that is attained instead. As has been discussed, this was recognised by the 1948 Criminal Justice Act, formally recognising open prisons' role in 'untraining' prisoners from their institutionally acquired tendencies and retraining them for social life.

Before verifying the extent of Askham Grange's role in the abatement of institutionalisation, it is essential to briefly address the impact of institutional routine on a person's life. Goffman argued that this 'impact' is manifested through what he termed 'disculturation'; in other words, it brings about the 'untraining', albeit sometimes temporarily, from certain social skills.[642] This aspect might have wide psychological and social dimensions. For example, Haney argues that the 'disabling effects of institutionalisation' such as becoming 'dependent on institution structure and routines' may hinder a parent's ability to effectively organise family life and 'exercise initiatives and autonomous decision making that parenting requires'.[643] Haney further argues that other characteristics acquired or reinforced while in prison that may affect social reintegration are distrust and hyper-vigilant tendencies; for example, some prisoners might experience feelings of alienation or, alternatively, feelings of being 'emotionally over-controlled'. In turn, these might lead to social withdrawal and a sense of low self-worth and esteem.[644] In fact, Lowthian argues that institutionalisation leads to a wider problem faced by all imprisoned women, which is the damage to their well-being.[645] Wallace goes as far as reproaching society's support of Total Institutions, arguing that 'we allow totality to develop in an institution today, so that it may do the dirty work

---

[642] Goffman, p.23.
[643] C. Haney, *The Psychological Impact of Incarceration: Implications for Post-Prison Adjustment*, National Policy Conference (U.S. Department of Health and Human Services, 2001), p.15.
[644] Haney, p.15.
[645] J. Lowthian, 'Women's Prison in England: barrier to reform', in *Women and Punishment: The Struggle for Justice*, ed. by P. Carlen (Cullompton: Willan, 2002), pp. 155-181 (p.159).

for us good people [...].'[646] He further suggests that society ignores the fact, which was repeatedly identified by research, that 'inmates of Total Institutions are [...] fit candidates only for a total society.'[647]

Studies concerning the aspects of institutionalisation have mainly looked at the environmental characteristics of those institutions which might foster institutionalising routine; these places have been defined by Goffman as Total Institutions, who described them as places of:

> Residence and work where a large number of like-situated individuals, cut off from the wider society for an appreciable period of time, together lead an enclosed, formally administrated round of life.[648]

For Goffman, constituting the 'totality' of the institution are aspects such as the centrality of place and authority, forced group interaction and unity of treatment, routine and institutional aims. In the particular case of prisons, by following Goffman's analysis, it becomes apparent that 'total' goes hand in hand with 'control' where an authority must exist to regulate all possible aspects of life,[649] thus emphasising the sense of a collective regimentation of people. There is no doubt as to the 'total' nature of the mainstream closed prison;[650] yet, Goffman's approach, equating and generalising the nature of different institutions such as prisons, care homes for the aged and religious cloisters, makes an assessment of the essence of open prisons within this context problematic. Indeed, Tizard et al recognise that one of the weaknesses of Goffman's analysis is the excessive focus he placed on identifying 'an underlying unity' between the Total Institutions, where diversity was ignored.[651]

Undoubtedly, an open prison, despite being 'open', is nevertheless a prison, and it is certainly an 'institution' with its norms, culture, rules and expected behaviour. Possibly, by analogy, drawing upon less 'correctional' and disciplinary institutions such as care homes, it could be argued that the open prison can also be classified as a Total Institution. This, however, contradicts the open prison's core function and subsequent purpose, which is the

---

[646] S.E. Wallace, 'On the Totality of Institutions', in *Total Institution*, ed. by S.E. Wallace (USA: Transaction, 1971), pp.1-8 (p.4).

[647] Ibid.

[648] Goffman, p.11.

[649] Ibid., p.17.

[650] In that regard, see also M. Ignatieff, 'State, Civil Society and Total Institutions'.

[651] J. Tizard, I. Sinclair and R.V.G Clarke, *Variety of Residential Experiences*, ed. (London & Boston: Routledge & Kegan Paul, 1975), p.4.

abatement of institutionalisation to facilitate social integration. The need to understand the diversity of institutions and thus their different effects on their inhabitants' lives has been the subject of research since Goffman's study. However, according to McEwen, agreement as to common measurements to be used across the board has not proved fruitful.[652] In his review, McEwen identifies at least three broad categories (or 'dimensions of variation') which researchers have used to assess institutional totality, while within each category researchers have demonstrated differentiation in the measurements used.[653] None, however, specifically discuss the open prison.

Significantly, it appears that the majority of the research cited by McEwen does not seem to clarify whether an institution is total or not; rather, as argued by Wallace, the question should be (and it has been) 'how much totality' does the institution display?[654] It is less clear however, which variants should be taken to measure this totality, especially in light of the many and varied approaches presented by the research studies. Therefore, due to the limited empirical data, my assessment of the open prison's level of totality will follow the three broad categories identified by McEwen; these are organisational scope, organisational power, and the bureaucratic management of the residents.[655] These categories might overlap, depending on the characteristics considered within each; therefore, more specifically, my assessment of the open prison's organisational scope will look into the education programme as a means to maintain social contact with the outside;[656] discussion on the bureaucratic management of the residents will focus on Sykes' concepts of deprivation of liberty and deprivation of autonomy;[657] and finally, in relation to the category of organisational power, the question of prisoners' culture will be explored.

---

[652] C.A. McEwen, 'Continuities in the Study of Total and Nontotal Institutions', *Annual Review of Sociology*, 6 (1980), 143-185, (p.152).
[653] Ibid., pp.152-159.
[654] Wallace, p.2.
[655] McEwen, pp.154-161.
[656] Ibid., p.154.
[657] Sykes, pp.63-64. In addition to deprivation of liberty and deprivation of autonomy, Sykes has also assessed deprivation of goods and deprivation of security. These topics are not discussed here.

Organisational scope

McEwen identifies organisational scope as a measuring variant used by several researchers. For example, Goffman considered the 'barrier' placed by the institution on the residents' socialisation with the outside; Wheeler used the concept 'degree of separation', while Kanter referred to this as 'renunciation'.[658] The category of organisational scope is meant to measure the extent to which the institution allows for community contact and the type of this contact. For example, local and/or training prisons (which are closed prisons) will allow some level of contact with the outside world; this would usually be in the form of family and legal visits, receiving and sending mail, and making phone calls. However, the greater the level of social interaction, the smaller the chance, in Wheeler's terms, of a 'reality shock'[659] upon release.

When measuring organisational scope in relation to social interaction with the community, one of the first striking aspects of the open prison is indeed the active involvement of many of the prisoners with the outside world. Forming part of its social integration ethos, Askham Grange is committed to providing learning and work-related experience contingent upon the employment available outside. Indeed, the educational repertoire has been shaped through the years reflecting recognition of new jobs accessible to women, greater focus on specific needs, and more systematic teaching. For example:

1948	Painting and decorating; Cookery; Housewifery; Needlework.
	Handicraft: Toy making; Glove making; Slipper making; Dressmaking; Fine needlework; Embroidery.
	First aid; Infant welfare; Personal hygiene; Country dancing; Singing; English literature; Art; Current affairs.
1953	DIY; Cookery; Embroidery; Dressmaking.
	Handicraft: Cane-work; Rug-making; Lampshade making; Glove making; Slipper making; Leatherwork.
	Country dancing; Music appreciation; Art; Current affairs; Drama and English.

---

[658] Goffman 1961, Wheeler 1966, Kanter 1972, cited in McEwen, p.154.
[659] Wheeler 1966, cited in McEwen, p.155.

1984	Electronic writing skills. Home economics: Cookery; Time management; Hygiene; Nutrition. Basic skills (English and mathematics); Basic literacy; Basic numeracy. Commercial course: Typewriting; English; Mathematics; Bookkeeping. Horticulture; Child care development course; Self-development seminar; Typing; Dressmaking; Cookery; Yoga; Arts and crafts; Sociology; Philosophy; Guitar class.
2008	Family learning; Literacy and numeracy; Information technology; Customer service; Business administration and hairdressing; First aid; Food preparation and catering; Food hygiene; Health and fitness; Librarianship; ICT; Gym instructor; Professional cookery.

The table above describes the courses available through the years.[660] The courses clearly demonstrate an ongoing active engagement with the provision of learning and extracurricular activities; it also shows the development of more sophisticated learning and more job-related training, such as the electronic writing skills introduced in the 1980s.

A closer look at the correlated reports reveals additional information. For example, most of the 1947 courses were introduced based on availability and expertise of the teachers. Many of the first prison officers, including Mary Size, had experience and were trained in various handicrafts; some had worked as cooks in the women's services during the war; others were even qualified in housewifery skills through training taken before the war. Courses such as cookery, housewifery and dressmaking were subject to final examinations through the local education authority or the London City and Guilds, and the produce of some handicraft courses was successfully sold on various occasions, emphasising the bond created with the local community.[661]

---

[660] The data have been collected from the following sources: the course lists available just after the launch of Askham Grange in 1947; courses indicated during the two inspections of the Ministry of Education in 1953 and 1984; and finally, the provision of courses available when the data was collected for this study in 2008.
[661] *Askham Grange report*, 1947. In her report, Mary Size does not specify whom the handicrafts were sold to; possibly, they were displayed in the few events

The standard and quality of the education provisions were monitored in line with the open prison aim: facilitating an effective future social integration. For example, the 1953 Ministry of Education report reveals that, in fact, the activities available were delivered as recreational 'pastimes', rather than aiming at skills development and vocational training. The report concluded by urging the Prison Commission to reassess the purpose of education at Askham Grange.[662] Indeed, by 1984 the prison was able to provide a much more structured educational syllabus. It comprised old and new recreational courses; it formalised the learning around the gardening activities by adding an accredited horticulture course; and it kept in line with changing learning trends such as the introduction of the home economics course (replacing the housewifery training). Most importantly, it introduced vocational training in office-related work, which the inspectors expected to be 'a requirement in the manufacture of a wide range of industrial and commercial components', thus securing employment opportunities for many of the women.[663]

In recent years, Askham Grange's education department has developed a syllabus of learning and training that has demonstrated a greater pertinence to some of the employment skills learned inside the prison. Most of the courses available at the time of data collection were accredited by The Manchester College (some courses run by the Craren College and some by SOVA)—and students could reach level 3 and take examinations. Indeed, the Conference Centre and the Salonique (hair salon), which are open to the public, provide ample opportunity for practising the skills acquired. In 2008, Askham Grange was able to provide fashionable and modern courses such as information technology and gym instruction; the education manager interviewed for this study explained that she was in the process of assessing the feasibility of a permanent make-up course requested by one of the prisoners.

---

organised by the prisoners and members from Askham Richard village were invited to attend.

[662] *Report by HM Inspectors on Educational Activities at HM Prison Askham Grange*, Ministry of Education, York, 23 October 1953, p.11 (LNA, ED 149/98).

[663] *Report by HM Inspectors on Educational Activities at HM Prison Askham Grange*, Ministry of Education, York, 15-19 October 1984, p.6 (LNA, ED 114/1612/5).

Askham Grange was awarded Grade 1 (outstanding) under each of the Inspectorate of Education's criteria.[664] The above was backed up by the 2008 Inspectorate of Prison report,[665] which noted that the 'learning and skills provision was outstandingly good' and that 'the provision was responsive to the needs of women'; in addition, the 'development of the women's skills and confidence was excellent on all programmes and women produced work of high commercial standards'.[666] Of course, as explained by the Askham Grange education manager interviewed for this study, accommodating prisoners' requests will depend mainly on funding and course costs or distance from the prison. The education manager stressed the importance of the courses having nationally accredited qualifications to increase employability. Sometimes, however, despite support provided by a few charities such as the Prison Education Trust and WIP, the prison will not be able to accommodate all the requests, and thus, support will be given to the prisoners by way of developing their skills through the available education provisions inside the prison.

As for the impact of education and training on the women's life after release, the 2008 Inspectorate of Prisons report noted that the 'transition planning was very effective and reflected Askham Grange's ethos on preparing women for resettlement'; according to the prison's records, 'at least 50% entered education, training or employment on release'.[667] The small number of prisoners accommodated in Askham Grange makes an individual approach largely possible. The education manager interviewed for this study noted that every prisoner will be interviewed and assessed by the education department when arriving at the prison; thus, the education department also takes an important share in the social integration process. A great majority of women arriving at Askham Grange, according to the education manager, might have had a bad experience at school or simply a negative perception of education. Women's background, needs, and unresolved issues are taken into consideration and addressed appropriately first, so they can focus on their studies. According to her, the approach is holistic, aiming at increasing self-respect and confidence but also at increasing respect for each other,

---

[664] *Inspection Report for HMP Askham Grange*, 2008, p.6. The criteria assessed are: effectiveness; achievements and standards; quality of provision; capacity to improve; leadership and management; equality of opportunity.
[665] The Inspectorate of the prison report for 2011 was an unannounced short follow-up report; thus, it only assessed the achievement of recommendation provided in the 2008 report.
[666] *Inspection Report for HMP Askham Grange*, 2008, pp.45-47.
[667] Ibid., p.47.

members of staff and study equipment (such as computers, books, reading rooms, furniture, etc.).

However, it is worth mentioning that within this context of education, training and prison regime, previous writings on women's imprisonment, such as research conducted by Carlen and Dobash et al., have acknowledged a concern related to the stereotypical understanding of women's social roles, which has encouraged prison training emphasising domesticity. The problem highlighted by this perspective is not so much about the 'role' itself but the 'conflict between the need to financially provide for the family and the expectations to conform to a socially ascribed role [...] that does not prioritise employment.'[668] It cannot be denied that a socio-institutional tendency to promote women's domesticity was present even in the context of the unorthodox custodial institutions. For example, the accompanying instructions to the 1908 Prevention of Crime Act clearly stated that borstal girls, before pursuing any vocational training (while in the borstal), should first go through training in laundry work, housework, needle work and cookery,[669] although there was no similar requirement for boys. Similar expectations were voiced by Governor Mary Size in the 1947 Askham Grange prison's report; she noted that 'it is an amazing fact that few of the women received here are able to cook a simple meal properly. Four out of the five employed in the workroom the day it was opened did not know how to sew.'[670]

Undoubtedly, domesticity and family life have had a central place in Askham Grange's training agenda; but although housewifery might have been perceived as the ultimate social aim, it was dignity and gaining control over their own lives that was at the core of the training. Governor Mary Size believed that the aim of Askham Grange was to implant 'the seeds of self-respect, [and] moral integrity.'[671] She further considered that:

> We made every effort to help them to regularize their lives and to teach them how to live decently. They were taught the value of team work and efficiency, self-discipline and respect for the rights of others, their own importance in the community as wives and mothers, and the responsibilities which this entails.[672]

---

[668] Hardesty et al., p.32.
[669] Ruggles-Brise, *The English Prison System*, p.262.
[670] *Annual Report Askham Grange*, 1947, p.2
[671] Size, p.187.
[672] Ibid., p.189.

Moreover, the 1960 Prison Commission report noted that in Askham Grange, the prisoners 'gain new life and new hope' and that they 'prove to themselves that they can be useful and needed.' The commissioners believed that 'these feelings, often strongly held, that they have been "written off" and rejected by society are modified as they show themselves and others that they can achieve something in the outside world.'[673]

Not all the women released from Askham Grange became full-time housewives; many were able to acquire part-time paid employment (although most of the jobs were domestic related, such as cooking, serving or laundry work).[674] A woman released from Askham Grange wrote:

> I thought you would like to know that everything has turn out all right [...]
> I have got good part-time job, and work from nine to one o'clock, cooking
> for twenty students. I get £2 2s. a week, so you see I am saving all I can to
> get the children a decent home [*sic*].[675]

Mary Size's memoirs further indicate how useful was Askham Grange's training after the prisoners' release:

> [A woman], who almost wept when she was told she would have to learn
> shirt-making, wrote some weeks after she returned home to tell me that one
> of her first jobs was to make two shirts each for her husband and two sons
> adding: "I thank the good Lord and Askham Grange for what I was taught
> there".[676]

Another woman wrote to Mary Size to inform her that:

> Out of the profits she had made from toy-making and glove-making (both
> crafts learned at Askham), she was able to buy linoleum for her living room,
> curtains for her son's bedroom, and several gadgets for the kitchen. [She]
> attributed her success as a good housekeeper to the fact that she worked on
> a time-table she based on the one in use in Askham. The ability to
> supplement her husband's wages gave her a good deal of satisfaction, as well
> as increased comfort and happiness in the home.[677]

---

[673] *Report of the Commissioners of Prisons for the year 1960*, p.25.
[674] Size, p.163.
[675] From a letter sent to Mary Size by G.E. after her release (Size, p.173).
[676] Ibid., p.162.
[677] Ibid., p.163.

Bureaucratic management of the residents

This category of measurement has been identified by McEwen as particularly problematic, not least because researchers have addressed it by looking into different variants and failing to reach an agreement among themselves for the purpose of consistency.[678] It appears however, that the variants used by the researchers discussed by McEwen have in common aspects related to the notion of the pains of imprisonment. For example, King and Regan refer to the inflexibility of routine, regimentation and depersonalisation;[679] Moos looked into, for example, the aspect of autonomy, order and organisation;[680] while Toch's study specifically reflected Sykes' pains of imprisonment by assessing, for example, privacy, safety, social stimulation and freedom.[681] In relation to the bureaucratic management of the open prison, as reflecting issues related to the pains of imprisonment, in the following paragraphs I will assess the level of totality by focusing on the deprivation of prisoners' liberty and autonomy.

The deprivation of liberty is a significant variable of the bureaucratic management of the prisoners, although there is a clear overlap with the organisational scope measure. Indeed, confining the criminal to the institution, symbolically and physically, represents, according to Sykes, moral and legal rejection by the community.[682] However, in the case of the open prison this is not reflected in the same way because its aim is to encourage the opposite: that is, to facilitate prisoner-community interaction for future smoother social integration. This has occurred in Askham Grange via the implementation of an extensive range of purposeful activities. All prisons are required to provide some formal activities such as education, vocational training and work; yet the unique feature of an open prison is that the prisoners can also do these outside the prison 'walls'.[683] For example, in 2008, ten women were pursuing further education courses and four were in higher education, whereas 20 women were in paid employment and 22 in

---

[678] McEwen, pp.156-8.
[679] King and Rayner, 1968, cited in McEwen, p.156.
[680] Moos, 1975, cited in McEwen, p.156.
[681] Toch, 1977, cited in McEwen, p.156.
[682] Sykes, p.65
[683] It is important to underline that only prisoners eligible for a Release on Temporary Licence (ROTL), regulated by PSO 6300, as amended by PSI 36/2007, can benefit from work and education outside the prison. Being in an open prison does not automatically give a prisoner ROTL eligibility.

volunteer community work; all these activities were performed outside the prison.[684]

Moreover, it is the role of the open prison within the policy of prisoners' progression that should be addressed when discussing deprivation of liberty. Returning to Goffman's Total Institution, it is undeniable that the open prison will have a centrality of place and authority, routine and even forced group interaction, but its institutional aim is to endorse a purposeful relationship with the wider community. The first contact with outside employment, which laid the ground for future solid relations, was offered in 1948 by an agricultural college. Initially, the task required planting potatoes in the college fields; however, the word spread quickly as to the 'methods and energy' of the women, and soon the local farmers' demand for labour exceeded what Askham Grange was able to offer.[685] Currently, employment and community work can provide work experience in hotels, hairdressing and beauty therapy salons, housing agencies, advice centres and other commercial organisations.[686]

When addressing the variable of deprivation of autonomy, Sykes investigated the restricted ability to make choices, dependence on the prison's staff, and the laconic communication that staff had with the prisoners on any matter perceived as important by the prisoner (as if decisions were being made behind the prisoner's back). All these foster hostility because 'they do not "make sense" from the prisoner's point of view' and 'the frustration of the prisoner's ability to make choices [...] involves a profound threat to the prisoner's self-image because [it] reduce[s] the prisoner to the weak, helpless, dependant status of childhood'.[687] Carlen has suggested that, indeed, the prison system would typically relate to female prisoners in the above way.[688] This interrelation has been termed by Hardesty et al. as an 'external' control; this, in turn, may have major implications on the level of self-esteem, leading to its reduction, which

---

[684] *Inspection Report for HMP Askham Grange*, Office for Standards in Education (Ofsted), 2 October 2008, http://www.ofsted.gov.uk/inspection-reports/find-inspection-report/provider/ELS/52247 (last accessed 02 Sep 2013), p.4.
[685] Size, p.168.
[686] Inspectorate report, Askham Grange HMP, 2008, p.46.
[687] Sykes, pp.74-5.
[688] Carlen, *Women's Imprisonment,* p.90.

might be responsible for potential maladaptation upon release and subsequent reoffending.[689]

However, the above-described scenario might be in some contrast to the open prison regime, which is intended to provide a milieu where prisoners are encouraged to take responsibility for their own actions and for their own lives. In other words, as discussed previously, a core feature of the open prison agenda is the 'untraining' of prisoners from what Goffman has termed 'disculturation'. Indeed, it is the retraining for social skills which have been watered down through the process of imprisonment that the open prison is set to achieve. Thus, the deprivation of autonomy, typical of the closed prison environment, is mitigated by the open prison through prisoners' empowerment (such as being responsible for attending one's own work/study/medical appointments and commitments). However, it is essential to consider that understanding the concept of empowerment is not without ambiguities when discussed in the context of custodial confinement. For example, Barton argues that even in those institutions that are not inherently penal, an apparently empowering regime could still lead 'to the infantilisation of its residents';[690] this is due to the inevitable effect that institutional routine has on a person's life. Alternatively, Shaw and Hannah-Moffat, in reference to specific 'empowering agendas', have argued that the concept of empowerment is applied in its totality, shifting the whole responsibility for the success of the programme/regime/personal development on to the prisoners.[691]

Prisoners are expected to arrange their own visits, to request an appointment with one of the service providers available, to lodge a complaint, or to sign for a specific meal requirement; realistically, this is the maximum level of empowerment that prisoners can expect in closed prisons. However, the empowering nature of the open prison does not form part of a rehabilitative programme or a pretext for shifting responsibility; rather, it is simply the way of living. Inevitably, prisoners transferred to an open prison are expected to have reached the mental readiness to be able to carry the weight of responsibility that is the 'price to be paid' for greater degrees of liberty. The deputy governor interviewed for this study admitted that the Askham Grange regime is not as 'ingrained' as in a closed prison, and this might be

---

[689] Hardesty et al., 'Self-esteem and the Woman Prisoner', in *Women Prisoners: A Forgotten Population*, ed. by B.R. Fletcher et al. (Westport, London: Praeger, 1993), pp.27-44 (p.27-28).
[690] Barton (2005) cited in Heidensohn and Silvestri, p.353.
[691] Shaw and Hannah-Moffat (2000) cited in Heidensohn and Silvestri, p.353.

difficult when prisoners arrive at Askham Grange from a closed prison. The deputy governor clarified that Askham Grange's prisoners will be 'free to go around not escorted'; they will not be told 'what to do in the same way as in a closed prison'; they 'will not be in their rooms during the day unless for a particular approved reason; they will work or study'. The deputy governor also noted that 'people need to have a watch, otherwise they will not know when to go down to eat or to see the doctor'.

It is difficult to see in the above mundane and largely 'normal' actions anything as significant as 'empowerment'; yet this could symbolise the regaining of personal control over oneself which had been lost in the closed prison. However, 'empowerment' in the context of the open prison could have an additional connotation that is no less important: the repossession of dignity. Askham Grange's prisoners are, in fact, called 'Residents', and they were referred to as such by all the people interviewed for this study. This should not be perceived as a hypocritical suggestion that prisoners transferred to Askham Grange are not prisoners any longer; they still are. However, Askham Grange's regime gives the prisoner the opportunity to re-establish what Goffman argued she was stripped of upon entering the Total Institution: the conception of herself by way of reinstating her social legitimacy; in other words, the open prison regime is perceived as an aid to undo the labelling process of what has made them 'prisoner' beyond the walls of the institution. Hardesty et al. have argued that an enforcement of the 'internal control' which 'refers to the extent to which a person perceives life events as being contingent upon one's actions' increases self-esteem and reduces chances for reoffending.[692]

Organisational power

An initial overview of this measure might suggest a level of complexity as researchers have used it to measure, on the one hand, voluntariness of membership, while others have used it to assess the power of the organisation to choose and expel members.[693] However, more significantly, organisational power has also been used to assess the extent to which the institution allows its members to commit themselves to the institution; this is further accompanied by the level of ability or need of the institution to control its members' behaviour.[694] Here, the level of totality of an open

---

[692] Hardesty et al., p.28.
[693] McEwen, p.155.
[694] McEwen, p.155.

prison will be assessed through the extent and dynamic of the formation of an institutional culture as developed by those who reside in that institution.

First, it is essential to take account of the importance of criminalisation within the context of prison institutionalisation. 'Criminalisation' has been defined by Jones et al. as the 'acquisition of criminal attitudes, skills and associates, as a result of sustained and socially functional interaction with criminals'.[695] It will usually operate within the fertile ground of what Sykes has identified as the 'prisoners' culture',[696] which can be simply understood as a culture of survival aimed at turning prison life into a more bearable experience.[697] More specifically, Street observed that the 'culture' is 'built around norms and values of solidary [*sic*] opposition to the official system and to staff', which is 'potentially oriented towards ameliorating its members' deprivation' by minimising staff interference and facilitating access to and distribution of 'scarce values, both licit [like choice of jobs in the prison] and illicit [like contraband]'.[698] According to Street, 'so far as this system succeeds [...] inmates released from the institution may leave more "prisonized" [*sic*] than rehabilitated'.[699] In other words, prisoners will become institutionalised to prison life and will conform to its socio-institutional expectations rather than be reformed or 'rehabilitated' from their criminal tendencies.

However, as in most research studies concerning prisons, the above-described perspectives have been drawn from the male closed prison experience; in fact, there is little empirical data theorising female prisoners' culture, let alone prisoners' culture in open prisons. Therefore, the following analysis is based upon the assumption that women prisoners also tend to develop a prisoners' culture, although it might differ from a typically male one. Furthermore, the discussion draws upon the research by Jones et al. on

---

[695] H. Jones et al., *Open Prisons* (London: Routledge and Kegan Paul, 1977), p.6.

[696] See Sykes. The prisoner culture has been also labelled as 'solidarity opposition' and 'inmate system' by D. Street, in his research *'The Inmate Group in Custodial and Treatment Settings'*, *American Sociological Review*, vol 30, n.1 (Feb 1965) 40-55.

[697] According to Sykes, the 'culture' may encompass more than one prisoner's social interactions; there will usually be a balance between, on one hand, some sort of anti-regime culture and, on the other hand, a prisoners' solidarity culture. Thus, some prisoners might act with little regard to other prisoners, whereas others might form a net of prisoner support.

[698] Street, pp.40, 45.

[699] Ibid., p.41.

open prisons and is supported by other research studies, such as Street's,[700] conducted on treatment institutions. Although the treatment institutions are penal institutions but not open prisons, they have some characteristics in common which distinguish them both from the (closed) 'correctional institution'. In particular, they place less emphasis on surveillance and containment and provide a less deprived physical and psychological environment, where prisoners are encouraged to develop their self-confidence.[701]

Based on fieldwork data, Jones et al. have speculated, albeit inconclusively, that prisoners' culture in open prisons might showcase a different dynamic than the one in closed prisons. He suggested two ways in which this dynamic could materialise, as follows:[702] first, the prisoners' culture in the open prison is weaker because the 'pains of imprisonment' are fewer; or alternatively, the prisoners' culture is as intense as in the closed prison, yet it is not as visible as it lacks the typical custodial pressure applied on prisoners in closed prisons.[703] However, an analysis of Jones et al. perspective tested against Street's research findings demonstrates that the two options do not necessarily exemplify two different situations and they, in fact, express the same conclusion: that is, the open prison's prisoners' culture manifests itself to a much lesser degree than in a closed prison, hence suggesting a lower level of 'totality'. Indeed, Street's research indicates that there is a link between the institution's regime[704] and the development of prisoners' culture;[705] he further suggests that there are two environmental factors that may affect prisoners' response to the prison regime. First, a disproportionate balance between gratification and deprivation (e.g. deprivation of liberty and deprivation of autonomy) will set in motion an anti-prison attitude; second, high levels of prison staff's control and

---

[700] See also B.B. Berk, 'Organizational Goals and Inmates Organization', *American Journal of Sociology,* Vol. 71, n.5 (March 1966) 522-534.

[701] Street, p.43

[702] It is worth mentioning that Jones's research was not designed to assess prisoner culture, but the research findings encouraged him to reflect on this aspect. He thus urged the academic community to conduct further research to explore this issue.

[703] Jones et al., pp.229-30.

[704] Street's findings challenged the idea suggesting that it is not the institution's setting that affects prisoners' perception of the institution's life, but rather it is the prisoners' predisposition, i.e., the impact of criminal history, past institutional record, age, ethnicity, IQ, family background, urban-rural background and social class (p.49).

[705] Ibid., p.42.

authority, such as strict supervision, will 'facilitate the inmates' recognition of a common fate and their potentialities for collective problem solving'.[706]

Street argues that if the level of deprivation and the level of control differ from one institution to the other, the prisoners' response to the regime must vary as well.[707] Indeed, the open prisons, similarly to the treatment-oriented institutions studied by Street, place greater emphasis on providing incentives, objectives and positive living experience; they also exercise less control over prisoners' association and general freedom. Street's findings confirm that prisoners in treatment-oriented prisons 'often expressed positive attitudes towards the institution and staff, non-prisonised views of adaptation to the institution, and positive images of self-change'.[708] Indeed, the two options offered by Jones et al. can be applied here. The first option suggests a weaker prisoners' culture; this can be seen through a far more balanced level of deprivation (i.e. the pain of imprisonment) in the open prison, and thus, the levels of collaboration and communication between prisoners and staff are higher. Therefore, as the balance between gratification and deprivation is much more proportionate in an open prison, prisoners' solidarity might well be developed but not necessarily channelled against the official system. Moreover, prisoners might be well aware that an anti-prison attitude would compromise their chances to stay in an environment which is based upon low levels of security and high levels of trust.

The second option proposed by Jones et al. suggests that the prison culture in open prisons is as intense as in a closed prison but is not as visible due to the lower levels of control. In fact, Street's findings indicate that group integration and solidarity is higher in the treatment-oriented prison than in the closed prison, this being facilitated by the greater degree of prisoners' association and less oppressive control by the staff.[709] This suggests that prisoners' culture is still there, even to high degrees, but it is being fed by 'positive norms and perspectives and greater commitment to the institution and staff'[710] rather than being an adaptation of an anti-prison attitude. For example, the use of illegal drugs in the open prison, discussed in the first part of this chapter, well emphasises the relatively balanced, albeit delicate, social interaction between prison staff, prison regime and prisoners. Illicit

---

[706] Ibid., p.45.
[707] Ibid., p.42.
[708] Ibid., p.47.
[709] Ibid., p.52.
[710] Ibid., p.46.

drug use has been confirmed to be present in Askham Grange by the Inspectorate report,[711] but it has also been suggested that it does not cause major security distress in relation to drug trafficking, violence, threats and bullying.

*

In early 2009, Askham Grange's prison management was fused with the management of New Hall prison (New Hall being a local female closed prison).[712] This has raised many concerns, especially by the Independent Monitoring Board (IMB):

> There was some resentment and insecurity amongst staff at the perceived injustice of the abandonment of a successful governor [Alec McCrystal]. Likewise, there were concerns by residents, particularly those who had served their initial term of imprisonment at HMP New Hall who were aware of its different ethos.[713]

Indeed, the main concern that could undermine the whole operation of the open prison regime was that the new management 'may not have the background knowledge to readily continue the unique ethos of Askham Grange.'[714]

The fusion of Askham Grange open prison into the New Hall orthodox closed prison highlights the argument at the core of this study: the orthodox closed prison does not have the physical and ideological expertise to satisfy effective social integration after release, while Askham Grange has provided such a purposeful regime for more than 60 years. This was concisely expressed by the Secretary of State in the introduction to the prison department report for the year 1964:

---

[711] *Inspection Report for HMP Askham Grange*, 2008, p.35.

[712] As discussed in the previous chapter, New Hall started as a satellite working camp for Wakefield prison in 1933. In 1948, it was officially declared an open prison. In 1961, its function changed to accommodate young offenders (not as a borstal); and finally, in 1987, it assumed its current role (*New Hall*, Prison finder, HM Prison Service, Public Sector Prisons, Justive.gov.uk (last updated Aug 2013), http://www.justice.gov.uk/contacts/prison-finder/new-hall (accessed 29 Aug 2013).

[713] *The Annual Report for the Independent Board HMP/YOI Askham Grange, York (IMB)* (year ending June 2009), http://webarchive.nationalarchives.gov.uk/20110206195651/http://www.imb.gov.u k/reports/Askham_Grange_2008-2009.pdf (accessed 29 Aug 2013), p.5.

[714] IMB, *HMP/YOI Askham Grange 2009*, p.5.

There is a positive value also in the open prison as a form of custody. It puts the responsibility for his decision on the prisoner in a way which a closed prison cannot do [...] Immediately a prisoner comes out of prison he will be faced with choices, pre-eminently the choice whether to resort to crime again. In an open prison, a comparable choice and responsibility will have been thrown squarely on him; whether to walk out or not.[715]

Moreover, the importance of acquiring the 'right' social skills might manifest itself in more or less successful social integration. The European Commission research project has highlighted the concern that many imprisoned women have already suffered some level of social exclusion prior to their imprisonment; this is further intensified because of their prison sentence and inadequate transition and adaptation once released. However, women 'who were not socially excluded prior to their imprisonment' may risk exclusion upon release. [716] In fact, Fortune et al. argue that encouraging empowerment inside the prison is one thing, but then facing the 'stigma associated with incarceration' once released is another.[717] Goffman noted that the prisoner 'may find that release means moving from the top of a small world to the bottom of a larger one',[718] which, according to Fortune et al., inevitably intensifies the feeling of powerlessness and thus the 'risk of being socially isolated and excluded'.[719] Therefore, experiencing work and study outside prison while still serving a prison sentence might be significant not only for the mere acquisition of working experience but also, as advised by the European Commission research project, because it 'would make a real difference for many women prisoners both during the imprisonment as well as for future reintegration.'[720]

Dame Anne Owers in her last Inspectorate Report for Askham Grange emphasised exactly that:

Askham Grange [...] has always had positive inspection reports, but on this occasion its performance can best be described as outstanding. It is the only

---

[715] Forward by the Rt. Hon Henry Brooke, M.P. Secretary of State for the Home Department in *Report of the Commissioners of Prisons for the year 1964*, Home Office (London: HMSO, 1964-1986), p. ix (13).
[716] *Women, Integration and Prison*, see executive summary, pp.5-16.
[717] D. Fortuna et al., 'Social Justice and Women Leaving Prison: Beyond Punishment and Exclusion', *Contemporary Justice Review*, 13,1 (2010) 19-33 (p.19).
[718] Goffman, p.71.
[719] Fortuna et al., p.19.
[720] *Women, Integration and Prison*, p.11.

adult prison which we have assessed as performing well across each of our four tests of safety, respect, purposeful activity and resettlement.

Those assessments reflect an establishment that is doing a great deal more than simply meeting targets, or going through the correct processes.

Open prisons, despite their relatively compliant population, are not always positive and supportive environments: too often they are merely waiting rooms on the way to release. Askham Grange was far from that: it provided a holistic and individualised approach to managing the transition from custody back to the community.

It is also a message to the prison system about the kind of establishment and the kind of approach that most benefit prisoners, particularly women prisoners.[721]

This chapter focused on the regime of the open prison, examining HMP Askham Grange open prison for women as a case study. It further assessed the dynamic of the penal policy of 'training for freedom' as developed first by the borstal's advocates and later fulfilled by the open prison agenda. I argue that although the aim of the open prison has been to retrain prisoners for those social skills lost through the process of imprisonment, hence institutionalisation, the drawbacks and permanent state of crisis experienced by the mainstream closed prison have only slightly facilitated these prisoners' progression from the closed to the open prison, thus limiting the effective implementation of the open prison. This adverse relationship and the dependence of the open prison on the mainstream closed prison's functional logistics makes the open prison a Total Institution, with the typical characteristics found to foster institutionalisation. The totality of the open prison, however, is mitigated by the intrinsic and unique characteristics and ethos of the open prison regime and agenda.

---

[721] HM Chief Inspector of Prisons, Dame Anne Owers, in the latest report published in 2008: *Report on an announced inspection of HMP Askham Grange*, 23 September to 3 October 2008, HM Chief Inspector of Prisons, http://www.justice.gov.uk/downloads/publications/inspectorate-reports/hmipris/ prison-and-yoi-inspections/askham-grange/askham_grange_2008-rps.pdf (last accessed 29 Aug 2013).

CONCLUSION

Academic writings have criticised the lack of scholarly documentation of the lives and experiences of women prisoners. This has fostered a discourse suggesting that women prisoners have been 'invisible' in a criminal justice system whose core interest has been the male offender. Despite these concerns, however, there has been little engagement with primary historical records to understand whether the invisibility of women prisoners represents a real lack of commitment (policy and practical) and thus scant resources to construct historical narratives; or rather, whether the invisibility stems from poor criminological historical investigation. Historical records suggest that despite the indisputably small number of female offenders and female prisoners in comparison to their male counterparts, policy and practitioners were as concerned, at least proportionally, with the female prisoner as they were with the male prisoner.

The institutional development of women's prisons can have a historiography in its own right without needing to compare and contrast it with what has been constructed as the mainstream prison history, that is, male prison history. Histories by Smith, Dobash et al. and Carlen were the first to dedicate their full attention to women's experiences with penal policy. The problem with these historical analyses, however, has been taking well-established mainstream prison history at face value; in other words, women's prison histories have been written within the contextual knowledge and boundaries created by these histories. Such analysis has denied the construction of an authentic and independent women's prison history and has led to conflicting historical accounts. Scratching beneath the surface of an unchallenged prison history by uncovering primary historical sources that solely address the issue of women prisoners helps us to understand the unique historical dynamic of this specific prison population. It would be misleading to state that the development of women's prisons has been unrelated to that of men's prisons; and yet, denying the development of women's prisons its own historical ownership would replicate misconceptions and distort historical narratives.

This study has traced the experimental nature of imprisonment and how this has affected, on the one hand, the longevity of the penalty and, on the other hand, its permanent state of crisis. Until the mid-eighteenth century, prison was classified as a secondary penalty. However, drawbacks related to capital punishment and transportation meant that the system of punishment needed to be revised. The death penalty was becoming perceived as morally disproportionate and transportation, although economically conducive, saw the colonies reluctant to take on more criminals. In this context of uncertainty, suggestions and recommendations were made for a contingency plan, where eventually Parliament had to be persuaded to upgrade imprisonment to function as a primary penalty. Parliament was reassured that this was merely an experiment and that, once the limitations on transportation were lifted, the usual order of things would be restored. Historical records indicate, however, that the plans concerning prison upgrade were not well conceived and lacked coherence and agreement. Indeed, prison as a penalty was born out of a temporary emergency plan whose objective was not 'confinement' itself, but rather, the rationale was promoted upon the idea of prisoners' labour and thus perceived as an economic venture.

Due to the circumstances in which imprisonment was upgraded, its implications and effects (on the individual and society) were never tested; this, in turn, led to a system that was constantly failing to address the socio-penal concerns of the day. The prison system was portrayed and perceived as being in a constant state of crisis, but instead of rethinking the values and aims underlining (or undermining) the penalty, imprisonment was routinely reinvented; this was done by rationalising and legitimising the justifications for its use. Carlen has termed this vicious circular process 'carceral clawback', where rather than challenging the legitimacy of the use of imprisonment per se, the effective delivery and fulfilment of the aims of imprisonment were tested against and reshaped to reflect 'spur of the moment' socio-political concerns. Indeed, this leads to the submission that the concept of 'reforming' the prisoner has been shaped by policy and academic discourses but has had no basis in practice; hence, it is a myth.

The study demonstrates that despite 'prisoners' reformation' being a recurring theme in prison policy and prison reform (and it still is), the foundational drawback presented by the prison system has meant that, in practice, an effective implementation of the ethos of reformation was never a feasible task. Prison regimes were routinely reshaped and redesigned to better fulfil this aim of imprisonment; yet, limitations related to ineffective prison management and expensive administration as well as the presence of conflicting social aims and penal policies meant that prisoners' reformation could not be taken beyond its theoretical construction. Such recognition contributes to the understanding that prison policy and prison administration has been less systematic than is suggested by Revisionist histories. It could be argued that too much credit has been attributed to the prison as a social institution striving for social control; but, on the other hand, the anomalous relationship between imprisonment and reformation has been merely tested upon the prison's (un)successful endorsement of new and reshaped policies. Prison discourses and prison studies, as well as social perception, have been fixated with the aim of prisoners' reformation, but this has been taken at face value. Instead, the 'myth of reformation' perspective draws attention to prisoners' inevitable adaptation to institutional life, rather than their 'reformation' to what has been deemed desirable, that is, a law-abiding (free citizen's) social life. Prisoners 'reform' (or rather adapt) to the institutional social life and thus go through the process of institutionalisation. This in itself does not guarantee a successful future social integration, and if anything, it could hamper it.

Historical records indicate that this was acknowledged at times by penal and academic discourses, but it was only with the 1948 Criminal Justice Act that the alternative prison policy of 'training' was proposed (parallel to the orthodox prison system). The 'training for freedom' perspective embraced the understanding that to reform prisoners to become law-abiding social citizens, the training must take place outside the prison walls. Hence, borstals and, later, adult open prisons were conceived for this purpose. It appeared that for the first time, 'reformation' was a feasible prospect; prisoners were trained, rather than reformed, to acquire those social skills lost through the process of institutionalisation. In the case study of HMP Askham Grange I explored the relationship between 'reformation' and 'training' by examining the first open prison for women.

This study clarifies the role of the open prison in the context of prison policy, that is, being part of the process of prisoners' progression as devised by the Criminal Justice Act 1948. This unveils the conflict between the mainstream prison system and the open prison; it demonstrates that reforms of the system and within the system are not standalone enterprises, inevitably affected by the intrinsic drawbacks and permanent crisis in the orthodox closed prison. Therefore, this understanding reiterates an important consideration: any attempt at introducing schemes and projects aiming at 'reforming' the prisoner will be short-lived; reformation will maintain its status as a 'myth' unless a sincere, politically free assessment of the legitimacy of imprisonment takes place.

BIBLIOGRAPHY

Anonymous, *Startling Disclosures! Six Months of hard labour in the City Prison, Holloway, by one who was there, and remand to Newgate* (London: Curtice & Co, 1878)

Bachman, Ronet and Schutt, Russell K., *Fundamentals of Research in Criminology and Criminal Justice*, 2nd edn (London: SAGE, 2012)

Banks, Charlotte; Mayhew, Patricia; and Sapsford, R.J., *Absconding from Open Prisons*, (London: H.M.S.O, 1975)

Barman, S., *The English Borstal System* (London: P.S King and Son Ltd, 1934)

Beattie, J.M., *Policing and Punishment in London, 1660-1750: Urban Crime and the Limits of Terror* (Oxford: Oxford University Press, Incorporated, 2001)

Beattie, J.M., 'The criminality of women in Eighteen Century England', *Journal of social History,* 8, 4 (1975), 80-116

Beccaria, Cesare, *On Crimes and Punishments and other writings*, ed. by Thomas, A. (Canada: University of Toronto Press, 2008)

Bentham, Jeremy, *A view on the Hard labour bill* (London: T. Payne, T. Cadell, P. Elmsley & E. Brooke, 1778)

Becker, Howard S., 'Becoming a Marihuana User', *American Journal of Sociology*, 59, 3 (1953), 235-252

Beneett, R., 'The Meaning of Institutional Life', *Gerontologist*, 3 (1963), 117-125

Bentley, Michael, *Modern Historiography*, Taylor & Francis e-Library (London: Routledge, 2005; 1st edn 1999)

Berk B.B, Organizational Goals and Inmates Organization, *American Journal of Sociology,* Vol. 71, n.5 (March 1966) pp.522-534

Besant, Walter, *All Sorts and Conditions of Men: An impossible story* (London: Chatto & Windus, 1882)

Blackstone, William, *Commentaries on the Laws of England,* Vol. 1 (Oxford: Clarendon Press, 1765)

Bottomley, Keith and James, Adrian, 'From Experiment to Expansion', *Criminal Justice Matters*, 30 (1997/98), 27-28, https://www.crimeandjustice.org.uk/sites/crimeandjustice.org.uk/files/09627259708552791.pdf (accessed 22 June 2017)

Bourke, Joanna, *Women on the Home Front in World War One*, BBC History, 3 March 2011,

http://www.bbc.co.uk/history/british/britain_wwone/women_employm
   ent_01.shtml (accessed 13 Oct 2015)
Bourke, Joanna, *Working Class cultures in Britain 1890-1960* (London:
   Routledge1994)
Bradley, Trevor, 'Social Exclusion', in *The SAGE Dictionary of
   Criminology,* ed. by McLaughlin Eugene and Muncie John, 3rd edn
   (London: SAGE, 2013), pp. 428-430
Burke, Peter, *History and Social Theory* (Cambridge: Polity Press, 2005)
Butterfield, Herbert, *The Whig Interpretation of History* (NY: AMS Press,
   1931; repr. 1978)
Buxton, Thomas Fowell, *An inquiry, whether crime and misery are
   produced or prevented by our present system of prison discipline*, 6th edn
   (London: Black Horse Count, 1818)
Camp, John Michael Francis, *Holloway Prison- the place and the people*
   (London: David & Charles, 1974)
Carpenter, Mary, *Our convicts*, Vol. 2 (London: Longman, 1864)
Carlen, Pat and Worrall, Anne, *Analysing Women's Imprisonment* (Devon:
   Willan, 2004)
Carlen, Pat, *Women's Imprisonment: A Study in Social Control* (London:
   Routledge and Kegan Paul, 1983)
Carlen, Pat, 'The Case of Women's Imprisonment in Canada', *Punishment
   and Society,* 4, 1 (2002), 115-121
Casale, Silvia, 'Conditions and Standards. In *Prisons After Woolf: Reform
   through Riot*, ed. Player, Elaine and Jenkins, Michael (London and NY,
   Taylor & Francis E-Library, 2002), pp. 66-77
Cavadino, Michael and Dignan, James, *The Penal System*, 4th edn (London:
   SAGE, 2007)
Cavadino, Michael; Dignan, James; and Mair, George, *The Penal System*,
   5th edn (London: SAGE, 2013)
Clarke, John, 'Social Constructionism', in *The SAGE Dictionary of
   Criminology,* ed. by McLaughlin Eugene and Muncie John, 3rd edn
   (London: SAGE, 2013), pp. 417-419
Cohen, Stanley, *Folk Devils and Moral Panics* (London: MacGibbon and
   Kee, 1972)
Cohen, Stanley and Scull, Andrew, 'Social Control in History and
   Sociology', in *Social Control and the State*, ed. by Cohen, Stanley and
   Scull, Andrew (London: Basil Blackwell Ltd, 1983; repr. 1986) pp. 1-
   14
Corbin, Juliet M. and Strauss, Anselm, *Basics of Qualitative Research:
   Techniques and Procedures for Developing Grounded Theory*, 4th edn
   (SAGE Publications, 2014)

Corder, Susanna, *Life of Elizabeth Fry: Compiled from Her Journal, as Edited by Her Daughters, and from Various Other Sources* (London: W. & F. G. Cash, 1853)

Crewe, Ben, 'Gresham Sykes (1922-)', in *Fifty Key Thinkers in Criminology*, ed. by Hayward Keith, Maruna Shadd, and Mooney Ayne (Oxon: Routledge, 2010), pp. 134-138

Crew, A., *London Prisons of Today and Yesterday* (London: Butler & Tanner Ltd, 1933)

Cross, Wilbur Lucius, *The History of Henry Fielding* (New Haven: Yale University Press, 1918)

Davies, Pamela, 'Doing Interviews In Prison', in *Doing Criminological Research*, ed. by Davies, Pamela; Francis, Peter; and Jupp, Victor, 2nd edn (London: SAGE, 2011), pp.161-178

Devereaux, Simon, 'The making of the penitentiary Act', *The Historical Journal*, 42, 2 (1999), 405-433

Devereaux, Simon, 'In place of death: transportation, penal practice and the English state 1770-1830', in *Qualities of mercy: Justice, punishment and discretion*, ed. by Strange Carolyn (UBC Press, 1996) pp.52-76

Dobash, Russell P.; Dobash, Emerson R.; and Gutteridge, Sue., *The Imprisonment of Women* (Oxford: Basil Blackwell, 1986)

Du Cane, Edmond, *The Punishment and Prevention of Crime* (London: Macmillan and Co., 1885)

Eden, William, *Principles of Penal Law* (London: B. White and T. Cadell, 1771)

Englander, David, 'The Word and the World: Evangelicalism in the Victorian City', in *Religion in Victorian Britain: Controversies*, ed. by Parsons, Gerald, Vol 2 (The Open University, 1988; repr. 1997) pp.14-38

Field, H.E, *Re-building Character in Delinquent Youth* (London: Institute of Education, 1933, unpublished PhD)

Fielding, Henry, *An Enquiry Into the Causes of the Late Increase of Robbers*, 2nd edn (London: A. Millar, 1751)

Fielding, Nigel and Thomas, Hilary, 'Qualitative interviewing', in *Researching Social Life*, ed. by Gilbert, Nigel, 3rd edn (London: SAGE, 2008), pp. 245-265

Finch, Emily and Fafinski, Stefan, *Criminology Skills* (Oxford: Oxford University press, 2012)

Fine, Gary Alan and Manning, Philip, 'Erving Goffman', in *The Blackwell Companion to Major Contemporary Social Theorists*, ed. by Ritzer, George, 2nd edn (Oxford: Blackwell, 2003), pp. 34-62

Fletcher, Susan Willis, *Twelve months in an English prison* (Boston: Lee and Shepard, 1884)

Forsythe, Bill, 'Women prisoners and women penal officials 1840-1921', *British Journal of Criminology*, 33, 4 (1993), 525-540

Forsythe, William J., *The reform of prisoners 1830-1900* (NY: St. Martin's press, 1987)

Fortuna, Darla; Thompson, Julie; Pedlar, Alison; and Yuen, Felice, 'Social Justice and Women Leaving Prison: Beyond Punishment and Exclusion', *Contemporary Justice Review*, 13, 1 (2010) 19-33

Foucault, Michel, *Discipline and Punish: the Birth of the Prison* (London: Penguin, 1979; repr. 1991)

Fox, Lionel W., *The Modern English Prison* (London: Routledge & Sons Ltd, 1934)

Fox, Lionel W., *The English Prison and Borstal Systems* (London: Routledge & Kegan, 1952)

Fry, Elizabeth Gurney, *Sketch of the origin and results of Ladies' Prison Associations, with hints for the formation of Local Associations* (London: A & J Arch and Hatchard and Son, 1827)

Fry, Elizabeth Gurney, *Observation on the visiting, superintending and government of female prisoners* (London: A & J Arch, 1827)

Fry, Gurney Elizabeth and Gurney, Joseph John, *Report addressed to the Marquises Wellesley, Lord Lieutenant of Ireland* (London: A & J Arch, 1827)

Fry, Katharine and Cresswell, Rachel Elizabeth, ed., *Memoir of the life of Elizabeth Fry*, Vol. 1, 2 (London: J. Hatchard and son, 1848)

Fry, Margery, 'The Borstal System', in *Penal Reform in England*, ed. by Radzinowicz, Leon and Turner, James William, 2nd edn (London: Macmillan and Co., 1946), pp. 127-151

Garland, David, 'The Limits of the Sovereign State: Strategies of crime control in contemporary Society', *British Journal of Criminology*, 36, 4 (1996) 445-471

Garland, David, 'Women, Crime, and Victorian England. By L. Zedner (Oxford: Clarendon Press, 1991)', *British Journal of Criminology*, 33, 1 (1993) 113-115

Garland, David, 'The criminal and his science', *The British journal of criminology*, 25, 2 (1985), 109-137

Gatrell V., 'Execution and the English people', in *Key Reading in Criminology*, ed. by Newburn, Tim (Devon: Willan, 2009), pp. 22-24

Gelsthrope, Lorain, *Doing Prison Research: Qualitative Methods* (Milton Keynes: Open University Press, 1992)

Gelsthrope, Lorain, 'Feminist methodologies in criminology: a new approach or old wine in new bottles?', in *Feminist perspectives in criminology*, ed. by Gelsthrope, Lorain and Morris, Allison (Milton Keynes: Open university press, 1990), pp. 89-106

Genders, Elaine and Player, Elaine, *Grendon- a study of a therapeutic prison* (Oxford: Clarendon, 1995)

Gordon, Mary, *Penal discipline* (London: George Routledge & Sons, 1922)

Goffman, Erving, *Asylums* (Middlesex: Penguin Books, 1961; repr 1976)

Gore, Elizabeth, *The Better Fight: The Story of Dame Lillian Baker* (London: Bles, 1964)

Griffiths, Arthur, *Memorials of Millbank and Chapters in Prison History* (London: Chapman and Hall, 1884)

Grovier, Kelly, *The Gaol: The Story of Newgate- London's Most Notorious Prison* (UK: John Murray, 2009)

Gurney, Joseph John, *Notes on a visit made to some of the prisons in Scotland and the North of England in company with Elizabeth Fry* (London, 1819)

Haney, Craig, *The Psychological Impact of Incarceration: Implications for Post-Prison Adjustment*, National Policy Conference (U.S. Department of Health and Human Services, 2002)

Hardesty, Constance; Hardwick, Paula G.; and Thompson, Ruby J., 'Self-esteem and the Woman Prisoner', in *Women Prisoners: A Forgotten Population*, ed. by Fletcher, Beverly R.; Shaver, Lynda Dixon; and Moon, Dreama G. (Westport, London: Praeger, 1993), pp. 27-44

Harding, Cristopher; Hines, Bill; Ireland, Richard; and Rawlings, Philip, *Imprisonment in England and Wales: A Concise History* (London: Croom Helm, 1985)

Hardman, Philippa, 'The origins of imprisonment', *The Prison Service Journal*, 177 (2008), 16-22

Healy, William and Alper, B.S., *Criminal Youth and the Borstal System* (London: Oxford University Press, 1941)

Hedderman, Carol, 'Payment By Results: Hopes, Fears And Evidence', *British Journal of Community Justice*, 11: 2-3 (2013), 43-58

Heidensohn, Frances and Silvestri, Marisa, 'Gender and Crime', in *The Oxford handbook of criminology*, ed. by Maguire, Mike; Morgan, Rod; and Reiner, Robert, 5th edn (Oxford: Oxford University Press, 2012), pp. 336-361

Heidensohn, Frances, *Women and Crime* (London: Macmillan, 1985)

Henry, Joan, *Who lie in Gaol* (London: Victor Gollancz LTD, 1952)

Hont, Istvan, 'The Permanent Crisis of a Divided Mankind: Contemporary Crisis of the Nation State', *Political Studies*, 42 (1994), 166-231

Holford, George Peter, *Thoughts on the criminal prisons of this country* (London, 1821)

Howe, Adrian, *Punish and Critique* (London, NY: Routledge, 1994)

Howard, John, *The state of the prisons in England and Wales* (Warrington: William Eyres, 1777)

Hudson, Barbara, 'Critical Reflection as research Methodology', in *Doing Criminological Research*, ed. by Jupp, Victor; Davies, Pamela; and Francis, Peter (London: SAGE, 2000, repr. 2006), pp.175-192

Hugo, Victor, *The Last Day of a Condemned Man*, 2nd edn (Richmond: Oneworld Classics Ltd, 1832; repr. 2011)

Ignatieff, Michael, 'State, Civil Society and Total Institutions: A Critique of Recent Social Histories of Punishment', in *Social Control and the State*, ed. by Cohen, Stanley and Scull, Andrew, (London: Basil Blackwell Ltd, 1983; repr. 1986), pp. 75-105 [Also available in Ignatieff Michael, 'State, Civil Society and Total Institutions: A Critique of Recent Social Histories of Punishment', *Crime and Justice*, Vol. 3 (1981) pp153-192]

Ignatieff, Michael, *A Just Measure of Pain* (NY: Pantheon, 1978)

Innes, Joanne, 'Prisons for the poor', in *Labour, Law and Crime: An Historical Perspective*, ed. by Snyder, Francis G. and Hay, Douglas (London: Tavistock Publications, 1987), pp. 42-122

Jebb, C.B., *Report on the Discipline and Management of the Convict Prisons* (London: W. Clowes & Sons, 1851)

John, J., *Thoughts on the construction and policy of prisons, with hints for their improvement* (1785)

Jones, Howard; Cones, Paul; and Stockford, Richard, *Open Prisons* (London: Routledge and Kegan Paul, 1977)

Johnson, McNown Miriam and Rhodes, Rita, 'Institutionalization: A Theory of Human Behaviour and the Social Environment', *Advance in Social Work*, 8, 1 (2007), 219-236

Karmel, Madeline, 'Total Institutions and Self Mortification', *Journal of Health and Social Behaviour*, 10 (1969), 134-141

Kennedy, Helena, *Eve was Framed: Women and British Justice* (London: Vintage, 2005, 1st edn 1992)

King, Peter, *Crime and Law in England 1750-1840* (Cambridge: Cambridge University Press, 2006)

King, Peter, *Crime, Justice, and Discretion in England 1740-1820* (Oxford: Oxford University Press, 2000)

Lewis, Brain and Crew, Harry, *The Story of a House, Askham Grange Women's Open Prison* (Yorkshire: Yorkshire Art Circus and HMP Askham Grange, 1997)

Lowthian, Jackie, 'Women's prisons in England: barriers to reform', in *Women and punishment: the struggle for justice*, ed. by Carlen, Pat (Cullompton: Willan, 2002), pp.155-181

Madam, Martin, Reverend, *Thoughts on Executive Justice* (London: Pall-Mall, 1787)

Mainwaring, V., *Thoughts on the construction and management of prisons* (London, 1786)

Mandaraka-Sheppard, Alexandra, *The Dynamic of Aggression in Women's Prisons in England* (Aldershot: Gower, 1986)

Marsh, Josiah, *A Popular Life of George Fox: The First of the Quakers* (London: Charles Gilpin, 1847)

Martin, Carol, 'Doing research in a prison setting', in *Doing Criminological Research*, ed. by Jupp, Victor; Davies, Pamela; and Francis, Peter (London: SAGE, 2006), pp. 215-233

Marwick, Arthur, *The New Nature of History* (Hampshire: Palgrave, 2001)

Mason, Jennifer, *Qualitative Researching*, 2nd edn (London: SAGE, 2002; repr. 2005)

Mason, M.H., *Classification of girls and boys in workhouses* (London: Hatchards, 1884)

Matrineau, Harriet, 'Life in the Criminal Class', *Edinburgh Review* (1865), 337-71

Mayhew, Henry and Binny, John, *The criminal prisons of London and scenes of prison life* (London: Griffin, 1862)

Mawby, R.I., 'Women in Prison: A British Study', *Crime & Delinquency*, 28, 1 (1982), 24-39

McConville, Sean, *English local prisons 1860-1900: Next only to death* (London: Routledge, 1995)

McConvile, Sean, *A history of English prison administration*, 1750-1877, Vol 1 (London: Routledge, 1981)

McEwen, C.A., 'Continuities in the Study of Total and Nontotal Institutions', *Annual Review of Sociology*, 6 (1980), 143-185

McLaughlin, Eugene, 'Managerialism', in The SAGE Dictionary of Criminology, ed. McLaughlin, Eugene and Muncie, John, 3rd edn (London: SAGE 2013), pp-260-262

McLynn, Frank, *Crime and Punishment in the eighteen century England* (London: Routledge, 1989; repr. 2002)

McNown, Miriam and Rhodes, Rita, 'Institutionalization: A Theory of Human Behaviour and the Social Environment', *Advance in Social Work*, 8, 1 (2007), 219-236

Melossi, Dario and Pavarini, Massimo, *The Prison and the Factory: Origins of the Penitentiary System* (MacMillan, 1981)

Moseley, Sydney A., *Truth about Borstal* (London: Cecil Palmer, 1926)

Murji, Karim, 'Moral Panic', in *The SAGE Dictionary of Criminology*, ed. by McLaughlin, Eugene and Muncie, John (London: SAGE, 2013), pp. 271-273

Naffine, Ngaire, *Feminism and Criminology* (Cambridge: Polity Press, 1997)

Neild, James, *State of the prisons in England, Scotland and Wales, Justice of the peace* (London: John Nichols and Son, 1812)

Newburn Tim, *Criminology* (Devon: Willan Publishing, 2007)

Norrie, Alan, *Crime, Reason and History: A Critical Introduction to Criminal Law*, 2nd edn (Cambridge: Cambridge University Press: 2001)

Ollyfee, G., *An Essay Humbly offered, for an Act of Parliament to Prevent Capital Crimes, and the Loss of Many Lives: and to Promote a Desirable Improvement and Blessing in the Nation* (London: printed for J. Downing, 1731)

Owen, Barbara A., *In the Mix: Struggle and Survival in a Women's Prison* (Albany: State Universtiy of NY press, 1998)

Owen, Robert, *A New View of Society: Essays on the Formation of Human Character* (London, 1813)

Owen, Robert, 'Hints, Plans and Proceedings of Benevolence', The Literary panorama, 1806-1819, 6, 36 (1817), 989-994

Owen, Robert, *The Revolution in the Mind and Practice of the Human Race* (London: Effingham Wilson, 1849)

Paley, William, *Principles of Morals and Political Philosophy*, (London: Thomas Davison, 1785)

Paterson, Alexander, *Paterson on Prisons*, ed. by Ruck S.K. (London: Frederick Muller ltd, 1951)

Playfair, Giles William., *The punitive obsession* (London: Victor Gollancz LTD, 1971)

Player Elaine, 'Women's Prisons after Woolf'. In *Prisons After Woolf: Reform through Riot*, ed. Elaine Player and Michael Jenkins (London and NY, Taylor & Francis E-Library, 2002), pp.203-225

Priestley, Philip, *Victorian prison lives* (London: Pimlico, 1999)

Pozen, David E., 'Managing A Correctional Marketplace: Prison Privatisation in the United States and the United Kingdom', *Journal of Law and Politics*, XIX (2003), 253-284

Radzinowicz, Leon, 'The Waltham Black Act', *Cambridge Law Journal*, 9 (1945), 56-81

Radzinowicz, Leon, A *History of English Criminal Law and it Administration from 1750*, Vol. 1 (London: Stevens and Sons LtD: 1948)

Raphael, D.D., *Moral Philosophy* (Oxford: University press, 1994)

Render, H.W., *Through prison bars- the lives and labours of John Howard and Elizabeth Fry- the prisoner's friends* (London: S.W. Partridge & Co., 1894)

Rock, Paul, *Reconstructing a women's prison- The Holloway redevelopment project 1968-88* (Oxford: Clarendon Press, 1996)

Roberts, Helen, *Doing Feminist Research* (London: Routledge, 1981)

Roberts, Rebecca and Cain, Claire, *Holloway: the Beginning of a Revolution?* Centre for Crime and Justice Studies, 2015, https://www.crimeandjustice.org.uk/resources/holloway-beginning-revolution (accessed 25 June 2017)

Ross, Stewart, *At Home in World War Two: Women's War*, in association with the Imperial War Museum (London: Evans, 2007)

Rothman, David J., *The Discovery of the Asylum* (Boston: Little, Brown, 1971)

Ruggles-Brise, Evelyn, *The English Prison System* (London: Macmillan & Co Ltd, 1921)

Ruggles-Brise, Evelyn, *Prison Reform at Home and Abroad: A Short History of the International Movement since the London Congress 1872* (London: Macmillan, 1925)

Rusch, Georg and Kirchheimer, Otto, *Punishment and Social Structure* (NY: Russell&Russell, 2003; 1st edn 1968)

Schwan, Anne, *Representing Female Prisons: Women and Crime in England 1813-1870* (Birkbeck London University: unpublished PhD thesis, 2005)

Scraton, Phil and Chadwick, Kathryn, 'Critical Research', in *The Sage Dictionary of Criminology*, ed. by McLaughlin, Euene and Muncie, John, 3rd edn (London: SAGE, 2013), pp.107-108

Semmens, Natasha, 'Methodological Approaches to Criminological Research', in *Doing Criminological Research*, ed. by Davies Pamela, Francis Peter, and Jupp Victor, 2nd edn (London: SAGE, 2011), pp. 54-76

Shoemaker, Robert Brink, *Prosecution and Punishment: Petty Crime and the Law in London and Rural Middlesex, C. 1660-1725* (Cambridge: Cambridge University Press, 1991)

Size, Mary, *Prisons I Have Known* (London: George Allen & Unwin Ltd, 1957)

Smith, Ann, *Women in Prison* (London: Stevens & Sons, 1962)

Spencer, John C., 'The Use of Corrective Training in the Treatment of the Persistent Offender in England', *Journal of Criminal Law and Criminology*, 44, 1 (1953), 40-44

Spongberg, Mary, *Writing Women History since the Renaissance* (Palgrave Macmillan, 2002)

Street D., *The Inmate Group in Custodial and Treatment Settings*, American Sociological Review, vol 30, n.1 (Feb 1965) pp 40-55.

Sykes, Gresham M., *The Society of Captives: A Study of Maximum Security Prison* (Oxfordshire: Princeton University Press, 1958; repr. 2007)

Tizard, Jack, Sinclair, Ian, and Clarke, R.V.G, *Variety of Residential Experiences*, ed. (London & Boston: Routledge & Kegan Paul, 1975)

Tobias, John J., *Crime and police in England 1700-1900* (Dublin: Gill and Macmillan, 1979)

Tosh, John, *The Pursuit of History*, 4th edn (Pearson Education Ltd, 2006; 1st edn 1984)

Tosh, John, *The Pursuit of History*, 5th edn (Pearson Education Ltd, 2013; 1st edn 1984)

Von, Koerber Lenka, *Soviet Russia Fights Crime* (London: Routledge, 1934)

Wallace, Samuel E., 'On the Totality of Institutions', in *Total Institution*, ed. by Wallace, Samuel E. (USA: Transaction, 1971), pp.1-8

Watson, J.A.F, 'The Prison System', in *Penal Reform in England*, ed. in Radzinowicz, Leon and Turner, James William, 2nd edn (London: Macmillan and Co., 1946), pp. 152-169

Webb, Sidney and Webb, Beatrice, *English prisons under local government*, Vol. 5 (London: Longmans, Green, 1922)

Wedderburn, Alexander Rosslyn, *Observation on the state of English prisons, and the means of improving them*; communicated to the Rev Henry Zouch a Justice of the Peace (London, 1793)

Weinstein, Raymond M., 'Goffman's Asylums and the Social Situation of Mental Patients', *Orthomolecular Psychiatry*, 11, 4 (1982), 267-274

Wiener, M.J., 'Women, Crime and Victorian England by Lucia Zedner', *Victorian Studies*, 37, 1 (1993), 186-190

Wilson, David, 'Social Control', in *The SAGE Dictionary of Criminology*, ed. by McLaughlin, Eugene and Muncie, John, 3rd edn (London: SAGE, 2013), pp. 421-423

Whitman, James Q., *Harsh Justice* (Oxford: University press, 2003)

Zedner, Lucia, *Women crime and custody in Victorian England* (Oxford: Clarendon Press, 1994)

Reports and research studies chronologically ordered

A Report from the Committee appointed to enquire into the state of the Goals of this Kingdom: relating to the Fleet Prison, Great Britain Parliament House of Commons (London: R. Knaplock, 1729)

Draught of a Bill to punish by Imprisonment and Hard Labour, Great Britain, Parliament, (London, 1790)

Report of the sub-committee respecting the improvements which have been lately made in the prisons and houses of correction in England and Wales (London, 1790)

Reports of the Directors of Convict Prisons, 1854, Brixton Prison (London: Spottiswoode, 1855)

Report on the Present State of Discipline in Gaols and Houses of Correction, Minutes of evidence, *Select Committee of the House of Lords,* Great Britain, Parliament, House of Lords (Dublin: Irish U.P., 1863)

Report of the Directors of Convict Prisons for the year 1873 (London: HMSO, 1874)

Second Report of The Commissioners of Prisons (London: HMSO, 1879)

Gladstone, Herbert John, Chairman, *Report (Minutes of Evidence) from the Departmental Committee on Prisons* (London: Parliamentary Papers. House of Commons, 1895)

Lushington G., Chaired, *Report to the Secretary of State for the Home department of the Departmental Committee on Reformatory and Industrial Schools*, Vol I (London: HMSO, 1896)

Report of the Commissioners of Prisons and Directors of Convict Prisons for the year 1896-1897 (London: HMSO, 1897)

Labour Research Department, *English Prisons To-Day: Being the Report of the Prison System Enquiry Committee,* ed. by F. Brockway and S.H. Hobhouse (London: Labour Research Department, 1922)

Prisons and borstals, Home Office (London: HMSO, 1945)

Annual Report for 1947 HM Prison Askham Grange, York, Mary Size

Prisons and borstals: Statement of policy and practice in the administration of the prisons and Borstal institution in England and Wales (London: H.M.S.O, 1950)

Report of the Commissioners of Prisons, Home Office (London: HMSO, 1947-55)

First UN Congress on the Prevention of Crime and Treatment of Offenders, Geneva, Switzerland 22 Aug – 3 Sep 1955, http://www.asc41.com/UN_Congress/1st%20UN%20Congress%20on %20the%20Prevention%20of%20Crime/first_congress.htm (accessed 13 Oct 2015)

Open Institutions- Recommendations adopted by Section II, Planetary Meeting, First United National Congress on the Prevention of Crime and the Treatment of Offenders, Geneva, 22 Aug - 3 Sep 1955, http://www.asc41.com/UN_Congress/1st%20UN%20Congress%20on %20the%20Prevention%20of%20Crime/009%20ACONF.6.L.2%20O pen%20Institutions.pdf (accessed 13 Oct 2015)

Report of the Commissioners of Prisons, Home Office (London: HMSO, 1956-62)

Report of the Commissioners of Prisons for the year 1964, Home Office (London: HMSO, 1964)

People in prison England and Wales, Home Office (London: HMSO, 1969)

Report on the work of the Prison Department, Great Britain, Prison Department (London: HMSO, 1964-1986)

Report on the Inquiry into Prisons Escapes and Security, Admiral of the Fleet, the Earl Mountbatten of Burma, Great Britain, Home Office (London: HMSO, 1967)

Community Service Orders: a first decade of promise, Howard League for Penal Reform, Pease K. (London: National Institute of Justice, 1981)

Crime, Justice and Protecting the Public: The Government's Proposal for Legislation, Home Office (London: HMSO, 1990)

The Woolf Report, Prison Reform Trust, 1991, http://www.prisonreformtrust.org.uk/Portals/0/Documents/Woolf%20r eport.pdf (accessed 22 May 2017)

Women Leaving Prison, Nacro (London, 1993)

Women In Prison: A Thematic Review, HM Chief Inspector of Prisons, London, Home Office, Crown Copyright 1997, https://www.justiceinspectorates.gov.uk/hmiprisons/wp-content/uploads/sites/4/2014/07/WOMEN-IN-PRISON-1996.pdf (accessed 05 June 2017)

Statistics on Women and the Criminal Justice system, Home Office, 1999, http://webarchive.nationalarchives.gov.uk/20100920143552/rds.homeo ffice.gov.uk/rds/pdfs/s95women.pdf (last accessed 02 Sep 2013 unavailable 2015)

Suicide is Everyone's Concern, A Thematic Review by HM Chief Inspector of Prisons for England and Wales, May 1999, https://www.justiceinspectorates.gov.uk/hmiprisons/wp-content/uploads/sites/4/2014/07/suicide-is-everyones-concern-1999-rps.pdf (accessed 22 May 2017)

Price David, 'The Origins and Durability of Security Categorisation: A
    Study in Penological Pragmatism *or* Spies, Dickie and Prison Security,
    British Society of Criminology Conference Selected Proceedings, Vol.3
    (1999; published 2000)
David Blunkett, *Reducing Crime- Changing Life*, Home Office, January
    2004,
    http://webarchive.nationalarchives.gov.uk/20080205174933/http://ww
    w.homeoffice.gov.uk/documents/reducing-crime-changing-
    lives?view=Binary (accessed 22 June 2017)
Report on an Announced Inspection of HMP/YOI Askham Grange, 15-19
    March 2004, HM Chief Inspector of Prisons Anne Owers, June 2004
Private Punishment: Who Profits? Prison Reform Trust, January 2005,
    http://www.prisonreformtrust.org.uk/portals/0/documents/private%20p
    unishment%20who%20profits.pdf (accessed June 2017)
*Women, Integration and Prison. An Analysis of the Processes of
    Sociolabour Integration of Women Prisoners in Europe*, Mip Project,
    European Commission, September 2005,
    http://ec.europa.eu/research/social-sciences/pdf/mip_en.pdf
    (last accessed 31 Aug 2013 unavailable 2015)
The Corston Report, Baroness Jean Corston, Home Office, 2007,
    http://www.justice.gov.uk/publications/docs/corston-report-march-
    2007.pdf (accessed 13 Oct 2015)
Report on an announced inspection of HMP Askham Grange, 23
    September- 3 October 2008, HM Chief Inspector of Prisons,
    http://www.justice.gov.uk/downloads/publications/inspectorate-
    reports/hmipris/prison-and-yoi-inspections/askham-
    grange/askham_grange_2008-rps.pdf (last accessed 29 Aug 2013
    unavailable 2015)
Women's Prison Allocation Strategy, Women & Young People's Group,
    HM Prison Service, Reed Elaine and Dichinson Helen, February, 2008
Inspection Report for HMP Askham Grange, Office for Standards in
    Education (Ofsted), 2nd October 2008,
    http://www.ofsted.gov.uk/inspection-reports/find-inspection-
    report/provider/ELS/52247 (accessed 13 Oct 2015)
*The Annual Report for the Independent Board HMP/YOI Askham Grange,
    York* (year ending June 2009),
    http://webarchive.nationalarchives.gov.uk/20110206195651/http://ww
    w.imb.gov.uk/reports/Askham_Grange_2008-2009.pdf (last accessed
    29 Aug 2013 unavailable 2015)
Statistics on Women and the Criminal Justice system, Immediate custodial
    sentences population into prison establishments, 2007, Ministry of

Justice, The Institute for Criminal Policy Research, School of Law, King's College, London, January 2009

Breaking the Cycle: Effective Punishment, Rehabilitation and Sentencing of Offenders. Ministry of Justice, (The Stationery Office Limited, 2010)

Women in prison - a short thematic review, 2010, http://www.justiceinspectorates.gov.uk/hmiprisons/inspections/women -in-prison-a-short-thematic-review/ (accessed 08 June 2017)

Bromley Briefings Prison Factfile (2010) Prison Reform Trust, http://www.prisonreformtrust.org.uk/uploads/documents/FactFileJuly2 010.pdf (accessed 08 June 2017)

The Annual Report for the Independent Board HMP/YOI Askham Grange, York (year ending June 2010) http://www.justice.gov.uk/downloads/publications/corporate-reports/imb/annual-reports-2010/Askham_Grange_2009-2010.pdf (accessed 13 Oct 2015)

Slopping out? A report on the lack of in-cell sanitation in Her Majesty's Prisons in England and Wales, National Council for Independent Monitoring Boards, August 2010, http://www.justice.gov.uk/downloads/prison-probation-inspection-monitoring/In-Cell_Sanitation_Report_V2_Aug_10.pdf (accessed 22 May 2017)

The Open Estate, Independent Monitoring Board, National Council Report, April 2011, http://www.justice.gov.uk/downloads/about/imb/imb-open-estate-report.pdf (accessed 13 Oct 2015)

Reforming Women's Justice: Final report of the Women's Justice Taskforce, Prison Reform Trust, 2011, http://www.prisonreformtrust.org.uk/Portals/0/Documents/Women's% 20Justice%20Taskforce%20Report.pdf (accessed 31 May 2017)

National Offender Management Service Annual Report 2011-12: Costs per place and costs per prisoner, NOMS, Ministry of Justice (25 October 2012) https://www.gov.uk/government/uploads/system/uploads/attachment_d ata/file/218336/prison-costs-summary-11-12.pdf (accessed 13 Oct 2015)

Panchamia, Nahal, *Competition in prisons*, Institute for Government, 2012, https://www.instituteforgovernment.org.uk/sites/default/files/publicatio ns/Prisons%20briefing%20final.pdf (accessed 22 June 2017)

Women offenders: after the Corston Report, House of Common Justice Committee Second Report of Session 2013-14, available in full at https://books.google.co.uk/books?id=wvt6IrCe8TIC&pg=RA1-PA121&lpg=RA1-

PA121&dq=NOMS+Women's+Team&source=bl&ots=uOVpyAI3m5
&sig=vQgQnAb1RtFZJHrSk0r0Wbsv_sQ&hl=en&sa=X&ved=0ahU
KEwi1pvbf2avTAhXsA8AKHYDYB9wQ6AEIOzAE#v=onepage&q
&f=true (accessed 31 May 2017)
Transforming Rehabilitation: A Strategy for Reform, Ministry of Justice,
    May   2013,   https://consult.justice.gov.uk/digital-communications/
    transforming-rehabilitation/results/transforming-rehabilitation-
    response.pdf (accessed 31 May 2017)
Third Aggregate Report on Offender Management in Prison, Findings from
    a Series of Joint Inspections by HM Inspectorate of Probation and HM
    Inspectorate of Prisons, December 2013.
    https://www.crimeandjustice.org.uk/sites/crimeandjustice.org.uk/files/
    offender-management-in-prisons.pdf (accessed 31 May 2017)
*Resettlement provision for adult offenders: Accommodation and education,
    training and employment,*. A joint thematic review by HM Inspectorate
    of Prisons, HM Inspectorate of Probation and Ofsted, September 2014,
    http://www.justiceinspectorates.gov.uk/cjji/wp-
    content/uploads/sites/2/2014/09/Resettlement-thematic-for-print-Sept-
    2014.pdf (accessed 31 May 2017)
Bromley Briefings Prison Factfile (2014) Prison Reform Trust,
    http://www.prisonreformtrust.org.uk/Portals/0/Documents/Bromley%2
    0Briefings/Factfile%20Autumn%202014.pdf (accessed 13 Oct 2015)
HMP Doncaster Payment by Results pilot: Final process evaluation report,
    Ministry of Justice Analytical Series, 2015,
    https://www.gov.uk/government/uploads/system/uploads/attachment_d
    ata/file/449494/hmp-doncaster-pbr-final-evaluation.pdf (accessed 16
    June 2017)
Outcome-based payment schemes: government's use of payment by results,
    Report by the Comptroller and Auditor General, HC 86 session 2015-16
    19   June   2015,   https://www.nao.org.uk/wp-content/uploads/2015/06/
    Outcome-based-payment-schemes-governments-use-of-payment-by-
    results.pdf (accessed 16 June 2017)
HMP & YOI Holloway, Report on an unannounced inspection, by HM Chief
    Inspector of Prisons, 5-15 October 2015, 2016, London: published by
    HM Inspectorate of Prisons
Contracted-out prisons, Justice.gov.uk, 30 January 2017,
    https://www.justice.gov.uk/about/hmps/contracted-out   (accessed   22
    June 2017)

News articles and media chronologically ordered

Cave E., ed., 'From an Enquiry into the Cause of the late Increase of Robbers', *The Gentleman's Magazine*, 21 (1751), 3-4

An Enquiry into the Causes of the late Increase Robbers, &c., *Universal magazine of knowledge and pleasure*, 8 (1751), 51

An Enquiry into the Causes of the late Increase of Robbers, *The Ladies Magazine*, 2, 7 (1751), 105-107

An Inquiry into the causes of the late increase of robbers, *The Magazine of Magazines* (1751), 135-144

'New Penitentiary, Millbank', *The Times*, 27th June 1816

'Reports of the Directors of Convict Prisons, England, 1861', *The Edinburgh Review*, 117.239 (1863), 241-268

Henry, M., 'The New Prison Rules and Plank Beds', *The Times*, Monday, Aug 12, (1878), 11, Letter to the Editor.

Tooley, Sarah T., 'The Prisoners' friends', *The Woman's Signal*, 1 November 1884

Ker, L.B. Marianne, 'The Girl with a Mission', *Young England*, 1 June 1885

Davenport-Hill, Florence, *Art II: Women Prison Visitors*, Paper Presented by request to the Third International Prison Congress, Rome, reported in *The Englishwoman's Review*, 15 December 1885

Du Cane, Edmond, 'Crime and Criminals 1837-1887', *Murray's Magazine*, 2, 9 (1887), 289-299

'Reforming The Prison System Of Great Britain; Winston Churchill Sees Galsworthy's Play, "Justice," And Then Institutes A Revolution', *The New York Times*, 7 August 1911

'Prison Life: Report on Committee of Inquiry', *Westminster Gazette*, 26 June 1922

Dyer, Clare, 'Top Judge Attacks Sentencing Reform', *The Guardian*, 22 March 1993

'Free the judges to jail the thugs'. *Daily Mail, 23* March 1993

Casey, John, "A wicked way to abuse our law; 'To defy the moral sense of law-abiding citizens brings criminal justice into disrepute and turns the law into a tyranny'." *Evening Standard*, 24 March 1993

'Justice Secretary plans 'radical' prison policy change', *BBC News*, 30 June 2010

'David Cameron launches Tories' 'big society' plan', *BBC news, Politics*, 19 July 2010

Travis, Alan and Mulholland, Helen, 'Prison system failing to tackle reoffending, says Ken Clarke'. *The Guardian,* 7 December 2010

Hotel killers: Three female convicted murders given jobs at same
Travelodge, *Mail Online*, 18 January 2011

'When Bankers were Good', Hislop, Ian (presented), Ford, Helena
(director), BBC 2, 23 November 2011, 11.50pm

Inwood, Joe, 'Leeds Prison set to introduce payment by results model', *BBC
Look North, BBC News*, 20 April 2012

'Housewives and Heroines: A 17th Century History for Girls', Lucy,
Worsley (presenter), Eleanor, Scoones (director), BBC 4, May 2012

Poyner, Chris, 'Prison Privatisation should be a national scandal', *The
Guardian*, November 2012

Lowe, Toby, 'Payment by results – a 'dangerous idiocy' that makes staff tell
lies', *The Guardian*, 1 February 2013

Crook, Frances, 'Who wins at 'payment by results'? Ask shareholders at
Serco, the company running Britain', OpenDemocracyUK, 5 March 2013,
https://www.opendemocracy.net/ourkingdom/frances-crook/who-wins-at-
%E2%80%98payment-by-results%E2%80%99-ask-shareholders-at-serco-
company-running- (accessed 16 June 2017)

Shiv, Malik, 'Vicky Pryce transferred to open prison in Kent',
theguardian.com, 17 March 2013,
http://www.theguardian.com/uk/2013/mar/17/vicky-pryce-transferred-
kent-open-prison (accessed 13 Oct 2015)

Rhodri, Phillips, 'Vicky's cushy new jail: Pryce moved to soft prison after
FOUR days', 17th March 2013, *The Sun*,
http://www.thesun.co.uk/sol/homepage/news/4845651/Disgraced-
Vicky-Pryce-is-moved-to-softer-open-prison-in-countryside-after-just-
FOUR-days-in-Holloway.html (accessed 13 Oct 2015)

Penrose, Justin and Wellman, Alex, 'Vicky Pryce moved to Cushy open
prison just three days after she was jailed', *Mirror News*, 17 March 2013,
http://www.mirror.co.uk/news/uk-news/vicky-pryce-moved-cushy-
open-1769457 (accessed 13 Oct 2015)

The End of Semi-Open Prison for Women- Preventing Family Contact,
Women in Prison, News (registered Charity No.1118727),
http://www.womeninprison.org.uk/news_show.php?id=31   (last
accessed 29 Aug 2013 unavailable 2015)

Bennett, Asa, 'Six Private Prisons Fact Chris Grayling doesn't want you to
know', *Huffington Post UK*, January 2014,
http://www.huffingtonpost.co.uk/2014/01/02/private-
prisons_n_4530768.html (accessed 22 June 2017)

'The First Georgians: The Germans Kings who Made Britain', Worsley,
Lucy (presenter), Sebastian, Barfled (series producer), and Michael Pool
(executive producer), episode 2, BBC 4, 12 May 2014, 10.35pm

Neilson, Andrew, 'Exploding the myth of "payment by results"', OpenDemocracyUK, 19 June 2015, https://www.opendemocracy.net/ourkingdom/andrew-neilson/uk-public-spending-watchdog-explodes-myth-of-%E2%80%98payment-by-results%E2%80%99 (accessed 16 June 2017)

Prisons Announcement, Written Statement to Parliament, 25 November 2015, Gov.uk, https://www.gov.uk/government/speeches/prisons-announcement (accessed 22 June 2017)

Saner, Emine, 'A woman's place? Why the closure of Holloway could bring a prison revolution closer', The Guardian, November 2015

Agbamu, Samuel, 'HM Prison Holloway is closed. What will become of the space?' *Revolutionary Socialism in the 21ˢᵗ century,* 14 December 2016, https://rs21.org.uk/2016/12/14/reclaim-holloway/ (accessed 25 June 2017)

Moor-Bridger, Benedict, 'Holloway prison: Campaigners to protest against plan to turn historic jail into luxury flats', *Evening Standard,* 16 February 2017

Other sources chronologically ordered

Hanging, Not Punishment Enough, For Murderers, High-way Men, and House-Breakers (London: Warwick-Lane, 1701)

Reformation necessary to prevent Our Ruin: A Sermon Preached to the Societies for Reformation of Manners, at St. Mary-le-Bow, on Wednesday, January 10th, 1727 (London: Printed and Sold by Joseph Downing, in Bartholomew-Close, near West-Smithfield, 1728)

'House of Lords Journal Volume 27: January 1751', *Journal of the House of Lords* Volume 27: 1746-1752 (1767-1830), http://www.british-history.ac.uk/report.aspx?compid=114316 (accessed 13 Oct 2015)

Grey B.H., *A letter to the common council and livery of the city of London: on the abuses existing in Newgate: showing the necessity of an immediate reform in the management of that prison,* 2ⁿᵈ edn (London, 1818)

The Pennsylvania Journal of Prison Discipline and Philanthropy, 3 (1847-8) (Philadelphia: E.C. & J. Biddle, 1848)

Churchill, Winston Spencer, *Abatement of Imprisonment* (London: Great Britain, Home Office, a Cabinet Paper, 1910)

Simone Edizioni Giuridiche, *Compendio di Criminologia* (Napoli: Cecom, 2000)

Amnesty International, *Death penalty: death sentences and executions in 2006*, 20 February 2008, http://www.amnesty.org/en/death-penalty (accessed 13 Oct 2015)

Prison Population Statistics, House of Commons Library, Berman G. (Version: 22 December 2010; 7 November 2011)

Dunn, Jane, 'Ellis , Ruth (1926–1955)', *Oxford Dictionary of National Biography*, Oxford University Press, 2004; online edn, Jan 2008 http://www.oxforddnb.com/view/article/56716 (accessed 13 Oct 2015)

Resettlement of released prisoners, Ministry of Justice, GOV.UK, Crown copyright (2012), https://www.justice.gov.uk/offenders/before-after-release/resettlement (accessed 13 Oct 2015)

Women Offenders: After the Corston Report, Second Report of Session 2013-14, House of Commons Justice Committee, Vol. I (London: The Stationery Office Limited, 2013), http://www.publications.parliament.uk/pa/cm201314/cmselect/cmjust/92/92.pdf (accessed 13 Oct 2015)

Categorisation & Assessment, National Security Framework, page 5 out of 15, available online http://a1538.g.akamai.net/7/1538/13355/v001/homeoffice.download.ak amai.com/13355/Doc/1016/10160005.pdf (accessed 13 Oct 2015)

Databases

Raithby, John, ed., *William and Mary, 1691: An Act to take away Clergy from some offenders and to bring other to Punishment* [Chapter IX. Rot. Parl. pt. 1. nu. 7], Statues of the Realm: Volume 6: 1685-94, (1819), 311-312 British History Online, http://www.british-history.ac.uk/report.aspx?compid=46363 (accessed 13 Oct 2015)

Clark, Richard, *Capital Punishment UK* (database originated in 1995) http://www.capitalpunishmentuk.org (accessed 13 Oct 2015)

Access to Public Records, July 2012, The National Archives, Crown Copyright 2012, http://www.nationalarchives.gov.uk/documents/information-management/access-to-public-records.pdf (accessed 13 Oct 2015)

Prison finder, HM Prison Service, Public Sector Prisons, GOV.UK, (last updated June 2012), http://www.justice.gov.uk/contacts/prison-finder (accessed 13 Oct 2015)

NACRO, 2013, http://www.nacro.org.uk/ (accessed 13 Oct 2015)

The Concise Oxford Dictionary of English Etymology, T. F. Hoad, ed. (Oxford: Oxford University Press, 1996 [published online 2003; last updated 2015])

http://www.oxfordreference.com/view/10.1093/acref/9780192830982.
001.0001/acref-9780192830982 (accessed 13 Oct 2015)
Oxford Dictionaries, (Oxford: Oxford University Press, last updated 2015)
http://www.oxforddictionaries.com/ (accessed 13 Oct 2015)
Contestable Market, Business Dictionary,
http://www.businessdictionary.com/definition/contestable-market.html
(accessed 22 June 2017)
Market Testing, Small Business Encyclopaedia, Entrepreneur,
https://www.entrepreneur.com/encyclopedia/market-testing (accessed
22 June 2017)
The Old Bailey Proceedings Online, 1674-1913, Hitchcock, Tim;
Shoemaker, Robert; Emsley, Clive; Howard, Sharon; and McLaughlin,
Jamie www.oldbaileyonline.org version 7.2, last updated March 2015
(accessed 13 Oct 2015)
London Lives, 1690-1800, Hitchcock Tim, Shoemaker Robert, Howard
Sharon and McLaughlin Jamie, *et al.,* www.londonlives.org version 1.1,
last updated April 2012 (accessed 13 Oct 2015)
Policy- Research Ethics http://www.bbk.ac.uk/rgco/policy/ethics.shtml as
approved on June 2010 (accessed 13 Oct 2015)
The Inspectorate Reports of Prisons, GOV.UK, 2012,
http://www.justice.gov.uk/about/hmi-prisons/ (accessed 13 Oct 2015)
Prison Population Figures, Statistics, Ministry Of Justice, GOV.UK,
version 2.0, Crown Copyright
https://www.gov.uk/government/publications/prison-population-
figures (accessed 13 Oct 2015)
Office for National Statistics http://www.ons.gov.uk/ons/index.html
(accessed 13 Oct 2015)
Internet Archives, 2001 http://archive.org/ (accessed 13 Oct 2015)
Scottish Prison Service, FQA, http://www.sps.gov.uk/faq.aspx#FAQno16
(accessed 13 Oct 2015)
Encyclopædia Britannica Online. http://www.britannica.com/ (accessed 13
Oct 2015)
d-maps.com http://d-maps.com/ Daniel, Delet (2007-2015) (accessed 13
Oct 2015)

Hansard

HC Deb 04 March 1811 vol 19 cc186-8
HC Deb 21 January 1812 vol 21 cc235-9
HC Deb 16 December 1819 vol 41 cc1189-217
HL Deb 26 February 1869 vol 194 cc332-50

HC Deb 25 July 1878 vol 242 cc216-8
HL Deb 29 July 1898 vol 63 cc404-15
HL Deb 14 December 1915 vol 20 cc609-36
HC Deb 27 July 1938 vol 338 cc3140-251
HC Deb 29 November 1938 vol 342 cc267-377
HL Deb 18 November 1952, cc318-72
HC Deb 25 February 1991 vol 186 cc659-73
HC Deb 16 March 2005, Vol 432, cc69-142

Acts

Debtors Imprisonment Act 1758 c.28 (32 Geo.2)
Discharged Prisoners Act 1774 c. 20 (14 Geo.3)
Health of Prisoners Act 1774 c. 59 (14 Geo. 3)
Criminal Law Act 1776 c.43 (16 Geo.3)
Transportation, etc. Act 1779 c. 74 (19 Geo.3)
Penitentiary House, etc. Act 1812, c.44 (52 Geo.3)
Criminal Law Act 1827 c.28 (7 & 8 Geo.4)
Poor Law Amendment Act 1834 c.76 (4 & 5 Will. 4)
Prison Act 1865 c.126 (28 & 29 Vict.)
Prison Act 1877 c.21 (40 & 41 Vict.)
Criminal Justice Act 1948 c.58 (11 & 12 Geo.6)
The Penal Servitude Act 1853 c.3 (20 & 21 Vict.)
Prison Act 1865 c.126 (28 & 29 Vict.)
Industrial Schools Act 1866 c.18 (29 & 30 Vict.)
Reformatory School Act 1866 c.117 (29 & 30 Vict.)
Prevention of Crime Act 1908, c. 59 (8 Edw.7)
Criminal Justice Administration Act 1914, c. 58 (4 & 5 Geo.5)
Criminal Justice Act 1948, c.58 (11 & 12 Geo.6)

Prison Service Orders/Instructions

PSI 39/2011 'Categorisation and re-categorisation of women prisoners',
    Issue date 26 Aug 2011
PSO 4800, 'Women Prisoners', Issue no.297, Issue date 28 April 2008
PSO 6300, 'Release on Temporary Licence', Issue 251, Issue date 29 Nov
    2005
PSO 0900, 'Categorisation and Allocation' (replaced by PSI 39/2011)

London National Archives references [LNA]

HO 20/1/59A
HO 20/4/31
HO 20/1/79
HO 45/23223
HO 45/10046[A62024]
HO 45/16224
HO 45/16456
HO 45/177768
HO 45/21911
PCOM 14/9, 14/10, 14/11
PCOM 9/1386
PCOM 9/156
PCOM 9/192
PCOM 9/139
PCOM 9/1989
ED 149/98
ED 114/1612/5